AFTER MEECH LAKE

LESSONS
FOR THE
FUTURE

AFTER MEECH LAKE

LESSONS FOR THE FUTURE

EDITORS
DAVID E. SMITH · PETER MacKINNON · JOHN C. COURTNEY

FIFTH HOUSE PUBLISHERS
Saskatoon, Saskatchewan

Design: Robert Grey, Apex Graphics

Canadian Cataloguing in Publication Data

Main entry under title:

After Meech Lake
Conference held Nov. 1-3, 1990, Saskatoon, Sask.
ISBN 0-920079-82-2

1. Canada - Constitutional law - Amendments - Congresses.
2. Canada - Constitutional history - Congresses. I. Smith, David E., 1936–
II. MacKinnon, Peter. III. Courtney, John C.

JL65 1991.A47 1991   342.71'03   C91-097018-1

This book has been published with the assistance of The Canada Council and the University of Saskatchewan.

Fifth House Publishers
620 Duchess St.
Saskatoon, Saskatchewan S7K 0R1

Printed in Canada

CONTENTS

Constitutional Challenges from Aboriginal Peoples and Women

The Future of Constitutional Reform

Introduction

The After Meech Lake Conference took place early in November 1990 in Saskatoon, but its genesis began the previous February. The organizers, from the College of Law and the Department of Political Studies at the University of Saskatchewan, took the view that whether or not the Meech Lake Accord was ratified by the 23 June 1990 deadline, it was time to pause to take stock of Canada's constitutional reform process. It was evident that regardless of what happened in June, there would be a legacy of grievance on the part of some Canadians who believed they had suffered as a result of the outcome. For reasons that had become endemic to Canada's view of itself as a united country, the constitutional reform process invariably nurtured division. The papers presented at the conference offered no evidence that such divisions had died with the Accord. If anything, events subsequent to the June deadline showed that the resolve of many of the competing players in Canada's continuing constitutional debate had been strengthened.

For three years, interest had been pitted against interest, region against region and, even, government against people. Where, in theory, at some point in the process constitutional change should evoke a spirit of accommodation and where, in fact, the agreement at issue was intended to promote national reconciliation, neither benefit was apparent. Nor was this the first time that this uncomfortable truth had been revealed: the process of constitutional reform, of which the Meech Lake Accord was depicted as the final chapter, had been conceived and adopted in an atmosphere of recrimination a decade before. Whatever its virtues—and they had grown faint by the beginning of 1990—the process appeared fatally flawed; not only would the Accord possibly fail but in the bargain the federation might be mortally wounded.

The conference organizers believed that perspectives on constitutional reform should extend beyond where most of the attention was then being placed—the question of Québec's relation to the rest of Canada. As important as that subject was, and is, to the future of the country, its answer could not escape acknowledging other pressing concerns. In the familiar words of section 91 of the Constitution Act—"for greater Certainty, but not so as to restrict the Generality of the fore-going"—these included the failure of Canadian federalism to embrace the multiple identities that are the raison d'être of federal government; the inability of Parliament and governments to articulate societal pluralism, most recently evident in the insensitivity of public institutions to the assertion of the politics of gender and Native peoples; the hesitant realignment of Canadian politics in response to the Charter of Rights and Freedoms and the community interests it has spawned that transcend territorially based concerns; and the determinative effect of the media that now intrudes on all political and constitutional discussion.

Through associating two disciplines—law and political science—and by inviting participants from eight of the 10 provinces and from each of the official language groups as well as from the aboriginal peoples, the organizers sought to present an informed and comprehensive understanding of the process of constitutional reform. At six sessions—A Decade of Constitutional Reform, Conflicting Views of the Constitution and Constitutional Reform, Constitutional Reform: Charter Rights and Freedoms, The Media and Constitutional Reform in Canada, Constitutional Challenges from Aboriginal Peoples and Women, and, finally, The Future of Constitutional Reform—participants, who included academics, journalists, former and present civil servants, a former provincial premier, a former attorney-general, and a leader of the Assembly of First Nations, were invited to comment on the course and conditions that affect the resolution of Canada's constitutional problems. They were not asked to recommend, and most of the papers do not offer, options for reform. As the British political scientist, Richard Rose, has said in another context: "In any fluid political situation the prizes go to the individuals who think up the *new* questions." Until this is done, until one stops and looks back and then, ahead, it is precipitate to talk of delegating power here, or expanding concurrency there. What *Globe and Mail* columnist Jeffrey Simpson calls "constitutional Lego-building" will fail unless we know what are the pieces and who are the players. Thus, those who want blueprints for the future will be disappointed with these papers, while those who want an inventory of the materials that will be needed to create a lasting constitutional structure will, we trust, be rewarded.[1]

As Alan Cairns and Tom Courchene demonstrate in their papers (and Courchene graphically in his appendix, entitled Political/Economic Factors Conditioning the 1980s Constitutional Climate), the past decade introduced new constitutional questions, new constitutional actors, and a new constitutional norm in the form of the Charter. The effect has been inherently antifederal, as federalism has traditionally been understood in Canada, with Canadians outside of Québec embracing the values of individualism and equality. Executive federalism, the preferred approach to resolving conflict for the last several decades, has fallen into disfavour, precipitously so once the unpopular Meech Lake Accord became identified as its product. Yet at the very time pan-Canadian sentiments are growing, countervailing national and international economic pressures are depriving Ottawa of its capacity to respond on a comparable level. Furthermore, the tension inherent in these contradictory developments is accentuated, says Courchene, by Québec's commitment to "goal-oriented" politics (which once typified all of Canadian politics) and by a new commitment elsewhere in the country to "means-oriented" politics. It is this last innovation, he says, which helps to explain the "unwinding [of] the legitimacy of the Commons, the Senate, and particularly executive federalism." Outlining the province of Manitoba's response to the 1987 constitutional accord, Kathy Brock concludes that Meech Lake failed more because it was seen as a threat by a variety of organized interests than because the rest of Canada was unable to respond to the opportunities for federal restructuring presented by Québec. To Allan Blakeney, the irreconcilability of three competing attributes of a constitutional amending formula (provincial equality, a Québec veto, and a measure of flexibility) underline the importance of considering the merits of asymmetrical federalism in future constitutional negotiations.

No wonder Alan Cairns says that major constitutional reform is not for the "faint-hearted," or that Peter Russell in his commentary agrees with him. For this reason, Russell proposes that the First Ministers Conference be replaced "by a forum with more democratic legitimacy." Another possibility, raised by Cairns as a question to be explored, is for referenda to become a part of the constitutional reform process. Agreement on such a proposal, however, might prove difficult to obtain if the differing views of referenda at the After Meech Lake Conference reflect the larger opinion.

In her paper on "Representation and Constitutional Reform," in the second session on "Conflicting Views of the Constitution," Jennifer Smith declares the current process flawed but not for the reasons critics often cite: the failure of the first ministers "to mirror" the characteristics of the general population. Instead, she advances the proposition that constitutional matters must be distinguished from ordinary political matters and that resolution of the former can only follow the action of "a legitimate constitution-making power." As the collapse of the Accord demonstrates, existing governments fail to meet that test. Citing Tom Paine—"the constitution of a country is not an act of government, but of the people constituting its government"—Smith asks how that popular source can be tapped, and she offers two possibilities: a popularly elected convention to propose major reform or a popular ratification process to approve it.

That the content of constitutional change may be as important as its process is a theme common to the papers of Edmond Orban and Guy Laforest. Both writers remind their audience that French-speaking Quebeckers passionately want the constitution to recognize their national community. To the extent that it does (and according to Laforest, this was the Accord's great virtue since it derived from the dualistic conception of Canada eloquently propounded by André Laurendeau), then "the legitimacy problem" of the Canadian federal regime in Québec would be solved. But both writers also acknowledge what Reg Whitaker in his comments makes explicit: the democratization of Canadian and Québec societies has inordinately complicated the realization of that cherished goal, because popular participation has revealed more starkly than traditional governmental practices ever did the existence of two "peoples." It is this reality, as much as any other, that leads Garth Stevenson to observe bleakly that Canada lacks "the necessary degree of social, economic, and political integration to support the institutions of a federal state."

An ostensible instrument of popular efficacy is the Canadian Charter of Rights and Freedoms. Yet even here, there is debate over whether its influence is benign or corrosive. In the third set of papers, on "Constitutional Reform: Charter Rights and Freedoms," William Lederman supports the first interpretation. The Charter, he says, "might help very significantly in the task of saving the Canadian federal union." As evidence that the courts and legislatures may operate as partners rather than rivals, he cites dextrous opinions of the Supreme Court of Canada in Charter cases which reflect judicial sensibility to the operation of parliamentary government. In this judgement and in his desire to see the elimination of section 33 of the Charter (the notwithstanding clause), he is joined by commentator Deborah Coyne.

In sharp contrast, Robert Martin, writing about "The Charter and the Crisis in Canada," indicts both the Charter and the Supreme Court for subverting parliamentary government and, ultimately, democracy. In significant part their influence over the last decade has made Canadian institutions less able "to address the democratic question and the national question." Not surprisingly, Martin adopts a positive view of section 33 of the Charter, believing it represents "the means of resuscitating parliamentary democracy in Canada."

One influence on the constitutional reform process that stands outside the formal institutions of government is the media. Nevertheless, Canadians who had access to television during the first three weeks of June could not be oblivious to that medium's influence on the process. As John Meisel and David Taras, two of the contributors to the session on "The Media and Constitutional Reform in Canada," state, the media became actors in the final attempts to salvage the Meech Lake Accord. David Taras goes further and argues that "television seemed to become another platform for negotiations among first ministers." Paradoxically, the constitutional reform process maligned by critics for its dependence upon secrecy has become enveloped by spectacle. The media's impact on the constitutional process became evident in 1981 as a result of the televised hearings of the Joint Committee of the Senate and the House of Commons on the Trudeau government's reform package. This time the coverage was both more intense and prolonged because of the protracted ratification period, and John Meisel demonstrates how, over this period, media reporting on the subject shifted. There were, as well, differences in coverage according to whether the source was public or private radio or television and whether it was via print or electronic media.

If the media shaped the constitutional process this is only retributive justice because, as Marc Raboy reveals in his canvass of Canadian broadcasting from Aird to the most recent legislation passed by Parliament late in 1990, broadcasting itself has, on occasion, been treated by the federal government "as a strategic weapon in its struggle against the rising and increasingly nationalistic movement in Québec." Dirigiste policies notwithstanding, broadcasting is "a microcosm of Canadian society," he concludes, because it reflects "the lack of consensus about the fundamental nature of Canadian nationhood."

Commentators Graham Fraser and Vaughn Palmer, both newspaper journalists, review the media's presentation of news and, in particular, the significance attached to the timing and sequence of events. They reject as unfounded the charge that the media were biased in their coverage of the constitutional reform process. If the media failed to promote national unity, then so be it: they are not in business to keep the country together. Moreover, it should be remembered, Palmer suggests, that "Meech failed not through lack of reporting, but because people did not like it."

Alan Cairns's paper had noted "a recurring pattern in the constitutional reform process—the tendency of those in charge to exclude, or try to exclude, other constitutional actors who stand in the way of agreement." In the session on "Constitutional Challenges from Aboriginal Peoples and Women," Beverley Baines and Ovide Mercredi corroborate that evaluation and testify to its serious consequences. Baines argues that gender representation is a legitimate issue of constitutional reform, but neither in the papers presented to the conference nor in constitutional discussions generally is it acknowledged as such, let alone examined. More disturbing still, she states, is "the lesson of Meech Lake and ... of all the constitutional exercises that preceded it," which is the assumption that "men can and should represent the interests of women."

Concern about exclusion and about a set of values which blinds constitutional architects to its consequences informs Ovide Mercredi's presentation. While the future of the First Nations must rest in the hands of the First Nations, that future need not mean aboriginal rejection of Canadian society. At issue, he argues, is whether Canadian people and their governments are ready to grant Native peoples new respect and acceptance. Speaking to the conference only two days after the creation of the Citizens' Forum, chaired by Keith Spicer, whose terms of reference failed to distinguish aboriginal peoples from individual "average" Canadians, Mercredi is not encouraged that traditional attitudes of government are about to change. Yet he confesses to believe that "we are [not] in a state of crisis in terms of the future of Canada," as long as the exclusion of Native peoples does not become irremediable, as the Meech Lake Accord threatened to make it.

The exclusion of women and aboriginal Canadians, which these authors cite, provides the text for Donna Greschner's reminder that federalism is supposed to "foster multiple identities." Instead, the institutions and processes of Canadian federalism, government, and constitutional reform are selective in the interests they embrace. This is why, she says, the Charter has such appeal for certain groups: it did not create them or the interests they possess, but it recognizes them and, by so doing, gives them a status and a legitimacy traditional structures deny. Her comments enlist a theme never far from the surface of all the papers in the book— the obstacles to participation in Canada's political process—and they underline again the central problem for constitutional reform: the perceived inadequacy of representation that many Canadians profess to experience.

The last session, on "The Future of Constitutional Reform," includes two papers, by Gordon Robertson and by John Whyte, along with the conference banquet speech, by Ian Scott. All three papers were distinct in that none of them had a formally assigned commentator; instead, members of the audience were invited to act as commentators or to ask questions, as they had at the other sessions.

All three authors agree that for Québec the status quo is dead and that the attitudes and values Canadians outside of Québec increasingly espouse complicate finding a new constitutional *modus vivendi*. The commitment to treat individuals and provinces equally, "to purge," in Whyte's words, "any rooted communitarianism," constrains political leaders in arriving at a mutually acceptable solution to the problem. As regards Québec, there are really only three broad alternatives, excluding separation: some form of special status, a generalization to all provinces of whatever status is determined for Québec (the Meech Lake Accord approach), or sovereignty-association. What option will find favour, and by what means, is still unknown. Robertson expresses "grave doubts" about the use of a constitutional convention since it has no basis in our political tradition; Scott sees some merit in the proposal because, among other virtues, it would reassure Canadians that "the public interest is being protected"; while Whyte believes that the constitutional commitment necessary to accommodate Québec's aspirations must originate at a sub-national level. At issue, as each author acknowledges by raising the subject, is the loss of "the requisite moral authority" once possessed by government to carry out so fundamental a task.

This concluding session of the conference concentrates particularly on the immediate question of Québec and its future relationship to Canada. That is understandable in light of the repercussions that have followed the collapse of the Accord. But what these authors say implicitly, and what some of the other contributors have said explicitly, is that there are many Canadians who feel themselves to be outsiders in their own country, who deserve full constitutional enfranchisement, and who seek assurances that their views will be sought as they too debate and weigh constitutional alternatives in the future. It is their sense of perpetually being in the background that explains the frayed ties of loyalty to a constitutional arrangement some see as moribund. For them, at least, Canada seems to be coming apart at the seams.

It was argued forcefully by conference participants that what is most needed at this stage is time—to cool tempers and to heal wounds. Whatever the merits of that claim, post-Meech Lake developments suggest that time is not likely to be a commodity in plentiful supply. But they do, however, make a persuasive case that lessons for the future must be learned quickly—for the cumulative conclusion of the papers presented here is that there will be no further chance.

David E. Smith
John C. Courtney
February 1991

---

1. Those who seek a bibliographic listing of the considerable literature on the Meech Lake Accord will be similarly disappointed. They could do no better than consult Dwight Herperger, "The Meech Lake Accord: A Comprehensive Bibliography," in Ronald L. Watts and Douglas M. Brown, eds., *Canada: The State of Federation* (Kingston, Ontario: Institute of Intergovernmental Relations, 1990), 271–289.

A DECADE OF CONSTITUTIONAL REFORM

The Charter, Interest Groups, Executive Federalism, and Constitutional Reform

ALAN C. CAIRNS

UNIVERSITY OF BRITISH COLUMBIA

Contemporary Canadians disagree on the role and function of the written constitution. To governments it remains what it always has been, an instrument of federalism. The division of powers, its interpretation by the courts, its management by intergovernmental machinery, and the process of its formal amendment comprise the vision of the written constitution that is natural to first ministers. From this governmental perspective, constitutional debate also focuses on intrastate federalism—the extent and nature of regional input at the centre, and the continuing propriety of what might be called intrastate federalism in reverse, the various instruments by which the federal government can insert itself into matters of provincial jurisdiction—disallowance, reservation, the declaratory power, and the spending power. From the perspective of what may be called the governments' constitution, the community basis of the constitutional order is found in the pan-Canadian community and the 10 provincial and two northern territorial communities. Canadians are to be thought of as Manitobans, Yukoners, or as citizens of a country-wide community.

Federalism provides rich constitutional fare. Until the arrival of the Charter, federalist discourse dominated our jurisprudence. Constitutional debate revolved around what the Fathers intended, generated the contested compact theory of Confederation, and praised or criticized the Judicial Committee of the Privy Council for its contribution to the evolution of Canadian federalism. It was natural in this tradition that such great state papers on the constitution as the Rowell-Sirois and Tremblay reports were, above all else, analyses of the past and future of federalism as a constitutional arrangement.

Federalism is no longer enough. It occupies a shrinking portion of our constitutional terrain. It is jostled by a rights discourse that preceded but was greatly stimulated by the 1982 Charter. Via the Charter the post-1982 constitution speaks

13

directly to Canadians in terms of citizen-state relations. The Charter also triggers various specific constitutional discourses—an ethnic discourse that responds to section 27 of the Charter from the vantage point of a society that is increasingly multicultural and multiracial; a discrete focus on the consequences of the sex division in society for the constitution, and vice versa, that is driven by the feminist movement and focuses on sections 28 and 15 of the Charter; an equality debate given constitutional stimulation by section 15 of the Charter and kept alive by what have come to be called "equality seekers"; [1] and a debate about the role of the constitution in relation to linguistic duality that draws from sections 16 to 23 of the Charter.

Yet another focus on the constitution, only peripherally linked to the Charter, addresses the question of the role and recognition of aboriginal peoples in Canadian society. What mix of special status and normal Canadian citizenship are they to enjoy? What differences, if any, should exist in the constitutional treatment of Indians, Inuit, and Métis? In one sense these are not new constitutional questions, as the appropriate relationship between aboriginal peoples and other Canadians has been a constitutional policy issue since Confederation. Clearly, however, the constitutional politics of aboriginal issues is now driven by a combination of numbers, self-confidence, indigenous nationalisms, a supportive international climate, and an enhanced degree of constitutional recognition since 1982 that no longer allows their relegation to the backwaters in which they formerly languished.

The written constitution has become, accordingly, a many splendoured much more comprehensive arrangement than was true of its spare predecessor, the BNA Act. It is, therefore, not surprising that Canadians disagree on the process of formal constitutional change, on who should participate and who should be in the audience. In the post-Meech Lake era Canadians are clearly in a state of constitutional transition, not only in terms of the Québec rest-of-Canada relationship but also in terms of the relationship of the Charter and aboriginal constitutional clauses to the traditional concerns of federalism. We disagree about the substance of the existing constitution, and about the procedures we should employ in trying to move to a new constitutional equilibrium.

We are now paying a heavy price for the prolonged constitutional immaturity that left the formal power of constitutional amendment in crucial matters in British hands until 1982. We too-long avoided the basic question of where sovereignty resided by leaving, formally, large chunks of it in the Parliament of the former imperial Mother country. This allowed us simultaneously to avoid the challenge of forming ourselves into a constitutional people, agreed on the fundamentals of our civic existence. [2] As a result, we now confront the issue of our constitutional future at a time when the Québec challenge to the federal dimension of our identity is supplemented by an aboriginal challenge to our Canadianism and by a nonterritorial pluralism drawing on the social cleavages of sex, ethnicity, race, disability, etc.

The written constitution has become a symbolic document of great importance. It hands out differential status to Canadians in terms of sex, ethnicity, language, indigenous status, and other social categories singled out for explicit constitutional attention. Meech Lake makes it clear that such questions as who is to receive constitutional recognition as a distinct society, and what are to be included in the constitution as fundamental characteristics of Canada are not dry technical matters but minefields of explosive emotions. Not surprisingly, the profound importance of our unanswered constitutional questions generates disagreement over the process we should follow in seeking answers. Our recent constitutional history confirms that constitutional process and constitutional outcome are closely linked.

HOBSON'S CONSTITUTIONAL REFORM CHOICE: FAILURE OR A PYRRHIC VICTORY

In the mid-sixties, when we began the constitutional soul-searching in which we have ever since been engaged, there was a tendency to assume that the task was relatively straightforward. In the midst of the counterculture climate, and the blossoming of new third world nations as ancient empires crumbled, the "out with the old and in with the new" did not seem a daunting task. Paper constitutions flourished and otherwise sensible people delighted in mocking the decrepit BNA Act as an anachronism whose imminent destination was the graveyard.

We now know better. Enthusiasm for constitutional reform is restricted to masochists and those who derive pleasure from Sisyphean tasks. The most likely outcome of a constitutional reform effort is failure. The demise of Meech Lake is simply the latest in a long list of failed attempts to change constitutional direction in a fundamental way. The historical evidence is depressing—the Fulton-Favreau amending formula of the mid-sixties, the Victoria Charter of 1971, Bill C-60 of the late seventies, and the four unsuccessful aboriginal constitutional conferences of the mid-eighties all join Meech Lake in testifying to the resilience of the discredited old order that so many would like to leave behind. Thus, defeat of reform efforts is the basic pattern.

The proposed federal government 1980–81 threat to proceed unilaterally to request an amendment from the British Parliament revealed an additional recurring pattern in the constitutional reform process—the tendency of those in charge to exclude, or try to exclude, other constitutional actors who stand in the way of agreement. The Trudeau unilateralism threat—a by-product of the unclear norms as to how much provincial government support was necessary for a "proper" request to Westminster—was designed to bypass provincial governments "unreasonably" opposing the proposed federal request. Further, the amending formula proposed by the federal government in the patriation package could have left up to four provincial governments in Atlantic Canada and western Canada on the losing side, or if the proposed referendum route were employed, theoretically 10 provincial governments could have been opposed to an amendment that would nevertheless be implemented on the basis of receiving the requisite voter support in the regions of Canada.[3] Although the threatened unilateralism route was not followed, and the proposed referendum route to constitutional change was not implemented, the actual 1982 Constitution Act left an embittered Québec government on the sidelines crying betrayal over its exclusion from the agreement.

That same 1982 constitutional outcome featured a last-minute erosion of the rights and recognitions that women and aboriginal Canadians thought they had won, that were only restored by applying extreme political pressure on the recalcitrant provincial premiers. The Meech Lake strategy, of course, was based on the thesis that a unanimous collective intergovernmental unilateralism could safely ignore the vehement opposition of Charter supporters and aboriginal elites who thought that their constitutional interests were being ignored or threatened. Had Meech Lake succeeded, accordingly, the vociferous cries of the aggrieved losers would have sullied the outcome in a manner analogous to the absence of the Québec government from the winner's circle in 1982.

Losers remember. They nourish their loss. It may be turned into a rationale for a more sympathetic constitutional round next time, as the "betrayal" of 1982 became the justification for the special Québec round called Meech Lake. It may feed a simmering politics of constitutional resentment, as among aboriginal peoples, after the failure of four aboriginal constitutional conferences was quickly followed by the seeming triumph of the Québec-sensitive Meech Lake Accord, a historical context that makes Elijah Harper's behaviour understandable. Or, as among feminist groups, the memories of past constitutional struggles suggest that without unceasing vigilance one's constitutional interests will be forgotten, ignored, or trampled upon. Thus, the difference between a constitutional "success" and a constitutional "failure" is less than meets the eye. Triumphs are not seen as such by the wounded losers. Defeats are not seen as such by those who opposed a failed constitutional package. Thus, both the category "triumph" and the category "defeat" contain winners and losers, albeit probably in different proportions. As the number of would-be constitutional players increases, the number of losers is likely to increase more than proportionately.

The high probability of failure, and the difficulty of including all of those whose interests might be affected account for the frequent resort to extraordinary stratagems to bring about constitutional change; hence the threatened unilateralism route of the Trudeau Liberals that would have required the British MPs to hold their collective noses and pass the federal government package in spite of the oppositionist tactics of some provincial governments and aboriginal organizations in London; hence also the attempt in the weeks leading up to Meech Lake to throw the media and constitution watchers off the trail by describing the pending Meech Lake meeting as exploratory only, rather than the setting for an attempted constitutional fait accompli.[4] Another indication that desperate constitutional times might require extraordinary constitutional measures was the Parti Québécois strategy decision to hold a referendum to generate and confirm the popular support for a fundamental constitutional change in Québec's status that could then be employed as a bargaining resource in the subsequent negotiations. For the nationalists, the referendum was a humiliating confirmation of the high risk of failure in constitutional reform efforts with which discussion in this section began.

Thus major constitutional reform is not to be undertaken by the faint-hearted, nor by those who seek a guaranteed return on their investment of time and energy; it is not to be undertaken by those who cannot tolerate the possibility that at the end of the day they might both be exhausted and worse off than before they began (the Parti Québécois after the referendum and the 1982 Constitution Act), nor by those who do not wish to risk the possibility that the constitutional order itself might be seriously damaged by a failure (as after Meech Lake).

Given these grim lessons, there are only three possible explanations for the quarter-of-a-century-long addiction of Canadians to constitutional reform: an overpowering necessity based on intolerable shortcomings of the existing constitutional order; an optimistic naiveté based on short memories; or the inability to stop a reform momentum that once begun can only be brought to a close by some kind of resolution. The last explanation is the most plausible, supplemented by intermittent doses of naiveté, and, for a handful of the participants, the intolerable nature of the status quo.

A BRIEF REVISIONIST HISTORICAL DIGRESSION

CONSTITUTIONAL EXECUTIVE FEDERALISM:[5]
THE GOLDEN AGE THAT NEVER WAS

The drama of Meech Lake is so recent and our emotional involvement with the roller-coaster of its fluctuating development was so intense that we are in danger of drawing lessons from it that are insufficiently steeped in history. One lesson, that is true in one version but misleading in another, is that Meech Lake was the occasion for the defeat of executive federalism in constitutional matters. The obvious truth of this assertion is that in intent Meech Lake was what Simeon calls a "text-book example of 'executive federalism,'"[6] and that it was administered a staggering rebuff by the varied constituencies of Charter supporters and aboriginal peoples. The correct interpretation of Meech Lake as a repudiation of executive federalism is, however, misleading if it is taken further to imply that prior to Meech Lake Canadians had enjoyed a golden age of executive federalism in constitutional matters. Nothing could be further from the truth.

The successes of executive federalism are found in the normal intergovernmental politics of working an ongoing federal system,[7] not in formally amending the constitution. In fact, the need for a pragmatic executive federalism of every day was justified by our collective inability to keep the constitution up-to-date by amendments. The First Ministers Conference to deal with the Rowell-Sirois Report in 1941 provided great theatre but broke up in disorder without seriously considering the Rowell-Sirois proposals.[8] For half a century, the executive federalism meetings of first ministers were unable to agree on a domestic amending formula, including the high-profile failures of the Fulton-Favreau formula and the Victoria Charter.

The replacement of the Judicial Committee of the Privy Council by the Supreme Court, the admission of Newfoundland, and the adoption of the limited domestic 1949 amending formula were all undertaken unilaterally by the federal government against the opposition of one or more provinces. With respect to the elimination of appeals to the JCPC, St. Laurent simply refused even to consult with the provinces because he knew Duplessis would never agree to such a change.[9] Thus Trudeau's threatened unilateralism in 1980–81, although perhaps unique in the extent of the constitutional changes he proposed, had a distinguished pedigree behind it.

The 1982 Constitution Act, and particularly the Charter, as is noted below, can only be described as a triumph of executive federalism by stretching the truth. Meech Lake, of course, a classic example of an attempt to amend the constitution by the instrumentality of executive federalism, was a catastrophic failure. In sum, the nontrivial amendments achieved by executive federalism in the last half-century are limited to a handful of discrete changes in the welfare field dealing with unemployment insurance and old age and disability pensions.[10] Meech Lake, therefore, should not be thought of as the defeat of an established tradition of constitutional executive federalism sanctified by its positive achievements. Meech Lake is more accurately thought of as a confirmation of the very limited capacity of executive federalism to grapple successfully with constitutional issues, a conclusion in agreement with Dupré's pre-Meech Lake pessimistic assessment of what he labels the " 'constitutional review model' of federal-provincial summitry."[11]

A ROLE FOR THE PUBLIC IS NOT NEW

Meech Lake was defeated because it clashed with the competing constitutional visions of aboriginal peoples, of English-speaking Canadians who identified strongly with the Charter, and of supporters of a strong central government. They made their views known before provincial legislative committees or task forces in New Brunswick, Ontario, and Manitoba, before the hearings of the Special Joint Committee of the Senate and of the House of Commons on the 1987 Constitutional Accord, and also before later separate Senate and House of Commons hearings. Provincial elections in Manitoba, New Brunswick, and Newfoundland replaced Meech Lake-supporting governments with successors who opposed Meech Lake. This legitimated opposition to the Accord by providing leadership to the anti-Meech Lake forces from within the political establishment. By the end of the three-year period in June 1990, dating from the Accord's ratification by the Québec National Assembly, the defeat of the Accord was in tune with public opinion.

As Lowell Murray and the prime minister ruefully observed, this was not at all what they had anticipated. They incorrectly thought that the agreement of 11 first ministers was an irresistible juggernaut that could easily deliver the goods of legislative ratification. As Mulroney reiterated, the first ministers gave their word, their word was their bond, and that was all there was to it.[12] This was, so to speak, an egregious error in understanding. The misunderstanding was many layered.

The first ministers failed to appreciate that the requirement of the 1982 Constitution Act amending formula for legislative ratification within a three-year period was not a simple formality, a mopping-up operation after the real business of getting the agreement of first ministers had been achieved. Under the 1982

18

Constitution Act amending formula the requirement for legislative ratification is a discrete second stage of hurdles that has to be overcome. As well, the organizers of Meech Lake failed to understand that the 1982 incorporation of a Charter of Rights into the constitution changed the constitutional culture of English-speaking Canada by giving various groups linked to the Charter a sense that they were legitimate constitutional actors with stakes in the constitution. More generally, the Meech Lake failure derived from an insensitivity to the potent new symbolic role of the constitution, especially the Charter, in English-speaking Canada. There was also a failure to appreciate the developing constitutional self-consciousness and constitutional ambitions of the aboriginal people, that were partly a by-product of the limited recognitions they had achieved in the Constitution Act, 1982, and of their frustration over the failure of four constitutional conferences from 1983 to 1987 to clarify their rights.

In these ways, the Meech Lake failure was the consequence of an inadequate short-term historical understanding or, slightly differently phrased, of an outdated constitutional theory that had not caught up with post-1982 constitutional realities. In fact, however, the weak sense of history went beyond the inadequate appreciation of the consequences of the Constitution Act, 1982, to a larger failure to appreciate the varied manner in which the public has played a role in constitutional politics since the 1960s.

In the mid-sixties, the Fulton-Favreau formula for constitutional amendment, agreed to at a First Ministers Conference, foundered on nationalist opposition in Québec that saw the formula as a straitjacket hampering Québec's future constitutional ambitions. A few years later, the Victoria Charter constitutional package, fashioned at a First Ministers Conference, also fell by the wayside—again because of Québec nationalist opposition, this time directed *inter alia* to the package's failure to respond to Québec's social policy goals.

In the late seventies, the Parti Québécois assumed that the major constitutional change of sovereignty-association that they sought was not simply a decision for the Québec government to make but required the referendum approval of the Québec people. The referendum campaign was passionate, the outcome deeply divisive, and the referendum question was not a model of clarity. However, the people spoke. Their verdict was negative, and it was respected by those who wished it otherwise.

The subsequent Constitution Act, 1982, and particularly the Charter, as previously noted, was only achieved because of the strong public support for the latter expressed in Special Joint Committee hearings and in poll results that overcame the opposition of most provincial governments to this unBritish repudiation of parliamentary supremacy. So the Charter was achieved in spite of executive federalism, not because of it. Further, both aboriginal organizations and women's groups engaged in massive political mobilization in order successfully to reinstate what they had lost in the final First Ministers Conference. This explains the feminist phrase, "The Taking of Twenty-Eight"[13] used to describe how

19

section 28, the sex equality clause, got into the constitution and was protected from the ambit of the notwithstanding clause.

The Constitution Act, 1982, sanctioned a further breach in executive federalism by its section 37 requirement to hold a First Ministers Conference to discuss aboriginal matters with representatives of the aboriginal peoples. Although the four conferences that were in fact held failed to achieve their objective, they clearly confirmed that pure executive federalism was an insufficiently comprehensive vehicle for the resolution of aboriginal issues that had a constitutional dimension.

These examples of public involvement and direct public influence on constitutional outcomes have been a recurring phenomenon, not an aberration. For 30 years Canadians have gone through a searing experience of constitutional consciousness raising. Thousands of briefs have been prepared and presented to the succession of royal commissions and task forces, parliamentary hearings, and provincial legislative committees that proliferated as Canadians lived through a seemingly unending period of constitutional introspection. To put it differently, it is not only governments that have been involved and have improved their constitutional understanding, but also the citizenry, especially of course the elites of the various groups, such as women, ethnic groups, and aboriginals who have developed constitutional knowledge to sustain their constitutional ambitions.

The nature of the public role has varied. Frequently it has been a blocking role, but that is mainly because the initiating role has been played by governments. Governments have not always welcomed public participation, because it often thwarts their constitutional objectives. The public role is not always incorporated into the process, but sometimes emerges in spite of it, as a reaction to what governments thought was a fait accompli. Occasionally, as in the making of the Charter, there is a clear alliance between one or more governments and an array of supportive interest groups. Normally, this is an attempt by governments to reach outside the circle of first ministers in order to increase their bargaining power in executive federalism. This, of course, was the object of the Parti Québécois referendum, although the assumption was that the subsequent bargaining would be one on one between Québec and Ottawa.

Whatever the nature of the public role, whether solicited or unsought by governments, whether supportive or opposed to the agenda of governments, the public response in the reform process, as in Meech Lake, has been tenacious and influential in the past three decades. It is not, however, a routinized role. It has been expressed in a diversity of ways. That is partly why its extent and significance have not been adequately appreciated.

THE CHARTER AND EXECUTIVE FEDERALISM: AN INEVITABLE CONFLICT

Much of the opposition to Meech Lake came from the varied constituencies of Charter supporters. They objected not only to the substance of Meech Lake, but also emphatically and truculently to the executive federalism process by which it was to be brought about. While much of this opposition was to the particulars of Meech Lake, there was a naturalness, almost inevitability to it, that derived from a larger opposition between Charter supporters and executive federalism that has roots in history and principle.

Initially, this opposition derives from the fact that the Charter is inherently an antifederal instrument, while executive federalism is the classic vehicle for empowering governments to speak for Canadians in terms of their membership in the territorial communities of province and nation. The Charter confronts the territorial identities of federalism with first, a stress on individual citizens, and second, a stress on the varied social categories singled out for specific mention—women, multicultural Canadians, official language minorities, the equality-seekers in section 15, and others. In other words, the Charter does not address Canadians in the language of federalism but in a mixed language of individual rights and nonterritorial social pluralism.

The Charter's message is not however indifferent to the distinction between provincial communities and the coast-to-coast pan-Canadian community. The Charter's message is a Canadian message. The rights it enshrines are Canadian rights. The community of citizen membership that it fosters is the overall Canadian community. It is the Canadianism of the Charter that explains the continuing lesser sympathy for, and the previous opposition to, the Charter by provincial governments. This differential pattern of empathy for the (or a) Charter by the federal and provincial governments is the source of the consistent pattern that emerges from the encounter between the Charter idea and federalism over the past three decades.

Federal government Charter leadership
The drive for a Bill of Rights and subsequently for a Charter were both led by the federal government. For both Diefenbaker and Trudeau this leadership role was a product of the nation-building function they attributed to rights. The 1960 Bill of Rights was the product of Diefenbaker's pan-Canadian one-Canada vision. His political purpose was to reduce the status difference between the British and French founding peoples and other Canadians, those who came to be called "Third Force" Canadians a few years later. The momentum that led to the 1982 Charter was consistently supplied by the federal government after Trudeau entered the Pearson cabinet. Its nation-building political purposes, to restrain centrifugal provincialism, and to keep alive a conception of French Canada extending beyond Québec have been analysed by Peter Russell and others.[14] In the contemporary period, the federal government has generally seen rights as a constitutional bulwark against provincialism.

Provincial government Charter opposition
One of the weaknesses of Diefenbaker's Bill of Rights, its nonapplicability to the provinces, reflected Diefenbaker's recognition that the provinces would not support a constitutional amendment that would apply the Bill of Rights to their jurisdiction. Trudeau encountered similar resistance from provincial governments. Bill C–60 in 1978 was a contorted attempt to have a Charter incrementally extend to the provinces as they individually opted in.[15] Provincial government support for the Charter

from the dissenting provinces was only gained in a tradeoff in which the Gang of Eight got their amending formula into the 1982 constitution package.

Provincial genesis of the notwithstanding clause

The pressure for a Charter-weakening notwithstanding clause came from provincial governments in western Canada, and was reluctantly acceded to by the federal government. Thus far the use of the notwithstanding clause has been restricted to provincial governments. The pressure to eliminate the clause disproportionately comes from federal politicians.

Interest group Charter support in hearings, provincial government opposition among first ministers

In the making of the Charter, a clear pattern emerged as discussion moved back and forth from the intergovernmental executive federalism arena to the public world of parliamentary hearings and interest groups. The initial federal government version of the Charter, emerging out of the 1980 summer of intergovernmental constitutional talks, was weak, reflecting the impact of the recent provincial government antipathy to the Charter on federal thinking. Subsequent pressure in the public arena of parliamentary hearings strengthened the Charter as the federal government realized that it might be better and easier to get strong public support for a strong Charter than limited provincial government support for a weak Charter. When the Charter moved back into the executive federalism arena for the last time, provincial pressure led to the section 33 notwithstanding clause and to encroachments on the rights of women and aboriginal peoples. The limited provincial government support for the Charter was reciprocated by the indifference of the interest groups that supported the Charter to provincial government concerns over the Charter's erosion of parliamentary supremacy.

This pattern of federal initiatives, public support, and the tendency of provincial governments to oppose the Charter sprang from the Charter's political purposes—clearly and specifically to set limits to the capacity of provincial governments to respond to their local situations in ways that offended against the constitutional norm of Canadianism enshrined in the Charter. The Charter was the Liberal government's answer to the Joe Clark definition of Canada as a community of communities. More fundamentally, it was an attack on the compact theory of Confederation that privileged provincial governments and provincial communities—especially the founding four of Ontario, Québec, New Brunswick, and Nova Scotia—as the building blocks of Confederation. As Duplessis used to say, the provinces are the parents and the federal government is the child, and children should not devour their parents. From the perspective of the Charter, the basis of the polity was not provincial governments and provincial communities but Canadian citizens. In the rhetorical language of the Kirby memorandum, the competing positions in the 1980–81 constitutional discussion could be summed up as the federal government's "People's Package" versus the (provincial) "Powers and Institutions Package," in which the Charter was the key component of the "People's Package."[16] At the time, the federal government succeeded in aligning supportive interest groups behind the Charter and against the opposing provincial governments. By the time of Meech Lake, the next generation of Charter supporting interest groups defended the Charter against both orders of government. The Meech Lake clash between Charter supporters and an executive federalism arena attuned to provincial government wishes was, given recent history, virtually inevitable.

THE CHARTER AND MEECH LAKE

While, as already noted, a public role in the constitutional reform process is not new, the public input in 1987–90 was qualitatively different for several reasons:

1) The initial attempt to freeze out the public, that subsequently unravelled, occurred against the backdrop of the 1980–82 exercise in which citizens' groups had unquestionably contributed decisively to the final outcome. Not only did much of the precise wording of the Charter derive from interest group suggestions, but the very existence of the Charter would have been problematic in the absence of strong public support. To some extent, therefore, the Charter came to be seen as their Charter by the many groups involved in its creation, and particular clauses as their clauses.

2) The positive group memories of having had an effect in the earlier process were supplemented by the fact that the Charter made them constitutional stakeholders. Thus the attempt to exclude them in Meech Lake was a constitutional indignity in a way that had been less true of their attempted exclusion in pre-Charter days. In this sense, the Charter delegitimated an executive federalism first ministers' monopoly of the constitutional reform process and legitimated citizen input. These mutually supporting tendencies might have been weakened had it been widely believed that the Charter had powerful and faithful defenders among the first ministers, particularly the prime minister. However, evidence to support this belief was lacking. This failure was viewed as a breach of faith, possibly because it contrasted with federal government leadership in the introduction of the Charter. It was seen as a failure of the federal government to do its duty of speaking for, strengthening, and defending the overall Canadian community of Charter rights holders. The participant impulse, accordingly, was stimulated by a lack of trust in elites.

3) The Charter structured the presentations of those who spoke on its behalf. This degree of consistency or appeal to a common document was much less possible in pre-Charter days when no such focal point existed around which citizen groups could coalesce and structure their constitutional thoughts. In 1980–81, the groups that appeared before the Special Joint Committee brought diffuse constitutional aspirations to their presentations. In 1987–90 they brought a Charter-inspired vision of Canadianism that was hostile to provincial variations in the availability of rights. Such variations were no longer the acceptable by-products of the territorial diversities that federalism reflects and nourishes. On the contrary, they had become violations of the rights of fellow citizens so that a simple appeal to federalism, or the assertion that the use of the notwithstanding clause was constitutionally legitimate, was an insufficient justification.

The everyday political or constitutional importance of the Charter, therefore, is that it gives citizens a Canadian constitutional norm to judge the behaviour of government in other jurisdictions. To put it differently, it psychologically involves all Canadians in the internal affairs of other jurisdictions when Charter rights are involved. Logically, this is more of a constraint on the provincial governments than on the federal government, for involvement in the affairs of fellow Canadians for matters under federal jurisdiction necessarily followed from the simple existence of the federal government and the Canadian community its policies served. For an individual provincial government, however, the Charter created critical external audiences who could now pass legitimate judgement as Canadians on government policies in other provinces. Thus Bourassa's use of the notwithstanding clause to pass his language of signs legislation was not just a Québec matter, but a constitutional issue for Canadians. In rights matters, accordingly, provincial politics is not insulated from external judgements by the division of powers. When Charter concerns are at stake, the watertight compartments of federalism disappear. Accordingly, that the notwithstanding episode gravely weakened support for Meech Lake outside Québec was to be expected.

The Charter's capacity to generate a roving Canadianism is not confined to normal politics, but inevitably inserts itself into the constitutional reform process if it appears that the Charter as such is threatened with a loss of constitutional status, or if particular rights appear to be weakened. The Meech Lake outcome, therefore, is explicable only if we appreciate how the Charter's taking root in English-speaking Canada has major consequences for the constitutional reform process.

The major source of opposition to Meech Lake in English-speaking Canada came from Charter supporters. Both the Manitoba Task Force Report and the New Brunswick Select Committee Report underlined the extent of Charter support in anglophone Canada. [17] For many, it has become the focal point of their constitutional identity, providing a vision of a country whose citizens possess equal rights.

Accordingly, the Charter restricts the range of acceptable constitutional variations in the treatment of the provinces. It sets constraints on what can be offered to Québec by limiting the manoeuvrability of executive federalism in responding to Québec demands for differential treatment. From the Québec perspective, such demands are likely to involve the Charter, for it has not taken root among the Québec francophone majority in the way it has elsewhere. [18] For Québec political elites, the Charter has an especially deleterious impact on Québec's language regime by restricting the choice of policy instruments available to protect a beleaguered linguistic minority. Thus, for the Bourassa government, Meech Lake's distinct society clause was an attempt to escape from the chafing constraints of the Charter. However, the Charter's linkage with the English Canadian conception of citizenship clearly makes it difficult for political leaders outside Québec to convince their citizenry that an asymmetric application of the Charter to Québec and the rest of Canada is sound constitutional policy. The Charter limits the constitutional policy flexibility of the federal government and the other provincial governments in the same way as Québécois nationalism does for Québec premiers.

Thus the anglophone rejection of Meech Lake is simply the rest-of-Canada counterpart of Québec nationalism's earlier rejection of Fulton-Favreau and the Victoria Charter. It is not a rejection of Québec, but the projection of a competing Charter-infused vision of Canada.

THE ABORIGINAL OPPOSITION TO MEECH LAKE

A distinct category of opposition to Meech Lake came from what section 35 of the Constitution Act, 1982, calls the "aboriginal peoples of Canada," defined as including the Indian, Inuit, and Métis peoples of Canada. The complex history that lies behind this aboriginal opposition can only be summarized here.

Six crucial historical developments or conditioning factors are central to the contemporary constitutional politics of the aboriginal peoples:

1)   The defeat of the 1969 assimilationist White Paper on Indian policy by status Indians eliminated one of the historic options in federal government Indian policy, the erosion of special status and the merging of Indians in the general population. [19] Consequently, some kind of special status regime no longer characterized by inferior treatment became the vaguely defined goal of Indian policy. [20]

2)   The constitutional broadening of the indigenous community from status Indians (section 91 (24)) to "aboriginal peoples" significantly enlarged and diversified the population seeking some kind of distinctive constitutional response. Although Inuit (formerly "Eskimos") had been included in the BNA Act definition of Indian since a 1939 judicial decision, [21] the 1982 inclusion of Métis in the new constitutional category "aboriginal" was a major constitutional change. It inevitably meant that the demands of status Indians, possessed of a land base on reserves, and a long history of unique policy treatment would spill over to the Métis. The Inuit, because of their small population, northern location, and historical separateness were clearly a discrete entity, although they too joined in the pressures for self-government.

3)   Throughout the seventies, aboriginal organizations supported by federal funding improved their political skills and enhanced their visibility at a time when stalemate prevailed in federal policy toward status Indians, and the larger category of aboriginal policy was inchoate. Aboriginal organizations aggressively and successfully fought their way into the constitutional reform process and achieved considerable recognition. Section 25 of the Charter guaranteed that its "rights and freedoms shall not be construed so as to abrogate or derogate from any aboriginal, treaty or other rights or freedoms that pertain to the aboriginal peoples of Canada." [22] By section 35 of the Constitution Act, "the existing aboriginal and treaty rights of the aboriginal peoples of Canada are hereby recognized and affirmed," and aboriginal peoples were defined in the way already noted. Section 37 of the Constitution Act also guaranteed the holding of a constitutional conference with an "agenda ... item respecting constitutional matters that directly affect the aboriginal peoples of Canada, including the identification and definition of the rights of those peoples to be included in the Constitution of Canada, and the Prime Minister of Canada shall invite representatives of those peoples to participate in

the discussions on that item." These were remarkable gains and recognitions for indigenous peoples who had long been relegated to the constitutional sidelines. Status Indians did not even get the vote until 1960.

4) Instead of one, four constitutional conferences with aboriginal leaders participating were held. While they failed to spell out aboriginal rights, and in particular to agree on the issue of self-government, the simple fact that they were held confirmed that the aboriginal peoples of Canada were not to be thought of as other Canadians. Their identity and present and future status did not and would not derive from the Charter, [23] but from their several unique historical backgrounds as the first Canadians, especially of course status Indians and Inuit.

The failure of the four conferences, the last of which just preceded the meeting of first ministers at which the Meech Lake deal was struck, angered aboriginal leaders who concluded that their demands had not been taken seriously.

5) Like other minorities, aboriginal peoples are especially sensitive to the symbolism of constitutional documents and of the manner and extent of their recognition or lack of it by those who hold positions of authority in the state. Thus the symbolism of Meech Lake defining Québec as a "distinct society," and "French-speaking Canadians ... and English-speaking Canadians" as constituting "a fundamental characteristic of Canada," but handing out no similar recognition to aboriginal peoples was received as an insult.

6) Finally, aboriginal peoples, especially of course their elites, are sustained in their political goals by their identification with an international movement of indigenous peoples and a supportive international climate. Canadian aboriginal leaders, in fact, are remarkably assiduous in exploiting the international environment in support of their domestic goals.

The preceding can be summed up in the statement that one of the key sets of players in Canadian constitutional politics is now found in the aboriginal peoples of Canada and the organizations that speak for them. Their language, like that of Québec nationalists, is a collective language of nationalism, self-government, sovereignty, and independence, although its applicability to the Métis is problematic.

In the same fashion as the anglophone supporters of the Charter, aboriginal peoples used the various Meech Lake hearings as platforms to protect and advance their interests. By my calculations, approximately 30 organizations and individuals explicitly speaking for aboriginal peoples appeared before the Special Joint Committee of the Senate and the House of Commons and the Charest Committee. [24]

CONCLUSION

The contribution of executive federalism to successful constitutional reform is, at best, limited. Meech Lake, therefore, does not represent the repudiation of a long-established successful practice that has earned the status of a cherished tradition. Further, the involvement of the public in the constitutional reform process, although erratic, and varied in its manner and its impact, has been a recurrent factor in the reform efforts of the last three decades. What was unique about Meech Lake was not the impact of the public, but the tenacity of the unsuccessful effort by the leading governmental players to render the public role ineffectual.

Nevertheless, the public role in Meech Lake did have certain distinguishing characteristics that derived from the Constitution Act, 1982. The Charter and the aboriginal constitutional clauses have generated a greatly increased cast of constitutional players. On the whole these new players, clothed with the legitimacy of constitutional clauses they identify with, express the social, ethnic, and gender cleavages of contemporary Canadian society. So accustomed have we become to seeing a parade of organizations representing women, aboriginal Canadians, and ethnic communities dominate the organized expression of briefs before legislative committees that we are in danger of forgetting that they represent only a particular slice of Canadian society. For example, by my count, and employing the categories used by the New Brunswick Select Committee, the Charest Committee heard 18 organizations speaking for aboriginal peoples, 11 linguistic lobbies, nine for women, six for commercial interests, three for multicultural groups (one of which was the umbrella organization, the Canadian Ethnocultural Council) and two for trade unions. What is striking is the limited participation in this kind of arena of the big battalions of business and labour, at least in terms of numbers of presentations. [25]

These statistics underline the extent to which the challenge confronting the constitution recently has been how to accommodate the federal dimension of our existence—the priority agenda of executive federalism—with the cleavages of an increasingly heterogeneous society whose component parts have highly developed particularistic forms of self-consciousness. The task, succinctly, is to find a constitutional *modus vivendi* responsive to the territorial communities of federalism, represented by governments, to the nonterritorial societal pluralism of the various groups that attach themselves to the Charter, and to the complexities of the aboriginal peoples, not all of whom live in organized communities on a discrete land base. The task is compounded because the executive federalism arena and the public hearings process respond to different segments of the totality whose constitutional synthesis is sought. What Robert Campbell said of Meech Lake reflects the very different mobilization of bias within executive federalism and within the public world of parliamentary hearings. He noted that although provincial government concerns dominated in the closed first ministers' meetings of Meech Lake and the Langevin Building, "these provincial issues and concerns all but disappeared [in the ratification process], pushed to the side as new players finally entered the process and articulated a bewildering and eclectic array of issues: women's rights, multiculturalism, national social programs, native rights, the status of the territories, language issues, the efficacy of the federal government, and so on." [26]

For the student of constitutional politics, observing where we have come from and where we now are, several questions beg for discussion beyond the central issue of the relationship between Québec and the rest of Canada:

1) Is the existing constitutional mobilization of bias, outside of governments, an appropriate counterweight to governments' domination of executive federalism?

In particular, is the minimal presence of capital and labour, business and unions, and the class division of society a deficiency that needs correcting? In the depression of the thirties, discussion flourished on the conflict between federalism and capitalism. In more recent constitutional discussions, concern for the economy has been little short of invisible with the exception of belated high-profile attempts by business organizations whose political bottom line is to favour whatever constitutional agreement will produce stability. The provincial government commission examining Québec's constitutional future has strong business and union representation. A move in that direction by the rest of Canada would be salutary for the next round of constitutional debates.

2)   One of the biases revealed by the Meech Lake process is how the Charter and aboriginal spokespersons have little sympathy for provincial governments. The provincial governments of English Canada, faced with this opposition, were unable to convince their provincial residents of the virtues of a province-strengthening constitutional package. Is the politics of constitutional discussion outside Québec biased against provincialism by the Charter in a way that does an injustice to provincial orientations that are not being tapped?

3)   How good are the democratic and representative credentials of those who speak for women, aboriginals, and others who feature so prominently in legislative forums? Can constitutional lobby groups develop the flexibility that allows some bargaining leeway or is the normal relation between leaders/officers and members such that their role is restricted to a rigid declamatory advocacy?

4)   Even if the answers to the preceding question are positive, what kind of constitution is likely to emerge from the clash of self-interested private organizational actors—who do not and cannot speak for the multiple constitutional concerns of a modern people—and equally self-interested governments? In this constitutional marketplace can we put our faith in an invisible hand that translates the competitive pursuit of constitutional profit into the public good?

5)   Can we continue with a constitutional reform process in which the presence or absence of nongovernmental constitutional actors, the role they play, and the reception they receive seem to result from the tension between governing elites who seek to control and manipulate and the struggle of private groups to be heard and taken seriously. A degree of procedural predictability erring on the side of openness would surely mute some of the rancour and ill-temper that now derives from attempted exclusion, insecurity, and uncertainty.

6)   Is there a role for referenda in our constitutional reform process of the future? An automatic Pavlovian rejection of such a proposal as not the Canadian way should be restrained while we ponder the dismal reality that there is no Canadian way, and that referenda might be a salutary check on the competition between governments and organized interests that otherwise is likely to prevail.

I began this paper with the assertion that federalism is no longer enough. I conclude it with the thought that in the process of constitutional reform we may be driven to conclude that to add up those who speak for federalism, for the Charter, and for aboriginal constitutional concerns does not satisfy the representational requirements of a legitimate process.

Whatever the answer to such questions, the student of the constitutional politics of the future must examine and analyse the new constitutional actors generated by the Charter and aboriginal constitutional clauses with the same rigour that is applied to the study of governments. The constitutional politics of the Assembly of First Nations and of the National Action Committee on the Status of Women deserve some of the attention we have previously devoted to executive federalism, courts, and amending formulas. The organizers of Meech Lake ignored these new constitutional players to their serious detriment. It is an unhelpful form of flattery for scholars to imitate the errors of those temporary office-holders who are our servants.

NOTES

1. Jill M. Vickers, "Majority Equality Issues of the Eighties," *Canadian Human Rights Yearbook 1983* (Toronto 1983), 67.
2. Peter H. Russell, "The Politics of Frustration: The Pursuit of Formal Constitutional Change in Australia and Canada," *Australian Canadian Studies* 6 (1988): 14.
3. The details of the proposed federal amending formula, the changes as it evolved, and the complex process by which it would become part of the constitution are discussed in Alan C. Cairns, "Constitution-Making, Government Self-Interest, and the Problem of Legitimacy," in Allan Kornberg and Harold D. Clarke, eds., *Political Support in Canada: The Crisis Years* (Durham, North Carolina, 1983), 423–28.
4. "PM invites 10 premiers to discuss Québec constitutional proposals," *The Globe and Mail*, 18 March 1987.
5. By constitutional executive federalism I mean the application of the practice of executive federalism to the constitutional reform process, known as First Ministers Conferences on the Constitution. Donald Smiley, who coined the phrase, defined executive federalism as "the relations between elected and appointed officials of the two orders of government in federal-provincial interactions and among the executives of the provinces in inter-provincial interactions." *Canada in Question: Federalism in the Eighties*, 3rd ed., (Toronto 1980), 91. In the following discussion, I apply the phrase executive federalism to First Ministers Conferences on the Constitution held before the phrase became part of the working terminology of Canadian federalism.
6. Richard Simeon, "Meech Lake and Shifting Conceptions of Canadian Federalism," *Canadian Public Policy* 14 supplement (September 1988): S22.
7. Although, even here the record is mixed. "In summary," wrote Donald Smiley a decade ago, "the institutions and processes of executive federalism are disposed towards conflict rather than harmony." *Canada in Question*, p. 116. An excellent discussion based on case studies is provided by Frederick J. Fletcher and Donald C. Wallace, "Federal-Provincial Relations and the Making of Public Policy in Canada: A Review of Case Studies," in Richard Simeon, ed., *Division of Powers and Public Policy* (Toronto 1985), vol. 61 of the research studies of the Royal Commission on the Economic Union and Development Prospects for Canada. Ronald Watts provides a valuable

comparative perspective in "Executive Federalism: The Comparative Perspective," in David P. Shugarman and Reg Whitaker, eds., *Federalism and Political Community: Essays in Honour of Donald Smiley* (Peterborough 1989).

8. Dominion-Provincial Conference, 14–15 January 1941 (Ottawa 1941).

9. Keith G. Banting, "Federalism and the Supreme Court of Canada: The Competing Bases of Legitimation," mimeo, revised, 21 (to appear in a forthcoming Ontario Law Reform Commission volume.)

10. Technically, the 1940 unemployment insurance amendment was not a product of executive federalism, strictly defined, as agreement was reached by correspondence. Paul Gérin-Lajoie, *Constitutional Amendment in Canada* (Toronto 1950), 107.

A brief flurry of amendments emerged from the 1983 First Ministers Conference on aboriginal matters. The prime minister, provincial first ministers, and aboriginal representatives agreed in 1983 to a constitutional amendment requiring "at least two [additional] constitutional conferences" (s.37.1 (1 & 2)) on aboriginal matters. Two additional clauses were added to section 35 by constitutional amendment, clause (3) providing greater certainty to the definition of treaty rights, and (4) guaranteeing aboriginal and treaty rights equally to both sexes. A new section 35.1 committed governments to giving aboriginal representatives the right to participate in the discussion at future constitutional conferences of constitutional amendments made to aboriginal constitutional clauses. Paragraph 25 (b) of the Charter protecting aboriginal, treaty, or other rights and freedoms against derogation or abrogation by the Charter was also strengthened. See Bryan Schwartz, *First Principles, Second Thoughts: Aboriginal Peoples, Constitutional Reform and Canadian Statecraft* (Montréal 1986), passim, for a detailed discussion. With aboriginal representatives present and participating, this was clearly executive federalism with a difference.

Various tidying-up amendments since WWII can be traced in the footnotes to the Constitution Acts, 1867 to 1982, reproduced in Richard J. Van Loon and Michael S. Whittington, *The Canadian Political System: Environment, Structure and Process*, 4th ed. (Toronto 1987), Appendix. Without exhaustive research, it is not possible to tell how many of these were preceded by provincial consultation or were discussed (and agreed to) at First Ministers Conferences. Russell identifies five minor amendments dealing with parliament undertaken by the federal government on the authority of the unilateral federal amending power assumed in 1949. "The Politics of Frustration," 7 and 25, n. 13.

11. J. Stefan Dupré, "Reflections on the Workability of Executive Federalism," in R.D. Olling and M.W. Westmacott, eds., *Perspectives on Canadian Federalism* (Scarborough, Ont., 1988), 247. The components of the "constitutional review model" that impede agreement are succinctly described on pp. 247–48.

12. Graham Fraser, "Premiers who oppose accord 'desire a solution,' minister says," *The Globe and Mail*, 8 January 1990; "Meech discord report rouses PM," *Vancouver Sun*, 8 March 1988; Graham Fraser, "PM says 1982 flaws removed 'flexibility' in Meech Lake talks," *The Globe and Mail*, 13 June 1988.

13. Penny Kome, *The Taking of Twenty-Eight: Women Challenge the Constitution* (Toronto 1983).

14. Peter H. Russell, "The Political Purposes of the Canadian Charter of Rights and Freedoms," *Canadian Bar Review* 61 (March 1983).

15. "[T]he Charter would become part of the Constitution immediately so far as matters within federal competence are concerned, and would become constitutionalized in respect of a province when adopted by that province. The Charter would become an *entrenched* part of the Constitution (and henceforth alterable only pursuant to a constitutional amending procedure) at such time as it is endorsed by a formal process for amendment of the Constitution." Hon. Otto E. Lang, *Constitutional Reform: Canadian Charter of Rights and Freedoms* (Ottawa 1978), 4. (emphasis in original)

16. The "Highlights of the Kirby Memorandum" are reproduced in Appendix 2 of David Milne, *The New Canadian Constitution* (Toronto 1982), 219–37. The same antithesis was repeated by Trudeau in his anti-Meech Lake speeches and writings in which he summed up the constitutional struggles

of the previous two decades as "much more than the struggle between two levels of government. It had been a struggle to establish the sovereignty of the people over all levels of government." Donald Johnston, ed., *With a Bang, Not a Whimper: Pierre Trudeau Speaks Out* (Toronto 1988), 94.

17. Legislative Assembly of New Brunswick, Select Committee on the 1987 Constitutional Accord, *Final Report on the Constitution Amendment 1987* (Fredericton 1989), 42, 44; Manitoba Task Force on Meech Lake, *Report on the 1987 Constitutional Accord* (Winnipeg 1989), 4, 25–7.

18. Some of the factors behind the different responses that had developed to the Charter among the Québec francophone majority and in anglophone Canada by the late eighties are discussed in "The Lessons of Meech Lake," chap. 4, in Alan C. Cairns, *Constitutional Change in Contemporary Canada: Interpretive Essays* (a revised version of the MacGregor lectures delivered at Queen's University, March 1987, publication forthcoming).

19. See Sally M. Weaver, *Making Canadian Indian Policy: The Hidden Agenda 1968–1970* (Toronto 1981) for an excellent case study.

20. Douglas Sanders, "The Renewal of Indian Special Status," in A.F. Bayefsky and M. Eberts, eds., *Equality Rights and the Canadian Charter of Rights and Freedom* (Toronto 1985).

21. *Re Eskimos* [1939] S.C.R. 104.

22. These included "(a) any rights or freedoms that have been recognized by the Royal Proclamation of 7 October 1763; and (b) any rights or freedoms that may be acquired by the aboriginal peoples of Canada by way of land claims settlement."

23. The conflict between the Charter and aboriginal values is sensitively explored in Mary Ellen Turpel, "Aboriginal Peoples and the Canadian *Charter*: Interpretive Monopolies, Cultural Differences," in Michelle Boivin *et al.*, eds., *Canadian Human Rights Yearbook* (Ottawa 1990).

24. *The 1987 Constitutional Accord: The Report of the Special Joint Committee of the Senate and the House of Commons* (Minutes of Proceedings and Evidence, No. 17, 9 September 1987), Appendix "A"; *Report of the Special Committee to Study the Proposed Companion Resolution to the Meech Lake Accord* (the Charest Report) (Minutes of Proceedings and Evidence, No. 21, 8–15 May 1990), Appendix A.

25. *Report of the Special Committee to Study the Proposed Companion Resolution to the Meech Lake Accord*, Appendix A. As organizational names are sometimes ambiguous, another researcher might produce slightly different totals. However, the basic orders of magnitude would not change. To facilitate comparison, I have used the categories employed in the New Brunswick Select Committee *Final Report*, immediately noted below.

Similar trends emerge in the group presentations to other Meech Lake committees. For example, the New Brunswick hearings had the following breakdown, using the Select Committee's own categories: aboriginals 3, linguistic lobbies 6, women 14, commercial 5, multicultural 3, unions 5. New Brunswick Select Committee, Final Report, Appendix F.

Applying the New Brunswick categories to the Manitoba Task Force presentations generates the following: aboriginals 23, linguistic lobbies 3, women 28, commercial 7, multicultural 14, unions 4. Manitoba Task Force, *Report on the 1987 Constitutional Accord*, Appendix A.

The Senate heard from the following in its Committee of the Whole and special Submissions Group hearings: aboriginals 10, linguistic lobbies 4, women 9, commercial 1, multicultural 4, unions 2. Senate of Canada, *Committee of the Whole on the Meech Lake Constitutional Accord, Third Report* (June 1988), Appendices IV and V. The Manitoba and Senate data contain some double counting. The caveat on the precision of the data expressed at the beginning of this footnote bears repeating.

26. Robert M. Campbell, "Eleven Men and a Constitution: The Meech Lake Accord," in Robert M. Campbell and Leslie A. Pal, *The Real Worlds of Canadian Politics: Cases in Process and Policy* (Peterborough 1989), 290.

Forever Amber

THOMAS J. COURCHENE

QUEEN'S UNIVERSITY

With the victory of the NO forces in the 1980 Québec referendum and with Trudeau's promise of "le fédéralisme renouvelé," Canadians and our governments had every expectation that the constitutional signals were finally flashing green. In an important sense they were. In 1982, nine provinces and Ottawa found a way through the constitutional intersection. And with the historic 1987 compromise, the way was set to bring Québec across the constitutional threshold as well. But apparently this is not the Canadian way. We seem to have an incredible ability to ensure that the future of our federation remains continually in the balance. Thus, with "assistance" from all players we engineered Meech Lake through a highly sophisticated kamikaze exercise. Then, in those heady days in Québec immediately following the Meech debacle, it appeared the signals were flashing red: the momentum and the societal cohesion in Québec pointed toward a quick exit. However, this is apparently not the Québec way either. Kahnesatake and Kahnawake burst Québec's sovereignty euphoria, at least for the near term, and combined with the recession and internal politics associated with Québec's Parliamentary Commission imply that Québec will not likely be able to forge a unified nonpartisan position. Hence, as we enter the 1990s we are back, albeit with a more complicated agenda and process, at our familiar constitutional crossroad. Moreover, the signals are also looking increasingly familiar: forever amber.

With this as backdrop, the purpose of this paper is to review the 1980s constitutional record both in its own right and in terms of what it might portend for the 1990s. I am giving a very broad definition to the "constitutional record," specifically those forces internal or external that impinge on federal-provincial, interprovincial, or citizen-state relationships. The principal background material is an appendix table that records and assesses selected events in the 1980s in terms of their implications for this triad of relationships.

In more detail, the first section focuses on the domestic political agenda and its impact on the institutional and constitutional framework. The analysis will be conducted in terms of the three political "mandates" in the 1980s—Trudeau's "Second Coming" and the two Mulroney administrations. Necessarily, this will draw on existing treatises, e.g., Milne (1986) and Simeon and Robinson (1990). The third section of the paper then deals very briefly with the way in which developments in the global economy are likely to influence the evolution of Canadian federalism. In the concluding section these various forces are brought together in order to isolate selected challenges and choices facing us in the 1990s.

DOMESTIC POLITICS AND THE CONSTITUTIONAL FRAMEWORK

TRUDEAU'S "SECOND COMING"

From the perspective of the 1977 block-funding of the established programmes and the Liberals' very generous constitutional proposals of 1978 (which, incredibly, the provinces rejected), Trudeau's "Second Coming" represented nothing less than a complete philosophical reversal. In Trudeau's own words, from a CTV Christmas 1981, interview:

> I think that the turn of the pendulum or the swing back of the pendulum [toward centralism] happened probably sometime between '78 and '81. I don't like to be too partisan, but I think that we had that short period of the Conservative party that was preaching the community of communities and I think it brought forth rather clearly when even Mr. Clark couldn't reach an agreement with Alberta, after he'd given up Loto Canada, after he'd given away the offshore and after he'd been making many other promises to decentralize to that community of communities, I think it became obvious to more and more people that that was going too far and then I began to feel that I had support for stopping the pendulum (quoted in Milne 1986, 23).

And stop the pendulum he did. Virtually the entire Liberal agenda—the National Energy Program (NEP), the intentions to strengthen the Foreign Investment Review Agency (FIRA)[1] and Canadian ownership, the Constitution Act, 1982, the termination of the revenue guarantee, and the "reconditioning" of post-secondary education transfers, the 1984 Canada Health Act, etc.—can be interpreted as deliberate initiatives designed to strengthen the federal presence, power, and visibility not only vis-à-vis the provinces and regions but also with respect to the forces of "assimilation and integration" emanating from south of the border.

Whether one refers to this as "defensive expansionism" following Aitkin (1959) or as the Liberals' "new federalism" (Milne 1986) or the "nationalist-centralist-interventionist agenda" (Courchene 1989), the implications were profound. At the highest level of generalization, by alienating the regions and provinces (the West with the NEP and the Canada Health Act, and Québec with the constitution), the Americans (intended changes in FIRA and the discriminatory features of the NEP), and the business community (galloping deficits and the fear that Canada would, for its anti-U.S. policies, be caught in any U.S. protectionist wave), Pierre Trudeau became, indirectly at least, the "author" of both Meech Lake and free trade. Phrased differently, it was almost inevitable that the Trudeau agenda would trigger powerful countervailing forces. And for the constellation of interests associated with the Free Trade Agreement (FTA), the Trudeau policies were overturned with a vengeance, i.e., well-nigh "constitutionalized" in the Canada-U.S. Free Trade Agreement. But other aspects of the "new federalism" have been anything but overturned. Foremost among these is the Charter which, as Alan Cairns noted as early as 1979 with respect to an early version of the Charter as proposed by the Trudeau government, has not only "democratized" the constitution (by "entitling" new groups such as Natives, the disabled, linguistic minorities, women, multicultural groups) but has also created a "nonterritorial" or pan-Canadian component to constitutional federalism:

> At a more profound political level ... the Charter was an attempt to enhance and extend the meaning of being Canadian and thus to strengthen identification with the national community on which Ottawa ultimately depends for support ... The resultant rights and freedoms were to be country-wide in scope, enforced by a national supreme court, and entrenched in a national Constitution beyond the reach of fleeting legislative majorities at either level of government. The *consequence, and a very clear purpose, was to set limits to the diversities of treatment by provincial governments, and thus to strengthen Canadian as against provincial identities.* Rights must not be dependent on the particular place where an individual chooses to reside (Cairns 1979, 354, emphasis added).
>
> The language of rights is a Canadian language not a provincial language. If the Charter takes root over time the citizenry will be progressively Canadianized (Cairns 1984).

The challenge the Charter poses to the traditional operations of Canadian federalism was highlighted by my colleague John Whyte when he noted that, in a charter-based society, citizen-state relations become "systematized, centralized, uniform, constant, unilateral and direct" while in a federal system they are "diverse, filtered, diluted, subject to mediation and complicated" (cited in Simeon and Robinson 1990, 281–2).

Ironically, however, the Charter is fundamentally offside with respect to the Liberal agenda (although perhaps not with Trudeau's personal philosophy). It is inherently "republicanizing" in the sense of undermining aspects of the essence of parliamentary government by introducing a checks-and-balances component (the courts) fully into our governing machinery. More intriguingly, it is inherently "Americanizing" in the important sense of moving us closer to embracing aspects of the individualism underlying the American creed.[2] Seymour Martin Lipset was correct, in my view, when in a *Maclean's* interview, 30 October 1989, he argued that the Charter, not the FTA, has the greater potential for bringing us into the American orbit and ambit. Evidence of this can be found in the Charter-influenced

35

position adopted by Premiers Wells, Filmon, and McKenna in the countdown to Meech to the effect that no province should have special powers.[3] This is quintessentially American, not Canadian, since asymmetric powers have long characterized our federation and important aspects of asymmetry are central to the Constitution Act, 1867.

Meech Lake may have been the first attempt to adjust to the insertion of the Charter into our governance structure. But it will not be the last, and before full accommodation is achieved the Charter will have touched deeply many aspects of the Canadian psyche including, for example, executive federalism (Courchene 1990a). On this score, David Milne raises an issue or puzzle that promises to be an academic gold mine for historians and political scientists alike: why should an essentially conservative people, with little inclination to distrust governments on principle, have decided to bypass governments and entrust so many of its rights, especially language rights, to judges and not to politicians? (Milne 1986, 52).

The Canadian Economic Union as Catalyst

What was the conceptual and/or operational catalyst that triggered this 1980–84 agenda? The answer, I think, was Chrétien's 1980 "Pink Paper" (*Securing the Canadian Economic Union in the Constitution*).

To attempt to demonstrate this, it is critical to recognize that what was novel about the 1980–82 constitutional round was the inclusion of the concept of the Canadian economic union (henceforth, CEU). Almost immediately, the nature of the bargaining process altered dramatically. Most of the provinces (or perhaps more correctly the provincial premiers) had long been viewing the patriation process as the vehicle by which to enhance their powers. This was especially the case in the spring of 1980, given the victory of the NO forces in the referendum and Trudeau's promise of a "renewed federalism." But the CEU had such potential for centralization (see Simeon 1982–83) and it was so well received by Canadians that the provinces suddenly realized that they would be lucky to escape from the process with their *existing* powers intact, let alone any enhanced powers.

The provinces found themselves in a truly awkward position: to argue their side they had in effect to challenge the free flow of goods, services, capital, and people across provincial boundaries. Not surprisingly, Trudeau made full use of the provinces' dilemma. On the opening day of the televised constitutional conference in the fall of 1980, after each premier had his say, it was the prime minister's turn:

If we look at the agenda ... there are eight items of the twelve where the provinces are either attempting to increase their powers or to reduce the federal ones, and this ... in the most decentralized federal form of government in the world. Now against these eight items ... where the provinces are asking for more power for themselves there is one item, the one called Powers over the Economy [effectively, the CEU issue] where, respectfully we are not asking for more powers for ourselves, the federal Canadian government, we are just asking that the constitution reflect what all of us wish and many of you said you wished—to have in Canada a common economic market (Trudeau 1980, 95).

36

Critical to the constitutional process was that Ontario immediately threw its support behind the federal proposals. History may record this as a nation-building, Canada-first initiative on Ontario's part. However, it is also the case that the introduction of a thorough-going CEU was very much an "Ontario-first" policy (Hudon 1983, Courchene 1989). Recall that this was the very time frame of the projected $210 billion of megaprojects, many of them energy related. A full-blown CEU (e.g., no purchasing preferences on the part of the Alberta government) would ensure full access by Ontario industry to these projects. Moreover, if this could in addition be combined with an overall "buy Canadian" preference, then the benefits to Ontario would be even more significant. Hence, it is perhaps not surprising that Ontario's Industry and Tourism Minister, Larry Grossman, argued just this (i.e., a CEU and a "buy-Canadian" preference) in *Policy Options* in the fall of 1980 and his department issued a formal Ontario position paper (the so-called "Purple Paper") to this effect in 1981. In effect, this would represent at long last the full realization and culmination of Macdonald's 1879 National Policy. The timing could not be more opportune. Moreover, this Ontario-Ottawa symbiosis meant, for example, that intentions designed to put more teeth into FIRA would find Ontario government support, and so on.

To be sure, the CEU acted principally as a catalyst in all this, since Trudeau agreed to *enshrine the right to impede* the CEU (preferential hiring for Newfoundland's offshore and the right to mount indirect taxes in respect of natural resources for the West) and, more generally, backed off the implementation of provisions like enhancing the trade and commerce power in order to cement the constitutional accord in the fall of 1981.[4] Nonetheless, in the context of the 1980–82 environment, the so-called "people's package" (economic rights via the CEU and political rights via the Charter) provided a powerful rationale not only for the constitutional process but also for the entire "new federalism" agenda. For example, Milne offers the following comments with respect to the NEP:

> If the object of the Trudeau government's constitutional strategy was to throw up guarantees and symbols against separatism and regionalism that would only subtly consolidate federal power, its National Energy Program was more directly and boldly centralist. Steeped in intoxicating nationalist rhetoric that challenged both foreign multinationals and "selfish" provincialism in the name of Canadian "patrimony," energy security, and pricing fairness, the policy's primary purpose was the strengthening of the federal state. Just as it had done during the battle over the constitution, the government served up nationalism as a powerful doctrine for rebuilding federal power. Once again, the theory was advanced that the "people's" interests could only be furthered by promoting the Canadian state, by celebrating Canada as it might be expressed through federal instruments and agencies (Milne 1986, 70).

The link also can be made in the fiscal federalism area as well. Under the guise of a "fiscal imbalance" (i.e., the federal government was shouldering too large a share of aggregate government deficits), Ottawa pared back the value of the

Established Programs Financing (EPF) grants by the two tax points that were part of the 1977 block-funding arrangements (and were designed to compensate for the termination of the revenue guarantee). At roughly the same time Ottawa moved, again unilaterally, to "recondition" the 1977 EPF transfers and began to argue that the provinces were "underfunding" post-secondary education. This approach of going over the heads of the provinces and appealing directly to Canadians reached its apex with the 1984 Canada Health Act: in effect, the federal government adopted the role of "guarantor" and, in some areas, ultimate arbitrator for aspects of the provincially run, health-care programmes (Courchene 1984).

Finally, the Liberals' approach to bilingualism and biculturalism whereby English- and French-speaking Canadians can feel at home anywhere in Canada resonates much more with the CEU and the Charter than it does with the "collective-rights" approach to language and culture espoused by successive Québec governments.

However one interprets this constellation of initiatives, it is clear that they represented a dramatic shift in both the traditional attitudes and traditional structures of the federation. As Breton (1985) notes, parliamentary government in Canada accommodates and even encourages these massive pendulum swings. Enter the Mulroney Tories.

MULRONEY I: NATIONAL RECONCILIATION

On 4 September 1984, Canadians resoundingly rejected the "new federalism," admittedly with some help from Prime Minister John Turner. As impressive as the magnitude of the Tory sweep (211 out of 282 or three-quarters of the seats) was its generality (at least 70% of the seats in each region) (Simeon and Robinson 1990, 301). While "national reconciliation" lay at the core of the Tory's campaign message, it is probably more appropriate to portray the message as an attempt at "rebalancing" the federation and, in particular, reaccommodating some traditional elites—business, the Americans and, above all, the provinces.

Rekindling Cooperative Federalism
From Mulroney's Sept Îles campaign speech (6 August 1984):

> Our task is to breathe a new spirit into federalism ... A Progressive Conservative government will be guided by the principle of respect for provincial authority (Simeon and Robinson 1990, 301–2).

From the vantage point of 1980–84, this is, however, really breathing the "old" spirit back into federalism, namely that federalism is first and foremost a relationship among and between governments. This aside, Mulroney certainly acted quickly on this commitment. Interstate (or executive) federalism flourished. Comparing the first year of the Mulroney mandate with the 1980–84 annual average reveals a dramatic increase in "federal-provincial diplomacy": first ministers' meetings (13 v. 5), ministers' meetings (353 v. 82), deputy ministers' meetings (72 v. 45) for an overall total of 438 v. 132 (Milne 1986, 222).

In terms of substance, rather than process, the Mulroney Tories negotiated both the Atlantic Accord and the Western Accord during their first year in office. The Atlantic Accord was particularly illustrative of the new environment: "Despite a unanimous decision from the Supreme Court in March 1984 awarding Ottawa the exclusive right to exploit and develop the offshore, the Mulroney government less than a year later granted to Newfoundland equal management powers, a decisive say on the mode of development on the offshore, and all rights to apply royalties and taxes 'as if these resources were on land, within the province'" (Milne 1986, 99). [5] Likewise, while the Western Accord may not have "gutted" the NEP, it did mark a "retreat of federal interests in the energy field, a reversal of the older policy of slanting federal energy policy towards Ottawa's own narrower state interests, and a joint intergovernmental decision to return oil and gas to the more or less normal operation of the marketplace." (Milne 1986, 112).

The FTA has been viewed as driving the final nail in the NEP philosophy, since it effectively "enshrines" market prices and, therefore, prevents the diversion of western energy rents via "made-in-Canada" prices. This is true. But it does not protect energy rents from the operations of the federal tax-transfer system. Not much political capital is spent in deregulating energy prices in the context of collapsed resource prices, as was the case for the 1985 Western Accord and even the FTA. The real challenge will come if and when energy prices spiral again. At the time of writing, oil is touching $40 a barrel. Should the price continue at this level, all the old pressures for rent-sharing will be rekindled. Other initiatives that qualify as resurrecting cooperative federalism would include ACOA (Atlantic Canada Opportunities Agency) and WDO (Western Diversification Office), both of which represented an increased provincial-regional say in development initiatives.

The FTA

The overt anti-Americanism of the 1980–84 era (sabre-rattling on FIRA, see note 1, and the NEP) became much more problematical in the mid-1980s when the Americans began to run record balance-of-payments deficits. Protectionist sentiment mounted, particularly in Congress, and the fear was that for our earlier sins we would not be exempt from any American "turning-inward." Hard evidence was not long in coming—U.S. trade remedy actions against Canadian steel, fish, softwood lumber, shakes and shingles, fishermen's UI, etc. Moreover, with the dollar dipping at one point below 70 cents, Canadian business was making important inroads in the U.S. market and free trade would "lock in" this market access. The fact that Europe 1992 was already launched and the fears (in this time frame) that it might become "fortress Europe" implied that, alone of the "G7" countries, Canada would not have access to a "domestic" market of at least 100 million. Finally, but not exhaustively, the Macdonald Commission's strong endorsement for a Canada-U.S. free trade agreement found a ready audience both in terms of substance and timing. Relaxing the FIRA provisions was a first step, but the window of opportunity opened for something much more grandiose—the FTA.

In terms of the Tories' policy of "national reconciliation," the FTA was a natural. In one fell swoop, Mulroney catered to all the parties who felt aggrieved by Trudeau's 1980–84 agenda—business, the Americans, and the provinces, particularly Québec (the constitution) and the West (the NEP). Moreover, the Québec-West business axis was fully in line with the Tories' political base. To be sure, Ontario was offside, but Mulroney cleverly isolated this province by including energy in the FTA: Alberta's support for the FTA stiffened in full knowledge that the FTA would prevent Ontario from ever again unloading an NEP on the West. Thus, whereas Trudeau went over the heads of business and the provinces to the people in implementing his agenda, the FTA reverses all this—Mulroney went over the heads of Canadians and appealed directly to business and provincial elites. The result was Canada's first recent election fought on "class lines," with Turner positioning himself and his party fully within the 1980–84 conception and with the traditional "class-party," the NDP, intriguingly relegated to the sidelines.

Meech Lake and Tax Reform

The high point of Mulroney's reconciliation efforts during his first mandate was surely the 1987 Meech Lake Accord. Euphoria prevailed for a while and the Accord was viewed as a historic compromise not just with respect to the Constitution Act, 1982, but also to the Constitution Act, 1867. Since interest centres less in its origins than in its dénouement, discussion of the Meech Lake Accord will come in the next section of this paper.

The Tories launched into a thorough tax reform midway through their mandate. Some of this (base broadening and lowering marginal rates for income taxation) was triggered by the U.S. tax reform. The remainder, essentially the proposed Goods and Services Tax (GST), was designed not only to replace the federal manufacturers' sales tax but as well to shift taxation from income to consumption. For electoral purposes, the Tories split up the overall package, in effect loading all the "goodies" (lower rates, base broadening, and conversion of exemptions to credits) into the first round and leaving the GST to be implemented in their next mandate. Foresight, let alone hindsight, questioned the political wisdom of a two-stage implementation procedure (Carmichael 1988; Courchene 1988).

MULRONEY II: DRIFTING INTO COUNTRY WARP

On November 1988, the Mulroney Tories won the free trade election and by year's end the FTA legislation received royal assent. Thus, as of 1 January 1989, the Tories were in a unique position: the single issue of the election was now behind them and they had a full term in front of them with effectively no *new* electoral commitments. To this point, nearly two years later, they have enunciated no new agenda (this is apparently due in early 1991) and they have instead presided over an unbelievable unwinding of their preexisting agenda, replete with profound implications for federal-provincial, interprovincial, and citizen-state relations, not to mention implications for the Tories themselves with the popular support for the prime minister running roughly at the level of the prime rate.

The Dénouement of Meech

The rise and fall of the Meech Lake Accord is far too complex to be dealt with in any comprehensive manner in the present context.[6] A few comments must suffice. Obviously, the election of Wells, Filmon, and McKenna complicated matters. None of them had signed the original Accord and two of them (Wells and McKenna) campaigned against it. So, too, Bourassa's recourse to the notwithstanding clause in the context of the sign-language legislation (Bill 178) complicated matters. Immediately, Filmon joined Wells and McKenna in opposing the Accord. However, in my view, what eventually stymied the Accord, and what has catapulted Canada into a profound constitutional crisis, was and is the clash of two conflicting views of what federalism and constitutional amendment are all about.

The conflict involved both substance and process. In terms of the latter, I have already noted that the democratization of the constitution via the Charter and the consequent "entitling" of Canadians (individuals and selected groups) increasingly discredited an amendment procedure limited to 11 (male) first ministers. Perhaps the most revealing incident in the whole process was the lavish praise from fellow premiers and the prime minister showered on Ontario's David Peterson (in the televised "second" accord in the late hours of 9 June 1990) for "magnanimously" offering Ontario Senate seats to clinch the "new" accord, while individual Ontarians were, on the whole, adding this initiative to the list of reasons for punishing Peterson at the polls. The Charter had more than taken root in English Canada. It was redefining what English Canada was all about and this redefinition did not include "eleven men ... around a table trading legislative, judicial and executive powers as if engaged in a gentlemanly game of poker" (Deborah Coyne 1987, 8, cited in the Joint House-Senate Committee Report 1987, 130).[7] In a sense, Meech Lake was hoist on its own petard. The essence of Meech was asymmetrical treatment for Québec (the distinct society clause) embedded in a symmetric ratification formula. Under the "equality" thrust of the Charter and the amending formula some provinces simply exercised their equality or symmetry right to defeat the Accord.

In the final analysis, it was Elijah Harper and the Natives that drove the final nail into Meech Lake, but multicultural or women's groups in English-speaking Canada would have done the same had they the opportunity. All first ministers have now recognized that the Meech process was seriously flawed.

Substance is far more complicated. Québec's Meech Lake demands were couched more in symbol than in substance. Given the humiliation attached with the rejection of this approach, the next set of Québec demands will surely be steeped in substance and will embody a conception of Canada in terms of decentralization that will go well beyond what most English Canadians deem acceptable. This is particularly the case given that the current mood outside Québec runs exactly in the opposite direction—toward a strong central government, a uniform application of the Charter throughout the land and, hence, toward a *rescinding* of the notwithstanding clause. However, while concerns about the post-Meech Lake scenarios are admittedly uppermost in some quarters, there are other concerns contributing to the general malaise in the population.

Fiscal-Driven Decentralization

Despite the fact that many non-Québec Canadians tend to look to Ottawa to play a greater role, the reality of the last few years is that the federal deficit and debt burden is driving Canada into unprecedented decentralization. Leading the way is the current two-year freeze in established programmes' financing (EPF) after which growth in EPF payment will be pegged at the growth of gross national product (GNP) minus 3%. Since the financing of EPF is a combination of tax transfers and cash transfers, what this means is that the tax transfer component will progressively account for more of the total transfer. Indeed, estimates suggest that cash transfers to Québec will fall to zero before the year 2000 and those for the rest of the provinces sometime before 2010.[8] Thus the roughly $20 billion of federal transfers will eventually fall to zero. This can be viewed as decentralizing on three counts. First, if the provinces maintain service levels by increasing their taxes, the ratio of provincial to federal taxes will increase. Second, if the provinces react by cutting back these programs or redesigning them, this also would be decentralizing in the sense that these "national" programs will progressively be designed provincially. The third reason is closely related to the second: when the federal cash transfer falls to zero, how does or can Ottawa insist on any standards at all? Less dramatic, but nonetheless significant, are the selected freezes in the 1990 federal budget on the Canada Assistance Plan (for the "have" provinces) and the tightened regulations for unemployment insurance (which, for the poorer provinces, will transfer unfortunate citizens from "federally financed" UI to jointly financed welfare).

All this focuses on "expenditure-shifting" as it were. On the revenue side, the GST invades the sales-tax area traditionally viewed by the provinces as their home turf. Intriguingly, there have been two polar responses to this. On the one hand, Québec has decided that it will integrate its sales tax with the GST (and will collect it for Ottawa and presumably will, at Ottawa's expense, employ Québec civil servants rather than "feds" in the process) and thus will take advantage of the broader base to lower its sales-tax rate. On the other hand, the western provinces, at the Western Premiers' meeting in Lloydminster in July 1990, have argued that the resulting revenue constraints may require that they develop, à la Québec, their own, separate, personal income tax (PIT) system (Western Finance Ministers, 1990). While this initiative has been viewed as a flexing of Western muscle in the post-Meech era, it is significant to note that the 20-page document espousing a separate PIT made no mention at all of Meech. Rather it was driven by the issues and concerns raised above.

In any event, whereas the 1980–84 squeeze on intergovernmental transfers was part of an overall framework to increase federal visibility and enhance national standards, the current squeeze is fiscally driven and, if anything, will lead in the direction of increased and/or enforced provincial autonomy over the design and delivery of the social envelope.

FTA Implications

Somewhat related to this are two implications arising from the FTA. The first of these has to do with the political economy of east-west transfers under increasing north-south integration. As long as trade flowed largely east-west, with Ontario the principal north-south conduit, the second-round spending impacts of interregional transfers generally came to rest somewhere in Ontario. Under full north-south integration for all of Canada's regions, this may no longer be the case. Some of the regional payments imbalances with the centre will now shift south, with the result that the second-round impacts of regional transfers may no longer come to rest in Ontario but rather in, say, North Carolina or California. At a political level, this will surely erode support for these transfers, particularly those that privilege "place" rather than people.

This may or may not be viewed as decentralizing, but what is clear is that sheltering significant regions of the country from market forces is going to become progressively more difficult both economically and politically.

The second implication relates to north-south integration itself. What this means is that the provinces and regions will now pay more attention to their competitive position vis-à-vis their cross-border regions. Thus, the provinces will take umbrage at federal policies that for whatever reason place provincial economies at a disadvantage, north-south. The result may be that the provinces will demand more say in economic policy affecting their region and may imply that wage behaviour across regions will become more diverse, perhaps even to the point of having wages for federal employees based more on regional than national scales.

In economic parlance, all this can be restated as follows: the optimal currency area is no longer the nation but the cross-border regional economies. One implication is that as north-south integration proceeds the appropriate exchange-rate policy will be one that favours fixity over flexibility. To delve into this in any detail (Courchene 1990) would take me too far afield. Suffice it to say that the Québec Chamber of Commerce (1990) submission to the Québec Parliamentary Commission on the province's political and constitutional future devotes considerable time to rethinking the framework for the conduct of monetary policy.

Institutions in Decline

Never has the popularity of a governing party fallen so low. This in itself is raising some major concerns about the nature of representative government. In this progressively information age, where direct democracy (e.g., referenda) is now increasingly feasible and when five years is easily equivalent to several mandates earlier in this century, should there not exist mechanisms for triggering elections or at least mechanisms such as referenda where the government must achieve some minimum level of support (say 25%) to forestall an election? What this would mean is that the nature of "responsible government" would become two-fold: in the normal course of events it would be defined as usual (support of elective representatives), but in abnormal times the "responsibility" would also have to carry over to citizens. What generates these concerns is, of course, the GST debate. Here we have the incredibly ironic situation where the unelected Senate is attempting to reflect the democratic will of the *people* (not the elected representatives). To be sure, this does run counter to parliamentary democracy and perhaps to the spirit of the constitution, but it does not run counter to the formal word of the constitution nor to a more general interpretation of democracy. If the Senate has any moral role in the legislative process, it is precisely at times when a government with 15% national support is attempting to push through a significant measure that roughly 80% of Canadians oppose.

However, for purposes of this paper, the real issue is not the low popularity of the Tories but rather the incredible degree of cynicism that has developed with respect to our traditional institutions of national governance—the House, the Senate, national parties, executive federalism, etc. Some of this began in Mulroney's first mandate (e.g., the CF–18 fighter contract) and was certainly advanced in the more recent budget where Via Rail cuts and military closures were concentrated (perhaps unavoidably, but the issue is perception not reality) in provinces that opposed either or both Meech Lake and free trade (New Brunswick, Newfoundland, and Manitoba). More recently, the appointment of the eight special senators runs directly contrary to the aspirations of the West for Senate reform. This is particularly the case for Alberta, the principal "Triple-E" advocate, since the packing of the Senate is viewed by them as designed to unload the GST on Alberta. One not surprising result is the move toward regional parties, parties that *will* vote their regional (not national party) interests—Reform in Alberta, Bloc Québécois in Québec, and COR in New Brunswick, for example. Note that a decline in the role of national parties and the rise in regional parties is somewhat similar to the earlier suggestion for more direct democracy since the allegiances of the new parties are to the regions they represent and they would bolt from any "governing coalition" on an issue of such importance as the GST.

The second result is that the Mulroney Tories have by now almost completely unwound any "national reconciliation." In terms of the impending constitutional challenges, the timing could not be worse since there is literally no one in the system now who has the moral authority to speak for English (or non-Québec) Canada. [9]

Native Issues
With Elijah Harper in Manitoba and with the fallout from events in Québec in the summer of 1990 (Oka/Mercier), aboriginal rights have now been catapulted to the top of the constitutional agenda, at least for English Canada. As my colleague John McDougall has noted, Canadians are finally coming to the realization that land is to the Natives what language is to the Québécois. However, there is a worrisome undertone to all this, namely that English Canada might be privileging aboriginal rights as an instrument in the ongoing Québec-Canada clash. In this regard, Premier Rae's very strong commitment to meaningful negotiations on aboriginal issues is particularly welcome.

What all this means is that it will be extremely difficult for English Canada even to contemplate consideration of a new set of constitutional demands from Québec unless, among other items, aboriginal rights and issues are an integral part of the package. Meech Lake spelled the end, at least for the foreseeable future, of incremental (single-issue) constitutional change. I doubt whether Québec realizes this or is willing to accept this—yet another challenge for the 1990s in terms of our constitutional future.

GLOBAL DETERMINISM

Thus far, the thrust of the paper has been, implicitly, that the forces driving future change in federal-provincial, interprovincial, or citizen-state relationships are *internal* forces. This is far too narrow a conception. Indeed, I would suggest that the forces of globalization will have more impact on the triad of relationships in the millennium than will internal factors.

Drawing very briefly from other work I have done (1990b), it seems to me that globalization and the telecomputational revolution will affect the role of national governments in at least four ways. Two of these relate to a transfer "upward" of some of the traditional functions of national governments. The first is the growing importance of transnational corporations. Unlike the old multinational corporations that entered countries subject to a host of "commitments," transnationals enter under "national treatment" conditions (i.e., the rules that apply to domestic corporations must also apply to foreign-owned corporations). Moreover, it is the transnationals (i.e., the private sector not the public sector) that are now driving globalization. This has enormous implications. For example, one can no longer meaningfully speak of a "national" production economy. Production is international and this poses major concerns for national welfare states since they were, in general, geared to "national" production machines. Second, and related, national governments are increasingly finding that activities that used to be done at the national level now have to be passed "upward," partly as a countervail to the globalizing transnationals. The Bank for International Settlements (BIS) capital-adequacy rules for financial institutions are a good example. This tendency toward international regulations and international standards is bound to expand and multiply.

The two other forces pass "power" downwards. First, the information revolution is privileging citizens. They are garnering enormous power as a result and this complicates old-style governance (for unitary or federal state alike). One way to view the information revolution is to note that "transmitters" used to control the information flow: increasingly, the "receptors" are in the driver's seat. Second, and more intriguing, globalization is spreading across the world through a network of "international cities." Nothing much has changed over the last decade in the relationship between the federal government in Ottawa and Bonn, except that soon it will be Berlin. But much has altered in the relationship between Toronto and Frankfurt. Yet our international cities (Toronto, Montréal, and Vancouver) are "constitutionless." They are creatures of their respective provincial governments. Given their role as the engines of expansion, this poses jurisdictional problems

45

because Saskatchewan's international city is not in the province and the Maritimes' international city (Boston/New York) is not even in the country.

I shall limit myself to only one implication from all this. In the face of a diminished role in the economic and regulatory sphere for national governments, citizens will increasingly view "sovereignty" as the ability to influence how they live and work and play. One can argue whether this is the role of government at the city or provincial level, but under the existing distribution of powers, it is *not* the national level. Are "distinct societies" the way of the future?

What all this evokes is the McLuhan vision of the "global village," or the "think globally, act locally" slogan of environmentalists. With the emphasis on markets, with the information revolution empowering citizens and with national governments attempting to "federalize," internationally, it is difficult not to view all this as inherently decentralizing.

THE 1990s AND THE CONSTITUTION

From the perspective of 1980, we are almost unrecognizable as a society. The institutions and the compromises that brought us through our first century are now no longer in vogue, let alone tolerated. Meech Lake and its distinct society clause is the best example of this. In an important sense it was rooted in the spirit of the Constitution Act, 1867—a society struggling to maintain its identity in the face of a "sea of anglos" and seeking to secure this through a lot of symbol and a slight extension of existing substance. Implicit, if not explicit, in the Meech Lake process was an olive branch (indeed, a carte blanche) offered by Québec to EBQ (everybody but Québec)—please take advantage of this opportunity to restructure yourselves in your likeness and image so you too can mount a bulwark, should you wish, against the sea of Americans. Where Meech Lake went off the rails is that EBQ never responded to this challenge. There was a period earlier this year when Premiers Filmon, Wells, and McKenna could have utilized their potential Meech Lake veto, *not* to subject Québec to this or that condition, but rather to devise a new deal for EBQ. For reasons elaborated earlier, this did not materialize. The fact remains that Québec was, and still is, profoundly indifferent as to how EBQ restructures itself internally, provided only that Québec acquires certain powers.

My personal view, and really one of the conclusions of this paper, is that this remains the real constitutional opportunity for the 1990s. No province would be happier if this would occur than Québec. Thus, the real challenge facing EBQ is not so much to focus on what Québec wants, but rather to focus on what the rest of us, collectively and individually, want from Canada. If we could settle on this first, then whether or not our goals are consistent with Québec's would be clear cut. If they were, then integration between EBQ and Québec might still be complicated in practice, but not in principle. It is in this sense that the ball is now in our court.

If the above analysis serves as a guide, however, the prospects are not good. In 1980, EBQ was incredibly apprehensive about a Québec referendum. No longer.

Setting the "we've had enough" arguments aside, there are several reasons why this is the case. Foremost among these is the FTA. The prospects of a breakup in 1980 could have been devastating in economic terms: Ontario would have been forced, literally, to plead to be the 51st state. Not so now, since we (presumably) have guaranteed access to the U.S. market. But this works in "boomerang" fashion as well: with guaranteed access to the U.S., why cater to *any* Québec proposals since, in the event of a breakup, we can always mount some sort of free trade agreement with Québec. Everybody in the world is doing this. Thus, the economics of a potential breakup is no longer the critical issue that it was in 1980 for EBQ (more correctly, for Ontario and the West since an independent Québec would pose significant problems for Atlantic Canada).

Having thus set aside the economic issue for EBQ, the major change ushered in by the events of the 1980s is that EBQ has come an enormous way in terms of defining itself: we are a "Charter" nation. As I have elaborated above, at base this is quintessentially American. However, it is appropriate and important to recognize that our *value system* through which the Charter is interpreted remains, thus far at least, quite different from the American creed. But, it is also the case that "life, liberty, and the pursuit of happiness" resonates better with the Charter and the FTA than does "peace, order, and good government." Phrased somewhat differently, whereas Canada was traditionally "goal oriented" while the U.S. was more "means oriented," the Charter is driving us quite dramatically in the direction of "due process" (means), perhaps at the expense of goals. Put yet another way, Québec's approach embodies a collective rights agenda that is not only inherently goal-oriented and resonates well with "traditional" Canadian ways (crown corporations, "place" prosperity, equalization, etc.) but runs directly counter to any individualist or due-process mentality. In turn, this emphasis on due process or appropriate process is unwinding the legitimacy of the Commons, the Senate, and particularly executive federalism, and is finding recourse in regional parties and punishing leaders like Peterson who were actively engaged in "traditional" processes like executive federalism.

One can of course argue that the solution lies in electing a new "group" or in implementing new institutions such as a Triple-E Senate. I do not wish to argue that these are not potential solutions. But it is also critical to recognize that Canada has embarked on a wholly novel and exciting venture, namely integrating a charter society with a parliamentary society. At the underlying philosophical level, the Charter is, as yet, inconsistent with our traditional notion of parliamentary government and is surely inconsistent in its process dimension with executive federalism and particularly with the executive federalism amending procedure. Accommodating these institutional/philosophical conflicts is challenging enough without having them overlaid with proposals from Québec that will surely be seen as seeking special status. But this is our fate in the 1990s.

Two final comments are in order. The first is that under the influence of, among other things, the Charter, the push for a Triple-E Senate and the amending formulas (particularly in Meech but also in the Constitution Act, 1982), there is

47

a view emerging in EBQ that the appropriate conception of constitutional federalism is one that has identical powers across all provinces, i.e., symmetrical federalism. Apart from the fact that this represents an incredibly revisionist view of our 120 years of history, it may be a recipe for disaster. Québec will argue for, and in my view requires, some powers that would be patently foolish to give to all other provinces. Consider manpower or human-capital policy. It may have gone unnoticed, but Québec has long had substantial control in this area and in any set of proposals it probably will want even more control. How does EBQ respond? Symmetry is a nonstarter: no one would suggest that my home province, Saskatchewan, ought to have its own, independent, human-capital policy. One logical response to symmetry is for the West and Atlantic to merge themselves into "regional" provinces: a human-capital policy for Canada West and Atlantic Canada may make sense, but not along existing provincial lines. Thus, if symmetry is to prevail it implies a realignment such that the new provinces have a sufficient economic and population base to meaningfully utilize such powers. Premier McKenna's recent proposal for improved Maritime economic union might be best viewed in this context.

However, this degree of change is unlikely in the near future. Elsewhere (Courchene 1990b), I have argued that there is an alternate approach to the symmetry issue. The first step would be to allow all provinces equal powers (symmetry in principle) but then let EBQ utilize section 94[10] of the Constitution Act, 1867, to "pass upward" some of these powers, either to Ottawa or to an EBQ "super level" (i.e., asymmetry in fact). This is "opting in," in contrast to Québec's "opting out," which generated much of our existing asymmetry and is (apparently) no longer acceptable. I believe that this is more than a gimmick: it incorporates a conscious exercise in constitution making on the part of EBQ and, as important, this procedure is rooted, not in some novel recommendation, but right in the original BNA Act.

The second observation relates to Québec. EBQ will have substantial trouble with the request for greater powers on the part of Québec. After all, isn't this the province that went through not one, but two, societal revolutions since 1960—the Quiet Revolution and what I have referred to as "market nationalism" (Courchene 1989)? Moreover, Québec has gone its own way in terms of tax policy, financial institutions, the role of the "caisse de dépôt," and laws relating to language and culture. And now, thanks largely to Québec, we have the FTA. So the question in EBQ becomes: given that Québec has been able to do *all this under the existing constitution*, how can they be dissatisfied? Do they not already have a version of sovereignty-association, albeit within the constitutional framework? Are not any additional demands really disguised demands for separation, in which case they will be never-ending?

These are indeed critical questions. I have no answers but I do have some responses. First, the fact that Québec was excluded from 1982 was not a major issue for Quebeckers (as distinct from their government), *at that time*. They were engaged elsewhere, developing their entrepreneurial class and information networks in French. Even at the time of Meech Lake, much less than 10% of Quebeckers had any interest in the substance or process. (Moreover, Quebeckers paid much *less* attention to the substance of Meech Lake than did the rest of Canadians.) The Québec government was concerned, however, and I think the reason was that the Charter-cum-constitution had potential for not only restricting future Québec accomplishments on the cultural-socio-economic front but as well for rolling back *existing* accomplishments. With hindsight, even if Québec was excluded from 1982, it would have been useful to "grandfather" the sorts of initiatives that they had been undertaking unless they ran directly counter to the Charter. This has always been my personal rationale for supporting Meech—enshrining the "distinct society" clause would allow Québec to continue its dramatic post-1960 evolution. It is in this sense that Meech was really more about symbol than substance, since it was not immediately evident, even to Quebeckers, *where* and *how* the Constitution Act, 1982, would bite.

But EBQ rejected this symbolism. Now the name of the game has altered dramatically. Québec is forced to restate its case *in terms of substance*. This is going to be difficult for Québec. The tendency will clearly be to cast the net quite broadly. Added to this is the fact that Québec will not want to place itself once again in the Meech Lake position where there is no fallback position. Thus, unlike in Meech Lake, Québec will *not* table a set of *minimal* demands.

My second general comment is that Québec was humiliated by the Meech Lake process. In 1980, Québec said yes to Canada. In EBQ's "referendum" (Meech Lake), EBQ said no to Québec. Earlier, I noted that the FTA among other things implied that EBQ would be less concerned (than in 1980) with an independent Québec. The reverse is also true. The remarkable *épanouissement* of the Québec business sector during the 1980s engendered a sense of confidence among all Quebeckers that they could "go it alone" if EBQ was unresponsive to their concerns.

My last comment in this context is at the heart of the pending Québec-EBQ impasse. The next round of Québec proposals will be driven largely from a business-economic-global perspective, with of course due recognition to language and culture. The cochairmen of the parliamentary committee are (for the Liberals) Michel Belanger, retiring chairman of the National Bank and (for the PQ) Jean Campeau, retiring chairman of the Caisse de dépôt, by far the largest investment fund in the country. They may have differing political ideologies when it comes to the appropriate "constitutional" setting for Québec within North America, but they are unlikely to differ much in terms of the nature of the measures required to ensure that Québec remains viable economically in the FTA and global context. Moreover, Bourassa's own statement on 23 June 1990 was that Québec would not embark on any venture that would endanger the economic livelihood of Quebeckers. Hence, what will emanate from Québec in the new year is an economics-driven agenda.

However, unless things change markedly, our response will be a *sociopolitical response*,[11] conditioned largely by the values of the Charter and provincial symmetry. Canadians are caught in a time warp. English Canada and particularly Ontario, is only now going through its own "Quiet Revolution." Québec knows where it wants to go and is determined to get there, Canada notwithstanding. EBQ is still wrestling with where it wants to go. Part of the problem here is that EBQ, and particularly Ontario, has always been so well-positioned economically that the sorts of global economic concerns that influence Québec elites have never permeated the minds of Ontario citizens. And if they did, this is what Ottawa is for, isn't it? Queen's Park plays nowhere near the role for Ontario-based business that Québec City plays for Québec-based business.

In any event, the underlying message is that it would be a tragedy of monumental magnitude to reject an economics-driven package from Québec on the basis of sociopolitical concerns only to realize a decade or so down the road that British Columbia, too, wants a similar package of "distinct society" proposals because it is fully Pacific Rim oriented and, perhaps, largely Pacific Rim peopled.

In lieu of a formal conclusion, I want simply to reiterate some of the major forces that will be at play in the 1990s. First and foremost, we must be aware of the way that global forces are shaping not only Canada but all nation states. I may be wrong to suggest that these forces imply a declining role for national governments and an increasing degree of consumer and citizen "sovereignty," but I am not wrong to suggest that it is utter folly to swim against the globalization tide. In this context, EBQ may aspire to a stronger role for the federal government, but if this is the case it must be a *different* role than Ottawa has traditionally played. And it behooves EBQ to begin defining this new role now. Elsewhere (Courchene 1990b) I have suggested that one obvious role for government in a globalizing world is to privilege citizens in the pursuit and development of their human capital potential. This is good social policy and it is also effective economic policy since knowledge is increasingly at the cutting edge of global competitiveness.

Second, Québec and Ontario (and perhaps EBQ as well) are at quite different phases of socio-political-economic philosophy. Québec has had its cultural or Quiet Revolution whereas Ontario is only beginning. The challenge here is, somehow, to see the future through all this when evaluating any new constitutional proposals. Third, even if the Charter may be "Americanizing," Canadians not only have a markedly different value system than the Americans but this is an integral part of what defines us as a society. Yet much of this value system has been conditioned over the years by the role of Québec in the federation—regional policy, equalization, multiculturalism. Both the FTA and globalization are exerting enormous pressure on this value system. Before we jettison Québec (and what we will likely perceive as its outlandish demands come spring 1991) we should be sure that we have put in place some mechanisms to anchor these values.

This leads me to the final point of the paper. Observers of the Québec scene have a reasonable sense of the nature of the demands that will emanate from that province over the next year or so—control over manpower, telecommunications, language, culture, perhaps research and development, plus a significant "disentanglement" in terms of overlapping functions, etc. On the surface, the issues in play in EBQ will be "symmetry," the Charter, and centralization-decentralization. However, in order that these proposals can be fully addressed, EBQ must begin the admittedly difficult process of sorting out its own cultural-economic priorities

50

vis-à-vis Québec, the Americans, and the rest of the world and the reference point for all this must be the year 2000 or beyond and not 1990 or 1991. Québec is conveniently providing the window of opportunity for precisely this exercise.

It is unlikely that we shall be so lucky as to have the constitutional lights ever again flash green. Our best hope is to keep our wits about us, to focus beyond the intersection and, when the time is ripe, to "run the amber."

NOTES

* It is a pleasure to acknowledge the many conversations with, and comments from, John McDougall in the preparation of this paper. Robert Young also contributed valuable suggestions.

1. It may seem ironic that although FIRA was established in 1973, it did not become a bilateral issue until 1981. As Leyton-Brown (1985, 33) notes:

   FIRA and the NEP came to be referred to in a single breath for three reasons: first, because of FIRA's apparent association with the NEP; second, because of the cumulative effect of FIRA's recent regulatory practices; and third, because the Canadian government's announced intention of broadening and expanding FIRA's powers in a fashion the United States saw as discriminatory.

   These "intentions" were advanced in the 14 April 1980 Throne Speech and included expanding FIRA's powers to publicize foreign takeover bids, to seek Canadian counterbidders, and to conduct performance reviews of existing foreign-owned companies (Leyton-Brown, 41). Canada eventually backed off these intentions.

2. One important aspect of this is the degree to which the Canadian Supreme Court relies on U.S. decisions in adjudicating cases under the Charter (see Manfredi, 1990).

3. The intent is not to argue that the trend toward provincial equality stems from the Charter. Clearly, the emergence of the principle of equality of provinces can be traced to such events as the return of control over public lands to the western provinces, the evolution of the various amending formulas toward equality and the movement toward a "Triple E" Senate. Milne (1990) traces this evolution of provincial symmetry. The point in the text is that the Charter enhanced this vision of equality, particularly in terms of the opposition to the distinct society clause in Meech.

4. Presumably in order to rectify this, one year to the day after the November 1981 Constitutional Accord, Trudeau launched the Royal Commission on the Economic Union and Development Prospects for Canada. While this (Macdonald) commission's final report did endorse the notion of a Canadian economic union, it did anything but embrace the 1980–84 nationalist, centralist-interventionist agenda. Opting for free trade ran directly counter to economic nationalism and the focus on "people prosperity" rather than "place prosperity" ran counter to the notion of a centralist-interventionist federal government. This is further evidence to the effect that the Trudeau agenda had generated powerful countervailing forces.

5. To be fair, Trudeau's "Second Coming" also took Atlantic Canada's concerns into account. Section 36 of the Constitution Act, 1982 enshrined equalization as well as provisions for equalizing regional opportunities. Moreover, the 1982 Nova Scotia energy accord went some direction toward recognizing Nova Scotia's interests, but nowhere near as far as the Atlantic Accord, especially after taking account of the 1984 Supreme Court decision.

6. For further discussion, see Watts and Brown (1990, chapters 1–3).

7. This provides yet another perspective from which to assess the "rolling of the dice" analogy utilized by Mulroney in the dying moments of Meech.

8. Québec has long received extra personal-income-tax points in lieu of cash transfers for post-secondary education funding. Thus, its cash transfers fall to zero before cash transfers to other provinces.

9. It is not obvious that the federal government could, even in the best of times, legally or constitutionally speak for English Canada since it also represents Québec. As one commentator put it recently, Ottawa speaks for 10 provinces and each provincial government can speak for only one. Thus, there is no formal or legal-constitutional institution that can speak for EBQ (everybody but Québec).

10. Section 94 reads as follows:

> 94. Notwithstanding anything in this Act, the Parliament of Canada may make Provision for the Uniformity of all or any of the Laws relative to Property and Civil Rights in Ontario, Nova Scotia, and New Brunswick, and of the Procedure of all or any of the Courts in Those Three Provinces, and from and after the passing of any Act in that Behalf the Power of the Parliament of Canada to make Laws in relation to any Matter comprised in any such Act shall, notwithstanding anything in this Act, be unrestricted; but any Act of the Parliament of Canada making Provision for such Uniformity shall not have any effect in any Province unless and until it is adopted and enacted as law by the legislation thereof.

Frank Scott argues that the role of this provision was to allow the original non-Québec provinces (and future non-Québec provinces as well) to "centralize" if and when conditions became more favourable (See LaSelva, 1983).

11. To be sure, there may be issues on which a sociopolitical response is fully appropriate. However, what I have in mind here is, for example, an adherence on the part of EBQ to a strong role for Ottawa (in the face of a decentralized Québec agenda) when the thrust of global forces is also decentralizing.

REFERENCES

Aitkin, H.G.J. 1959. *The State and Economic Growth*. New York: Social Science Research Council.

Breton, Albert. 1985. "Supplemental Statement," in Royal Commission on the Economic Union and Economic Development Prospects for Canada, Report, vol. III, Toronto: University of Toronto Press, 486–526.

Cairns, Alan. 1979. "Recent Federalist Constitutional Proposals: A Review Essay," *Canadian Public Policy*. Vol. 5, 348–65.

_____ . 1984. "The Politics of Constitution Making: The Canadian Experience" in K. Banting and R. Simeon, eds. *Redesigning the State: Constitutional Change in Comparative Perspective*. London: Macmillan.

Carmichael, Edward A. 1988. "Tax Reform: The Impact on Government Finances" in E.A. Carmichael, ed. *Tax Reform: Perspectives on the White Paper*. Toronto: C.D. Howe, 75–86.

Chrétien, Jean. 1980. *Securing the Canadian Economic Union in the Constitution*. Ottawa: Ministry of Supply and Services Canada.

Courchene, Thomas J. 1984. "The Canada Health Act and Federalism" in William Watson, ed. *Report of the Policy Forum on Medicare in an Age of Restraint*. Queen's: John Deutsch Institute.

_____ . 1988. "Tax Reform: Impact on Individuals" in E.A. Carmichael, ed. *Tax Reform: Perspectives on the White Paper*. Toronto: C.D. Howe, 11–48.

_____ . 1989. *What Does Ontario Want?* York University: The Robarts Centre for Canadian Studies.

_____ . 1990a. "The Tragedy of the Commons," forthcoming paper from the School of Policy Studies, Queen's University: School of Policy Studies.

_____ . 1990b. "Global Competitiveness and the Canadian Federation," paper prepared for the University of Toronto Conference, "Global Competition and Canadian Federalism," forthcoming.

Coyne, Deborah. 1987. Testimony before the Special Joint Committee of the Senate and House of Commons on the 1987 Constitutional Accord. Issue No. 14, (27 August).

Grossman, Larry. 1980. "Constitutional Renewal Requires a Canadian Common Market," *Policy Options*. (September/October), 9–11.

Grossman, Larry. 1981. *Interprovincial Economic Cooperation: Towards the Development of a Canadian Common Market.* Toronto: Ministry of Industry and Tourism.

Hudson, Raymond. 1983. "Québec, the Economy and the Constitution" in K. Banting and R. Simeon, eds. *And No One Cheered: Federalism, Democracy and the Constitution Act.* Toronto: Methuen, 133-153.

LaSelva, Samuel. 1983. "Federalism and Unanimity: The Supreme Court and Constitutional Amendment," *Canadian Journal of Political Science.* XVI:4 (December), 757-770.

Leyton-Brown, David. 1985. *Weathering the Storm: Canada-US Relations, 1980-83.* Toronto: C.D. Howe Institute.

Manfredi, Christopher P. 1990. "The Use of United States Decisions by the Supreme Court of Canada Under the Charter of Rights and Freedoms," *Canadian Journal of Political Science* XXIII:3, (September), 499-518.

Milne, David. 1986. *Tug of War: Ottawa and the Provinces Under Trudeau and Mulroney.* Toronto: James Lorimer and Company.

_____. 1990. "The Unresolved Struggle for Equality of Provinces," mimeo, Department of Political Studies, University of Prince Edward Island.

Simeon, Richard, and Ian Robinson. 1990. *State, Society and the Development of Canadian Federalism.* Vol. 71. Studies commissioned by the Royal Commission on the Economic Union and Development Prospects for Canada. Toronto: University of Toronto Press.

Special Joint Committee of the Senate and the House of Commons. 1987. *The 1987 Constitutional Accord.* Ottawa: Queen's Printer.

Trudeau, Pierre. 1980. Transcript of the Opening Remarks to the First Ministers Conference on the Constitution, 8-12 September. Ottawa: Document 800-14/083.

Watts, Ronald L., and Douglas M. Brown. 1990. *Canada: The State of the Federation 1990.* Kingston: Institute of Intergovernmental Relations, Queen's University.

Western Economic Finance Ministers. 1990. *Economic and Fiscal Developments and Federal-Provincial Fiscal Relations in Canada.* A report submitted to the Western Premiers Conference, Lloydminster, Saskatchewan, (26-27 July).

APPENDIX TABLE: Political/Economic Factors Conditioning the 1980s Constitutional Climate

Date	March of Events		Federal/Provincial Implications	Interprovincial Implications	Implications for Citizen/State Relationships
	Political	Economic			
Panel A: Trudeau's Second Coming					
Dawn of 1980s	Clark Interregnum	Resource Boom	Clark Tories willing to accommodate West in terms of energy prices (decentralization).	Economic centre of gravity moving west.	Demands rising to share Alberta's rents.
Feb. 1980	Trudeau's second coming		Appeal to Canadians, not provinces. Campaign against Clark's decentralist/privatization agenda.	Ontario lowers boom on Alberta. Premier Davis's words (not premier himself) feature prominently in Liberal campaign.	Final campaign swing through Ontario reveals nationalist/interventionist philosophy. Beginning of rift between business and Ontario government.
April 1980	FIRA proposals in Throne Speech		Beginning of economic nationalism.	Another Ontario-first policy. (Canadians do not have enough confidence to invest outside Ontario.)	Increasing concern by business about anti-U.S. policy.
May 1980	"No forces win referendum"		Trudeau promises "le fédéralisme renouvelé."	Provinces anticipate enhanced powers under renewed federalism.	Canadians breathe sigh of relief.
Summer 1980	1980–82 constitutional negotiations begin		"Economic Union" (Internal Common Market) provision very centralizing. Provinces caught by surprise.	Provinces view Ontario's support of Trudeau's package to be Ontario-first policy (Economic union gives Ontario access to energy projects). Ontario also argues for protecting domestic market from foreigners.	"Peoples package" (Charter and Economic Union) appeals to Canadians. Represents the beginning of people v. provinces clash that eventually rises to fore at end of decade.
Fall 1980	NEP (Budget)	NEP	Ottawa preempts western energy rents and transfers them to Canadians via lower-than-world prices. Diverts activity (via subsidies) from West to "Canada lands."	Viewed by West as an Ontario-Ottawa conspiracy. Strengthens West (Alberta)-Québec axis, since Québec supports West's position.	Raises issue of whether Canada is about people or provinces. Business community very concerned about anti-American aspects of NEP as well as interventionism (e.g., the "back-in" and the Canadian content provisions). Business concerned further by MacEachen's 1981 budget and its retroactive provisions.

Appendix Table (continued)

Date	March of Events		Federal/Provincial Implications	Interprovincial Implications	Implications for Citizen/State Relationships
	Political	Economic			
1981	Neoconservatism (Reagan, 1981; Thatcher, 1979)		Canada way off side vis-à-vis rest of world.	Resonates more with Canada West than with Ontario (especially in light of NEP).	Astonishing degree of antagonism toward Reagan philosophy, at least as reflected in *The Globe and Mail* op. ed. pages.
April 1981	Reelection of PQ		Stage is set for clash over the constitution.	Québec's embracing of an economic agenda will create substantial problems for other provinces (e.g., financial deregulation).	PQ drops sovereignty, pushes economic agenda. Beginning of Québec's embracing of the international economy, which culminates in overwhelming free trade support in 1988 election.
Fall 1981–Spring 1982	Midnight Accord and Constitution Act, 1982		The "gang of ten" isolates Québec and patriates the constitution. The West is brought in by a resource taxation amendment and the Notwithstanding Clause. Newfoundland obtains provisions for preferential hiring for off-shore employment. Thus, the "economic union" beginnings of the 1980–82 constitution process are sacrificed to repatriate the constitution, replete with the Charter. Québec invokes notwithstanding clause for all its legislation and withdraws from all further constitutional conferences.	Amending formula for most items is 7 provinces and 50% of population plus federal government. Québec "loses" veto here. However, for certain items, unanimity is required. This advances the concept of provincial equality (symmetry).	The constitution is "democratized." Aboriginals, linguistic minorities, multicultural groups, women (gender equality) have rights enshrined via Charter. Most significant constitutional change since Confederation. Flags fly at half-mast in Québec City, but Québec citizens largely indifferent, pursuing "market nationalism."
1981+		1981–82 recession and then auto-led recovery in Ontario and collapse of energy and raw material prices.	Interest rates peak at over 20% in depths of recession. Federal deficit mushrooms. The 6 and 5 programme initiated. Ottawa pares back transfers to provinces.	Ontario again king of the castle. Reverses 1970s and early 1980s where resource provinces acquired power. West falls on hard times.	Severity of recession increases citizen attachment to transfer system.

Appendix Table (continued)

Date	March of Events		Federal/Provincial Implications	Interprovincial Implications	Implications for Citizen/State Relationships
	Political	Economic			
1984	Canada Health Act		Arguably, the apex of Trudeau centralization. Ottawa will control standards and aspects of medicare. Unanimous Commons support, despite opposition of several provinces.	Several provinces incensed. Lays groundwork for spending power provision in Meech Lake.	Triumph for "national programmes." Citizens ignore constitution and look to Ottawa, not provinces, for maintenance of social programmes.
1984+		Record U.S. Twin Deficits (fiscal and trade)	Concern over fiscal deficits does not spread to Canada. Will create problems later. Fall in Canadian dollar enhances our penetration of U.S. markets—fuels U.S. protectionism v. Canada.	Ontario "spends" fiscal dividend unlike Alberta in '70s which banked its fiscal dividend in the Heritage Fund. Later, this forced the Bank of Canada to use high interest rates across Canada to control "Ontario" inflation.	Record balance of payments deficits leads to protectionist sentiment in U.S. Trading status quo in danger particularly in light of U.S. view of FIRA and NEP.
Panel B: Mulroney I.					
Sept. 1984	Mulroney Election		Business agenda (deficits and patching up relations with the Americans) and reconciliation agenda (with West in terms of NEP and with Québec in terms of 1982 constitution). Focus switches away from citizen interests toward provincial interests. Overall agenda is decentralist.	Development of Québec-West axis. But Tories also have 70% of seats in each region. Arguably, Mulroney government proves to be least responsive to Ontario's concerns in this century.	Citizen-state relationships alter dramatically. Tory concern is more with provinces (federalism) than with citizens. And at citizen level, interest centres on business rather than the "ordinary citizen" (as in Canada Health Act). Turner's patronage appointments are major factor in election. Voters anticipate new approach from Tories who deliver, initially, with the appointment of Stephen Lewis as UN ambassador.
1985	Western and Atlantic Accords		Resurrection of cooperative federalism.	Resource provinces gain greater control.	Little reaction, since easy to move to market pricing when resource prices are depressed.

Appendix Table (continued)

Date	March of Events		Federal/Provincial Implications	Interprovincial Implications	Implications for Citizen/State Relationships
	Political	Economic			
1985–87	Abortive Aboriginal Constitutional Deliberations		Negotiations on an amendment for aboriginal self-government break down.	Québec not at constitutional table.	Citizen involvement and concern minimal. Aboriginal loss here will reverberate on Meech Lake, although through unanticipated channels (Elijah Harper in Manitoba).
1987	Meech Lake Accord		Unexpected unanimous agreement on integrating Québec fully in the constitutional family. Viewed by Ottawa as historic compromise, not only with respect to 1982, but 1867 as well.	Initially, highpoint of Mulroney's reconciliation efforts. Atmosphere among premiers close to euphoria. Three-year ratification process proves too long to ensure passage. Several provinces initiate hearings.	Initial citizen reaction positive, but not euphoric. As process proceeds, Charter enshrined groups (women, aboriginals, multicultural groups, etc.) gain strength and challenge the legitimacy of a ratification procedure that rests solely within the realm of executive federalism.
1987+	FTA and 1988 Election		Tories sign FTA with U.S. 1988 election on FTA won, thanks to overwhelming Québec support. Opposed by Ontario, PEI, and Manitoba, although business interests deliver much of Ontario in 1988 election. The western provinces, historical free-trade advocates, very lukewarm to FTA, except Alberta. Reflected in election results. FTA transfers aspects of Canadian sovereignty upward to FTA tribunals. As of 1 January 1989 Tories have full mandate with no electoral commitments.	For Québec, FTA is just one more step in direction of "market nationalism." Alberta views FTA as guarantee against another NEP.	1988 election fought on "class" lines. BCNI very active and successful, particularly in Ontario. Surprisingly, NDP not a factor in this "class" conflict. Individual Canadians express concern about social programmes (viewed as essential component of glue that binds our polity).

Appendix Table (continued)

Date	March of Events — Political	March of Events — Economic	Federal/Provincial Implications	Interprovincial Implications	Implications for Citizen/State Relationships
Panel C: Mulroney II.					
1 Jan. 1989		FTA	Emphasis on markets is "decentralizing" in the important sense that all levels of government are constrained. Although the FTA applies largely to the federal government, the provinces will eventually be equally bound. The Supreme Court is likely to be quite intolerant of interprovincial barriers now that there is Canada-U.S. free trade.	Support for the east-west transfer system will likely decline now that economic integration along north-south lines will increase. As north-south integration proceeds, the Canadian regions will likely become less integrated east-west.	The "life, liberty, and pursuit of happiness" of the U.S. constitution resonates more with the FTA than the "peace, order, and good government" rhetoric of the Canadian constitution. Thus, the FTA (by emphasizing markets) and the Charter (by introducing the courts into our parliamentary system) introduce powerful "Americanizing" influences into Canadian politics and governance. The challenge is to maintain a Canadian polity in the presence of a north-south economy.
1987–89	Election of new premiers		New Brunswick (McKenna, Oct. 87), Newfoundland (Wells, April 1989) and Manitoba (Filmon, April 1988) have new premiers. Since they were not signatories to Meech Lake, they do not feel bound by the agreement.	Beginning of provincial split over Meech.	Individual Canadians delighted to find new avenues for combating Meech Lake. Premier Wells, in particular, is literally overwhelmed by anti-Meech Lake "support" from non-Newfoundland Canadians.
1989–1990	Erosion of National Reconciliation		Tories begin process of alienating almost everyone. 1989 budget punishes anti-free-trade provinces (PEI and Manitoba) and anti-Meech Lake province (NB) in terms of military base cuts and Via Rail cuts.	7-3 split develops over Meech.	National debates, such as that over the FTA, inevitably generate opposition. These measures, however, introduced a conception of cynicism, if not vengefulness, on the part of the Mulroney Tories. Opposition is particularly strong in the West (particularly Alberta) which promotes both Senate reform and the Reform party.

Appendix Table (continued)

Date	March of Events		Federal/Provincial Implications	Interprovincial Implications	Implications for Citizen/State Relationships
	Political	Economic			
Dec. 1989+	Bill 178 and the use of the Notwithstanding Clause		In wake of Supreme Court judgment, Bourassa utilizes notwithstanding clause, to promote use of French in terms of commercial signs. Mulroney and other original Meech signatories hold firm to Meech Accord. Begin to speak of "disaster" scenarios if Meech fails.	Reaction in rest of Canada stuns Québec. Manitoba, for example, rethinks Meech policy. Somewhat later, i.e., over Charest Report "Bloc Québécois" is launched, supported passively at least by the Montréal business community.	For citizens, Meech becomes a lightning rod for all manner of concerns about Mulroney Tories. Anti-French sympathies materialize, particularly in Ontario. More substantively, many Canadians and some premiers adopt positions that all Canadians and all provinces ought to be treated equally. Influence of Charter is evident here.
23 June 1990	Meech Lake Fails		"Second Meech Accord" falls apart under pressure from Manitoba (Elijah Harper) and Newfoundland. However, supposed negative capital markets implications of Meech do not materialize. Both Michael Wilson and Premier Bourassa move to calm international capital.	Tumultuous St. Jean Baptiste Day Parade in Québec. Later Bloc Québécois sweeps by-election. Québec constitutes two commissions to propose new constitutional arrangements. Suggests that in future it will deal with "Canada" only on a one-to-one basis. But who speaks for Canada? Ottawa and provinces contemplate their own constitutional commissions.	In a sense, triumph for Charter and "symmetrical" federalism.
Summer 1990	Oka/Mercier		Deflates sovereignty balloon. Raises general question of role of aboriginals in any Québec constitutional alternative. Catapults Native rights into forefront.	Focus is on Québec, but substantial implications for other provinces since most aboriginal claims are outside Québec. In general, citizens outside Québec more tolerant of Native demands.	Extremely complicated impasse, but probably the case that citizens outside Québec become less tolerant of Québec demands, constitutional or otherwise.
1990-		Monetary Policy	High interest rates and an overvalued dollar lead initially to charges that the rest of Canada is fighting the Ontario-triggered inflation. Later even Ontario suffers from tight money.	Québec Chamber of Commerce report to the Québec parliamentary commission on the constitution argues for substantial changes in the structure of the Bank of Canada.	Business increasingly concerned that the overvalued Canadian dollar is converting the FTA opportunity into an economic nightmare.

AFTER MEECH LAKE

Appendix Table (continued)

Date	March of Events		Federal/Provincial Implications	Interprovincial Implications	Implications for Citizen/State Relationships
	Political	Economic			
1990		GST and Senate Appointments	Ottawa pushes GST in spite of overwhelming opposition from provinces and Canadians. Québec finally comes on side in anticipation that it can collect and administer the federal tax. Senate threatens to withhold approval. Mulroney begins stacking Senate.	Packing of Senate stymies Senate reform process. Québec-West axis weakens as Québec supports GST.	Incredible cynicism pervades country. Senate appointments deflate western hopes for a reformed Senate.
1990–		Globalization	Ongoing globalization has substantial ramifications for the future of national governments. Powers transferred "upwards" to transnational enterprises and to supranational governmental bodies and "downwards" to consumers via the information revolution and an emphasis on markets.	Emphasis on markets likely to make regional transfers more difficult in future. Regions likely to become more independent of each other.	As globalization erodes role of national governments, citizens likely to pay more attention to community governments. How one organizes the way in which one lives and works and plays is about all that remains in terms of sovereignty. And for this the local governments are as important as national governments.
Dawn of 1990s			No obvious leader anywhere in English Canada that can command national respect. Spells trouble for dealing with pending Québec proposals. For the first time in constitutional debates the federal government finds itself as a player rather than an umpire since a more decentralized federation is among the range of possibilities.	Québec again withdraws from first ministers conferences. Bob Rae wins Ontario election. Citizen reaction to Meech Lake and executive federalism? Beginning of new approach to politics and policies?	Major conflicts developing. Non-Québec citizens increasingly influenced by Charter and its implications for equal treatment across citizens and provinces. Particularly concerned about the existence of notwithstanding clause. But western premiers, for example, are demanding greater powers. Is federalism a system for "provinces" (Mulroney) or "people" (Trudeau and Charter)? In either of these, the Atlantic provinces are the most vulnerable. Not surprisingly, NB Premier McKenna is now promoting closer economic integration for the three Maritime provinces.

COMMENTARY

ALLAN E. BLAKENEY

UNIVERSITY OF SASKATCHEWAN

One is forced to agree with Tom Courchene that as we enter the 1990s we are back, with a more complicated agenda, at Canada's familiar constitutional crossroad and the signals are looking increasingly familiar—forever amber. The Western Canada Concept of yesteryear has become the Reform Party of today, and the PQ has grown a federal political wing, the Bloc Québécois. But in many ways the situation resembles the late 1970s.

There are differences. We are experiencing even more sharply differing views on how to interpret recent history—Canada's history since the advent of the era of Pierre Trudeau. To continue the literary allusions, we see a rebirth of the Two Solitudes when we review the interpretations put on the events of the 1970s and 1980s.

There is certainly a disposition in western Canada, and I suspect elsewhere in Canada outside Québec, to regard Pierre Trudeau and the massive phalanx of MPs from Québec that he led during the 1979–1982 period as the voice of Québec in federal and constitutional matters. Trudeau's bilingualism initiative is seen as a Québec initiative pressed upon Canada by a federal government with massive support from Québec (74 of the 75 MPs in the 1980 election) and no support from western Canada. (In the 1980 election there were no government MPs from Saskatchewan, Alberta, British Columbia, and the Territories, and only two from Manitoba.)

The government of the province of Québec did not agree to the 1982 constitutional changes. But in Western eyes that was an intra-Québec division, not a Québec-rest-of-Canada division. Until the last cutting of losses during the negotiations of November 1981, an action taken because western provinces did not think they could totally stop the Trudeau initiative adorned as it was with the highly popular Charter of Rights, western provincial governments and most of the MPs from western Canada did everything they could have done to resist the Trudeau-Chrétien initiative. In Western eyes, to characterize the compromise reached in 1982 with the Trudeau-Chrétien juggernaut, supported as it was by a federal Liberal caucus over half of which came from Québec, as an English Canada rejection or, worse still, a "betrayal" of Québec, is surely to put a strange construction on the facts as we understand them.

Many will readily acknowledge that there were two points of view in contention in 1981. It is just that they were not represented by English Canada and Québec, but rather by the Trudeau vision of Québec and the Lévesque vision of Québec. The "nationalist, centralist, interventionist" agenda of Pierre Trudeau, as Professor Courchene describes it, was manifested long before 1980—with Petro-Canada, wage and price controls, the 1973 FIRA initiative, a proposed Charter of Rights in Bill C-60, and other moves. If this was unacceptable to the voters in Québec they did not act that way at the polls. The party of Pierre Trudeau never failed to get a majority of MPs from Québec, and usually a massive one: 1968 – 56 seats; 1972 – 56 seats; 1974 – 60 seats; 1979 – 67 seats; and 1980 – 74 seats.

Many Canadians outside Québec were entitled to believe, did believe, and do believe that the Trudeau vision and the Trudeau actions had very substantial support in Québec. If this circumstance has now changed, we need to deal with that fact but not because of the events of 1981 and 1982. Accommodations will need to be made, but not arising out of any sense of guilt. It was Prime Minister Mulroney's implied assertion that Canadians should accept the Meech Lake Accord to atone for their previous sins that provided part of the ire against the Accord.

In passing I want to agree with Tom Courchene and Seymour Martin Lipset that the Charter will turn out to have a profoundly "Americanizing" effect on Canadian society and will touch deeply many aspects of the Canadian psyche. It may well be that as our society becomes increasingly made up of people from backgrounds other than French or English, we can no longer rely upon the traditional unifying forces in Canadian society and need to have recourse to a new cast of symbols, heroes, and myths, in part enshrined in a Charter of Rights and Freedoms. But we should not be surprised if most people in Québec who have their own symbols, heroes, and myths are not warmly embracing the new challenger.

To return to my review of past events, I would suggest that we should let the ghosts of the past rest. We are not going to agree on what bodies were buried and who slew them.

The circumstances that gave rise to the demise of the Accord were three:

1) The 1982 amending formula, for the first time in our history, provided for the formal approval of provincial legislatures. This involved, in some provinces, public hearings, and in all provinces, potential delays. There can be no "done deal" when Parliament and 10 legislatures must approve the same text, and the representation of the Accord as a "done deal," unchangeable and carved in stone, provoked a reaction among legislators and especially among some members of the public.

2) The 1982 constitutional changes, particularly the Charter and section 35, created communities who believed they had a particular stake in "their" constitution. Aboriginal groups and women used the legislative approval process to mount their attacks by providing a legislative ratification requirement. They needed more. They needed public support legitimated by hearings or some other public process. They found that support.

3) The content of the Accord overreached itself. It contained a provision of high emotive content, the distinct society clause (which could have been introduced with the consent of seven provinces with 50% of the population) coupled with a change in the amending formula (with much less emotional charge) that required all provincial legislatures to agree. In hindsight it was tactically unsound to couple those two.

The 1982 changes represented a victory for the equality-of-provinces view of the federation over the equality-of-regions concept. Clearly, the equality-of-regions concept permits a veto for Québec on many matters that other provinces (except Ontario) do not enjoy. The provincial equality concept, carried forward into the Accord meant either no Québec veto or an amending formula requiring wholesale unanimity—the very problem that the Victoria Charter (by adopting the regional concept) and the 1982 amendments (by adopting the provincial equality concept with no veto) sought to address. To state the obvious, we cannot have provincial equality, a Québec veto, and a flexible amending formula. At least symmetric federalism cannot have all these attributes.

I predict that the merits of asymmetrical federalism, now widely scorned both by defenders of the federal power like Pierre Trudeau, and by provincial equality decentralists like Robert Bourassa and Don Getty, will be more fully appreciated as the difficulties of avoiding it mount.

But it will not be easy. One notable development of the 1980s has been the rise in the seeming legitimacy of a concept of classic federalism. Until a dozen years ago discussion of both amending formulas and a reformed Senate took place in a context of regional, as opposed to provincial, assumptions. The amending formula discussion switched concepts in 1980–82 and now the discussion of Senate reform is very much centred on equal provincial representation. These changes make it much more difficult to accommodate any arrangement that would apply to Québec but not to all other provinces.

There was a recognition, understood in previous periods of our history, that Canada was not a classic federal state and could not be, because of the English-French duality concept that was also part of the underlying basis or of the Canadian union. This recognition is fading.

Ontario opinion usually recognizes the duality concept as part of what Canada is. The four western provinces, growing in population and wealth, and now exceeding Québec on both counts, have been less willing to acknowledge this reality. The Prairie provinces, with a catalogue of grievances against the industrial heartland akin to Québec's sense of grievance against "les Anglais" are less willing to acknowledge the dualism.

The Prairies and Québec, each in its own way a colony of the English heartland, seem unable to understand the sense of grievance of the other. Each characterizes the other as part of the oppressors—the anglophone majority oppressors or the industrial heartland oppressors, as the case may be. Since each oppression is far less a fact than it previously was, reconciliation should be easier. But it will require time. "Je me souviens" is a motto that is as alive and well on the Prairies as it is in Québec.

I will add a comment on aboriginal issues. In referring to aboriginal issues I think it is important to consider the dynamics of a campaign for recognition and legitimacy by a people who regard themselves as oppressed. I suggest one way to look at such a campaign. Step one of the campaign usually involves identifying a common enemy who would be recognized as such by all members of the group sought to be rallied and energized for the fray. White society generally fills that role. Step two usually paints a vision of a better future couched in charismatic and imprecise language. (One thinks of Martin Luther King calling forth visions of having been at the top of the mountain and of having seen the "promised land.") Step three combines the vision-painting with an agenda of short-term attainable objectives that can be represented to the campaigners as steps toward the better future or the promised land.

In many ways the concept of aboriginal sovereignty is akin to the concept of the promised land—it is imprecise and, I suggest, deliberately imprecise. Each member of the oppressed group can give it his or her own content. This is a legitimate method of campaigning so long as there are also short-term objectives being pursued. Such objectives would include settling unfulfilled treaty land entitlement, or dealing with aboriginal claims to land in the Yukon, or confirming hunting rights in Nova Scotia or fishing rights in British Columbia.

This is not to suggest that aboriginal leaders and Canadian governments should not be attempting to put flesh on the concept of aboriginal sovereignty. It is, however, to suggest that we should not despair if it proves a little difficult to give precise content to an idea that in some respects is a rallying cry for a general campaign rather than a precise agenda for constitutional or legislative change.

I hope to add to what Alan Cairns has elsewhere labelled GNCT, Gross National Constitutional Talk. I refer to the idea of taboos—things that we have tacitly agreed not to discuss.

One that I do not believe he referred to is any discussion of the process of separation. Because there are so many dangers of conflict inherent in attempting to divide a country with a long history of unified existence, consideration should, in appropriate circumstances, be given to the constitutional basis of separation, to its practical basis, to steps in the process, and to the consequences of a failure to agree on the part of the negotiators. In very different circumstances, claims to sovereignty by the Mohawk Nation last summer were met with a total denial by authorities in Ottawa and Québec that the claim had any legitimacy. There should be no inhibition on Canadians in considering what our response might be to any claim to separate statehood by the government of Québec or by any discrete group of Canadians.

COMMENTARY

KATHY L. BROCK

UNIVERSITY OF MANITOBA

Alan C. Cairns and Thomas J. Courchene offer complementary approaches to understanding the record of constitutional reform in the 1980s and its implications for Canadian constitution making in the 1990s. Professor Courchene emphasizes the influence of the changing domestic and global economic environment on the process and content of constitutional changes. Professor Cairns analyses domestic institutional and social dynamics of constitutional change.

Professor Courchene's discussion of the economic realities shaping constitutional reform is illuminating. He explains that in the early 1980s, the inclusion of a concept of the Canadian economic union (CEU) in the patriation package influenced the outcome of the constitutional negotiations. Provinces opposed to the "people's package" tabled by Prime Minister Trudeau were placed in the uncomfortable position of defending their stance against such popular ideas as mobility rights. The CEU provided a compelling reason for Ontario to accept the constitutional package since it would benefit most from a strong national economy.

In the late 1980s and early 1990s, the economic pressures tend toward decentralization. Trends in federal-provincial fiscal relations, the impact of the Free Trade Agreement on east-west transfer payments, and the forces of globalization weaken the rationale for a strong federal government. Québec's demands for more autonomy are consistent with this pattern. Future constitutional reform is likely to conform to these realities.

Professor Courchene goes beyond economics to offer an intriguing account of the demise of the Meech Lake Accord. He attributes provincial opposition to the Accord to a Charter-influenced belief in provincial equality that is more consistent with American practices than the Canadian tradition of asymmetry between the provinces. Future constitutional demands by Québec will be rejected on this basis. He further suggests that the Meech Lake Accord failed because the rest of Canada was unable to respond to the opportunity presented by Québec to restructure itself to stave off American encroachments.

Another explanation of the failure of the Accord could be offered. First, provinces like Manitoba recognize the importance of provincial equality. Still, the Manitoba Task Force Report on the 1987 Constitutional Accord clearly acknowledges the distinct status of Québec as traditionally defined and its need for unique powers. However, the task force objected to an expansion of provincial powers to the detriment of the smaller, have-less provinces. This position, which became the official Manitoba government position, is consistent with the Canadian tradition of respecting rights unless they endanger others. Second, provinces like Manitoba began the process of restructuring presented by Meech Lake by attempting to balance the demands of Québec and other governments with citizen concerns expressed by aboriginal, female, and multicultural Canadians. The task force initiated a dialogue with the rest of Canada that was intended to reflect new social realities. (Due to time and economic constraints, the task force did not hear out-of-province presenters but accepted written submissions instead.) Given the public postures the Accord supporters had assumed, they could not respond. Thus, Meech Lake failed because it appeared to threaten too many other interests in Canada.

Professor Cairns traces the difficulties revealed in the Meech Lake Accord process in attempting to reconcile traditional governmental demands with societal demands. He observes that executive federalism is inadequate as a vehicle for constitutional reform particularly in the post-Charter era where there are new constitution stakeholders. Executive federalism empowers governments, not citizens. The denial of a public role in the Meech Lake process put the government agenda on a collision course with the public's perception of its interests. Professor Cairns concludes that the failure of the Meech Lake Accord underscores the need to find a "constitutional modus vivendi" that is responsive to the federal and provincial governments as well as Charter rights holders and aboriginal Canadians. He concludes by raising six questions to guide this search.

The only quibble I have with the Cairns paper lies within the six questions. Professor Cairns asks "How good are the democratic and representative credentials of those who speak for women, aboriginals, and others?" Earlier, he notes that public hearings are not fully representative of Canadian society but instead tend to be dominated by certain interests. He suggests that referenda might be a viable alternative. These concerns are valid. However, a study of American and Australian referenda reveals that this vehicle for reform is rife with problems. Perhaps a more satisfying answer rests in combining meaningful public hearings with a strengthened role for Parliament and legislatures. The legislators could represent both constituent and broader societal interests while societal groups could represent particular interests that have been overlooked in the past. A balance could be thus achieved.

The Cairns and Courchene papers offer insights into the daunting challenge facing Canadians in the 1990s. Perhaps one of the most important messages is one of the simplest they present: the process of constitutional change is dangerous and requires that we proceed with caution.

COMMENTARY

PETER H. RUSSELL

UNIVERSITY OF TORONTO

I agree with Alan Cairns that constitutional politics are not for the faint of heart. Constitutional politics are about first things. They raise questions of political justice expressed in symbolic terms that arouse deep moral passions. The symbolic terms of constitutional politics touch something more important than money or power—a person's sense of identity and self-worth. And the problem is, of course, that whether we like it or not, Canadians are divided—deeply divided—on those matters. Meech Lake revealed deep divisions between the majority of Quebeckers and the majority of Canadians outside Québec on what constitutional justice requires and on the essential meaning of what it is to be Canadian.

So I am a self-confessed constitutional chicken. I am afraid that by indulging in yet another round of constitutional politics we are more likely to tear our country apart than bind it more firmly together. Further, our absorption in constitutional politics will prevent us from tackling the serious economic and environmental problems that now confront Canada.

Polling data indicate that a majority of Canadians—both within and outside Québec—are also constitutional chickens. They would prefer that our political leaders put the constitution on the back burner for a while and deal with the crushing economic hardship so many Canadians are experiencing. Most of those people are not in this hall today. They could not care less about the constitution. If, despite these people, we plunge into another round of constitutional politics then we must proceed with caution. Those of us like tenured professors who are sheltered from the economic storm should do all we can to find ways of settling our constitutional differences that minimize the additional material hardship inflicted on those of our fellow citizens who are so vulnerable.

But I believe Alan Cairns is right and that, despite the hazards, we Canadians are hell bent for another round—perhaps a decisive round—of constitutional politics. The momentum of events, especially in post-Meech Québec, is carrying us irresistibly in that direction.

So if we must go on with constitutional politics, I prefer to be naively positive (or is that positively naive?) rather than cynical and negative. If we must indulge in constitutional politics we will have to find a new constitutional process—one that is compatible with the democratic ethos of our times. Already we are moving in this direction with the wide public discussion that is now going on prior to any negotiations. If and when we reach the negotiating stage, the First Ministers Conference will have to be replaced by a forum with more democratic legitimacy. So long as we are operating within the rules of the Constitution Act, 1982 (and I think it would be severely destabilizing simply to throw that rule book out), the best bet, I think, is a conference attended by all-party delegations from the constituent legislative assemblies with the results to be ratified by the legislatures.

There has been a good deal of talk about a referendum being the quintessential democratic instrument of constitutional change. Alan Cairns mentions such a possibility. In principle, for reasons of democratic theory, I too favour placing final custody of the constitution directly in the hands of the people. I should add that as a constitutional conservative I also like the practical results of the referendum process—at least in Australia where the people reject nearly all proposals for change.

But the sad truth is that we Canadians are not yet—and may never be—a people. We are at best a collection of communities competing for the status of founding peoples. We have never at the popular level rested the constitution squarely on the consent of the people. We cannot have a Canada-wide constitution referendum until we agree on what kind of a people we are. A simple majority-rule referendum would be utterly unacceptable to at least the Québécois and our aboriginal peoples. If through our existing constitutional machinery we could agree on which majorities in which communities must by referendum approve changes in the Canadian state, we would through that very act have at last agreed on what kind of a people we are. We would indeed have accomplished a social contract and become truly a self-governing constitutional democracy.

But we cannot pretend that we have reached that point yet. If the present Canadian population are to share citizenship with one another under a constitution based on mutual consent, there are some major differences on questions of political justice that must be overcome. One of these concerns the Charter. We Canadians will not be able to go on together if English Canada's "Charter patriots," to use Cairns's term, insist that Québécois must subordinate their aspiration to be a distinct society to the Charter.

I very much doubt that our constitutional differences can be resolved by Tom Courchene's neat ploy of having massive federal powers transferred temporarily to all the provinces, then hoping that all the provinces, except Québec, will, via section 94, hand the powers back to Ottawa. This smoke-and-mirrors method of accommodating Québec's demand for special status will not deliver the symbolic goods sought by the major participants in constitutional politics. Also I would question Tom's advice (which I may have misunderstood) that English-speaking Canada's response to Québec be couched primarily in economic terms. Free trade and Québec's economic self-confidence have removed the economic imperatives of Confederation. If we are to continue as fellow citizens it will have to be because we share some social and cultural ideals.

One constitutional issue that I hope we will tackle immediately and not hold hostage to this heroic quest for a Canadian social contract is aboriginal rights. In the comprehensive land claims process we have—potentially—a means of negotiating directly with aboriginal peoples who have never consented to be part of Canada. Inflicting our European hegemony by force and fraud on these peoples is our greatest constitutional injustice. Through a reformed land claims process we should get at this injustice immediately. By working out a just relationship with aboriginal peoples we Canadians may just find something constitutional we can celebrate together.

CONFLICTING VIEWS OF THE CONSTITUTION AND OF CONSTITUTIONAL REFORM

Representation and Constitutional Reform in Canada

JENNIFER SMITH
DALHOUSIE UNIVERSITY

During its short life, the package of constitutional amendments known as the Meech Lake Accord has been the subject of intense debate.[1] Initially, supporters and opponents were preoccupied with debating the meaning and wisdom of the Accord's provisions. But even before its demise in June 1990, when it failed the unanimity test of the amendment procedure, critics had turned on the process of constitutional change itself.

The failure of the Accord has fuelled criticism of the process. So what is wrong with the process? How valid are the charges levelled by the critics? I will argue that popular criticism of the amendment process is confused and misdirected, and that the real problem is a lack of congruence between constitutional process and the content of constitutional change. This accounts in large measure for the fact that the process leading to the adoption of the Constitution Act, 1982, and the process leading to the failure of the Meech Lake Accord of 1987 were both, albeit in different ways, procedural fiascos.

In the first section of the paper I examine the amending process and the charges made against it. The review of the charges is based on editorials, letters to the editor, and press reports of the opinions of individuals and groups. It is followed by an analysis of the amending process that distinguishes its formal and regulated elements from the informal and unregulated ones. The distinction is largely unnoticed in popular criticism, but it is an important one, and not simply because the informal process is governed by conventional practices that can be adapted more easily to pressure for change than the formal process. The informal process is a proposal-negotiation stage, while the rule-bound formal process is a ratification stage only.

In the second and third sections of the paper, I pursue the idea of reforming the amending process by working out the types of change that seem to follow from the logic of prevailing criticism. As vehicles for this purpose, I have chosen Alan Cairns's analysis of constitutional minoritarianism and Robert Vipond's discussion of the concepts of sovereignty and legitimacy.[2] Both writers offer coherent and original theories about the grievances that arose during the Meech Lake debate against the existing amendment process. In my view, however, their challenging and shrewd arguments do not yield acceptable reform proposals. Cairns, ironically, founders on the rock of representation. Vipond mistakes a crisis of legitimacy for a problem of sovereignty, and as a consequence fails to heed his own stricture on the need to distinguish between the ordinary and extraordinary uses of power. Yet it is in pondering their arguments that I am led to two conclusions. One is that it is necessary to distinguish between a constitutional amendment and a constitutional amendment "package." The other and related conclusion concerns the need to know when to distinguish the *pouvoir constituant* from the *pouvoir constitue*.

THE AMENDING PROCESS AND ITS CRITICS

THE CHARGES AGAINST THE PROCESS

Critics of the constitutional process made a number of points, and the focus of their attack ranged from the identity of the participants to the style of the proceedings. They noticed, for example, that the 11 first ministers are male and white, and concluded that this amounts to a denial of representation of those who are not. In the words of one letter writer, "Through all the Meech Lake coverage I wondered how women and native people felt about the fact that, as usual, a group of white males were (sic) hammering out an agreement to satisfy other white males."[3] The disdain for the closed federal-provincial conference, a staple of executive federalism, flowed from the same hostility to what are perceived to be exclusionary practices. According to a *Canadian Forum* editorial, the failure of the Accord "discredits 'behind closed doors' federal-provincial meetings, so called executive federalism."[4]

Ironically, the *in camera* first ministers' meeting was also under attack because of the style of the deliberations that are supposed to take place there—the style, that is, of horse trading, or, to use the favoured metaphor, of labour-management negotiations. One citizen wrote that the "eleventh-hour, pressure cooker approach" used in labour negotiations was inappropriate in the constitutional context because there were "too many issues and disparate perspectives involved and the stakes were too high." He regretted that a more participatory approach had not been adopted: "A collaborative and comprehensive set of discussions among all parties, scheduled to permit necessary consultations, might have resulted in the airing and resolution of some of Canada's most entrenched conflicts."[5] Whatever labour negotiators might think about this view of their work, the clear implication is that constitutional issues ought to be dealt with in a democratic and elevated way that resists comparison with bargaining, or even with compromise. Thus Premier Wells of Newfoundland was praised as a man of principle precisely because, in the words

70

of one letter writer, he kept his head and stood firmly opposed to the Accord, declining to explore actively a compromise solution. [6]

Taken together, these criticisms yielded the now-familiar lament about 11 men, each armed with a veto, meeting in closed sessions to wheel and deal on constitutional matters. The effect, the critics alleged, was to bar the public from the process. Even the prime minister appeared to support the allegation. Certainly he expressed it as clearly as anyone when he said, "One crystal-clear lesson is that a way must be found to ensure public involvement in the constitutional amendment process ... This explains why we are so anxious to review the amending procedure and the need for public hearings." [7] Assuming for the moment that the public was excluded from the amendment process as applied to the Accord, is that a necessary result of the formula? [8]

THE AMENDMENT PROCESS
Formal requirements
The Canadian amending formula is surely one of the most complicated to be found in any constitution in the world, since there are several formulas and each is applicable to different parts of the constitution. However, there are two important features that these formulas share. One is that they prescribe only ratification and dissent procedures—they do not regulate the way in which proposed amendments are devised. True, it is stipulated that amendment resolutions must be initiated in one of the country's legislative houses (the Senate, the House of Commons, or a provincial Legislative Assembly), and given the conventions of the parliamentary system, this gives a decided edge to the governing party. [9] But there is nothing to regulate the way in which the parliamentary party or its leaders arrive at the proposal. The American constitution, by contrast, outlines alternative methods of proposing amendments. One follows the congressional route, and requires the support of two-thirds of both houses of Congress. The other directs Congress to establish a constitutional convention for proposing amendments on the request of two-thirds of the states, a procedure that has never been used. [10] If it were, it would likely have the effect of taking control of the proposal phase away from Congress.

The second feature common to the formulas is that they require resolutions of assent from legislatures as opposed to governments. This is not a complete break with the past. The conventional practices developed and used between the years 1867 and 1982 required that both houses of Parliament request the British government to place a proposed amendment before the British Parliament. The provinces, on the other hand, had no formal role in the process, and federal consultation with them was confined to the provincial executives. The provincial executives, in turn, did not often consult their respective legislatures. [11] The real change, then, is the inclusion of a formal role for the provincial legislatures.

Cairns argues that the requirement of legislative ratification hardly makes a dent in an otherwise government-dominated process. The amending formula,

71

he writes, is "overwhelmingly an affair of governments" and the "very acme of executive federalism." It relegates citizens to the role of spectators. [12] Cairns does not draw an explicit distinction between the informal and formal phases of the process. That is why, in unintended irony, his account of the amending formula's exclusionary properties relies on the testimony of citizens who appeared before federal legislative committee hearings. The fact of the matter is that the legislative consent requirement propelled the establishment of legislative committees which in turn held hearings on the Accord. These hearings, held at both levels of government at various times over a three-year period, were hardly insignificant affairs. They exposed significant and growing opposition to the Accord outside Québec, and at the same time helped to mobilize this opposition by giving it a place in the process. They also offered critics like former prime minister Pierre Trudeau (who still has a high national profile) an unparalleled opportunity to publicize their position. As elements of a formal ratification process, therefore, the hearings proved to be powerful vehicles of public discontent.

Prior to 1980, legislative committee hearings on proposed constitutional amendments were unheard of practices. But in October 1980 the Trudeau government unveiled its constitutional reform package and then reluctantly agreed to refer it to a Special Joint Committee of the Senate and the House of Commons, initially for only one month. The period was extended to five months, and the joint committee undertook televised and widely reported hearings, listening to the views of individual Canadians, organizations, and interest groups. This set the precedent, referred to above, that was later followed—or at least partly followed—by governments in relation to the Accord. Before the Special Joint Committee had concluded its deliberations, the Trudeau government responded to a few of the suggestions that had been made to the committee in a revised constitutional package. Thus the hearings themselves had a direct effect on the substance of the government's proposals. In the case of the Accord, this was not possible, which is the reason Cairns dismisses the hearings as an interesting or important popular element of the process. But *why* was it not possible?

The answer is obvious as soon as the position of the Trudeau government in 1980 is compared with that of the Mulroney government in 1987. In October 1980, the Trudeau government, having failed to reach agreement on constitutional reform with the provincial governments, decided to proceed on its own—unilaterally. Therefore, it could respond easily to criticisms aired before the joint committee, in precisely the same way that it might respond to suggestions made by a Commons committee studying a government bill. It needed only to consult itself, because at that stage there were no other official parties to the constitutional bill. Much later in the increasingly tortured process, when the Trudeau government had gained the agreement of nine provincial governments to a different version of the bill, attentive groups keenly interested in particular provisions found that the government-legislative committee process in which they could participate had vanished, superseded by the conventions of executive federalism. Thus they had to resort to personal appeals to the principals, the first ministers. [13]

When the Mulroney government presented the Accord to the Canadian public following the Langevin Block meeting of first ministers in June 1987, all the participants were signatories to it. That was the initial success. The Accord was now a quasi-treaty, much like the resolutions produced at the Québec Conference in 1864 were deemed to be a treaty by one of the conference's leading participants, John A. Macdonald. As everyone knows, treaties normally are voted up or down. If one of the parties desires a change, that party has to get all the others to agree, which means starting over again. Thus the treaty is a take-it-or-leave-it proposition that feeds directly into a straight ratification process. The public debates that follow are not less important because they must culminate in a simple, decisive vote. On the contrary, for that reason they are terribly important and highly stressful. But they necessarily exclude the very different kind of debate that takes place in the informal stage of the process, the federal-provincial conference.

Informal arrangements
The ratification phase of the amending process is preceded by an unregulated, informal phase in which an amendment or package of amendments is devised. The parties initiating amendment ideas have always been governments. Whenever the subject matter is such as to require the approval of several governments, they undertake negotiations that often culminate in First Ministers Conferences. Thus the argumentation, discussion, and negotiation take place within the conventional institution that Donald Smiley aptly termed "executive federalism."

In earlier analyses of the First Ministers Conference, Smiley noted a degree of openness in recent constitutional conferences that seemed to stem largely from national televising of the proceedings. He also thought that the increasing number of participants militated against a high degree of secrecy. In any event, he seemed not to be exercised about the secrecy factor.[14] By 1979, he had concluded that executive federalism "contributes to secret, non-participatory, and non-accountable processes of government."[15] He argued that the secrecy and complexity of the processes of executive federalism discourage citizen interest in public affairs, and that the structure of these processes excludes citizen participation because it minimizes the role of political parties—organizations in which citizens can and do participate. Executive federalism is organized to serve the needs of politicians and senior officials, not to consult citizens, and this is as true for intergovernmental meetings on tax matters as it is for meetings on constitutional matters.[16]

Those who argue that citizens were excluded from the amendment process in the case of the Meech Lake Accord clearly have in mind the informal phase of the process—the executive federalism phase. Precisely because it is informal, however, this phase is flexible, and can be adapted to changing expectations. Thus Cairns recommends the establishment of opportunities for citizen participation here, where it is easiest. He suggests that legislative committee hearings be held at the federal level and in all the provinces before and after federal-provincial conferences; that governments publish serious position papers to aid public discussions; and that governments initially restrict themselves to provisional rather than treatylike agreements so that they may respond to public commentary.[17]

Cairns's suggestions are fascinating. By injecting citizens into the executive federalism stage, he would transform it into a legislative federalism stage. This is not likely to make executives happy, but it might make citizens *and* (noncabinet) legislators happy, which is quite a feat. Even more important, however, is the extent to which these processes are designed to garner consensus. If an amendment proposal, particularly one subject to the unanimity rule, went into the maw of consultative legislative federalism and actually came out the other end, the ratification process would be a formality, the chance for a last-ditch effort by a few sore losers.

Elaborate, consensus-building, consultative procedures might take forever, but they are inclusive, civil, and therefore appealing. However, there is a nagging problem: from which citizens is the consensus to be obtained? Under executive federalism, elite consensus means that the 11 governments agree, which means that the 11 political leaders and their respective cabinets and senior officials agree, if that does not cast the net too wide. What is a consensus in Cairns's consultative legislative federalism? Obviously only a limited number of citizens and citizen groups can appear before legislative committees. Which of them gets to be part of the consensus? Members of Charter minorities? If that is the answer, then the problem of representation immediately arises.

THE AMENDING PROCESS AND REPRESENTATION

ELECTORAL REPRESENTATION

Commenting on the criticism aimed at first ministers during the constitutional imbroglio, Stefan Dupré argues that it flows from nonparliamentary ideas of representation. He writes: "The values of parliamentary democracy and the primacy it assigns to party teams are besieged by those of pluralist democracy and the primacy it assigns to organized groups. The values of responsible government are besieged by those of representative government."[18] In the context of parliamentary theory, then, what is the proper role of first ministers in an amending process and how does it relate to the concept of representation?

The first ministers are heads of responsible governments. A.H. Birch identifies three meanings of the concept of political responsibility. It is used: (1) to describe a government that is "responsive to public demands and movements in public opinion"; (2) to invoke notions of duty and moral responsibility; and (3) to refer to the accountability of cabinet ministers, or cabinet as a whole, to an elected house.[19] As Birch points out, the representative system, by which he means the electoral and party systems, is the institutional mechanism of realizing the idea of responsiveness to the public as well as that of accountability to the legislatures. But responsiveness cannot be a simple matter of demand-supply. The representative system exposes a multiplicity of immediate self-interests that issue in conflicting demands. Thus a government's responsiveness is tempered by the need for compromise, policy coherence, and longer-term over shorter-term choices.

74

The meaning of "representative" that is consistent with responsible government hinges on procedural rather than behavioural or personal considerations. Following Birch, political representatives are freely elected members of the legislature. [20] They are not required to act as agents or delegates of their constituents, although for obvious reasons, reelection among them, they will want to advance the interests of their constituents whenever that is possible. Nor are they required to possess the personal characteristics of the people they represent—to "mirror" them, so to speak—although in some instances they would find it difficult to get elected if they did not.

On the basis of the theory of responsible government, then, first ministers are not only legitimate representatives in their own right. They are heads of governments charged with the responsibility of making public policy choices and gaining public support for them, and they can be held accountable for those choices. First ministers can be accused of not being sufficiently responsive to public opinion, or the opinions of some groups. They cannot be accused of being unrepresentative of a given group on the ground that they do not share the characteristics of the members of the group. The idea of mirror representation is not a relevant standard of representation in the system of responsible government. And yet it is precisely the standard now invoked to criticize the first ministers' role in the amending process. Otherwise, the idea that a First Ministers Conference is tantamount to the exclusion of some groups, who are then said to be unrepresented at the table, is unintelligible. But how strong is the standard of mirror representation on its own?

MIRROR REPRESENTATION

Cairns identifies the groups who felt left out of the Meech Lake process as Charter minorities. By this he means groups who consider particular provisions of the Charter of Rights and Freedoms to be relevant primarily to themselves. The list includes women, the disabled, aboriginals, official language minorities, third-force ethnic Canadians, and visible minorities. [21] According to Cairns, one of the great and probably unanticipated changes wrought by the Charter is that it has offered roles to these new constitutional actors. By naming them and conferring rights on them, it gives them constitutional status, and a constitutional interest to defend and augment. It encourages them to develop a unique vocabulary crafted for these purposes. Cairns observes that Charter minorities were all previously marginal in terms of a public identity and an admired social status. As a result, they are not only new to the constitutional play, they are in a competitive and hostile relationship with the established constitutional actors who have dominated it for years. The established actors, of course, represent the very territorially defined majorities against which the Charter is supposed to protect minorities. And that is why they are not regarded by constitutionally defined minorities as trustworthy representatives. According to Cairns, the minorities prefer the mirror concept of representation over a procedural concept based on the partial (to them) justice of numbers alone—majority rule. He writes: "They are suspicious of theories and practices of representation that imply or assert that representatives can be trusted to speak for

75

citizens/constituents when they lack the defining characteristics of the latter."[22]

Surely it can come as no surprise to Cairns or anyone else that a mirror theory of representation, whatever its demerits intellectually, is very convenient from the point of view of leaders of so-called Charter minority groups. Without it, they could hardly make the exaggerated and misleading claims of representation that they do. During the Meech Lake process, repeated use of the language of exclusion made this point painfully obvious. The letter writer who recited the "fact" that women and Native people were simply excluded, provides an example. He did not think to qualify the statement by referring instead to "their" leaders. Cairns is careful to do that and more. He writes: "Those who speak for the various groups that have won a constitutional niche for themselves are deeply suspicious of processes of constitutional change from which they are excluded."[23] He refers to spokespersons and does not say that they are elected. Who are these persons and for whom do they speak?

Let us consider the two groups named by the letter writer. From the point of view of a political strategist, there is a world of difference between them in terms of organization. Since Native peoples possess their own political organizations and have their own ways of deciding who will speak for them, it makes sense to say that they are not represented if their leaders are not present. At least it does so long as there are not individual Natives who prefer to be considered ordinary voters for purposes of political representation. In the case of women, on the other hand, there is nothing remotely resembling this situation. The leaders of women's groups who presented briefs on the proposed Accord before legislative committees, or gave media interviews, do not represent "women" in any procedural, electoral way. They represent themselves, and the members of the particular organization with which they are associated—altogether the smallest fraction of Canadian women. Therefore, the only general claim of representation that leaders of these organizations can make is a mirror claim, which amounts to the idea that they can speak *for* women (on what? women's issues? other issues?) because they *are* women—an idea unacceptable to any independent-minded citizen.

The same argument applies to the other Charter minorities that Cairns lists, with the exception, as noted, of Native peoples. Now none of this matters if these groups are considered to be interest groups, rather like the Consumers' Association of Canada or the Canadian Manufacturers' Association. In that case, consultation is a matter of political prudence—a two-way exercise in education, consensus-building, and legitimacy. Moreover, in the view of some theorists it is an increasingly important task for governments to undertake, particularly if political parties are less important vehicles of representation than ever before. Thus Bernard Crick argues that while parties are still the essence of parliamentary systems and inject some consistency into policy debates, they count for less than they used to. Interest groups, on the other hand, count for more, which is why governments have developed more methodical ways of consulting them before taking major policy decisions. Crick applauds this development because he thinks that modern governments cannot enforce the kind of social and economic policies they need to pursue without a relatively high level of popular support. [24]

Moreover, the background assumption about interest groups is that they pursue a partial interest—their own, at least as they conceive it—on particular issues. Governments, which face many interests, are expected to understand that at best the claims of these groups embody a partial concept of justice. This is a crucial point for citizens who do not identify with any one group. They rely on governments to save them from interest groups, not expose them even further to their claims. As Birch points out, the system of electoral representation is an important institutional check against interest-group influence. Based on territorially defined constituencies, it implies a notion of the public good which governments can use to evaluate competing demands. [25]

THE AMENDING PROCESS AND SOVEREIGNTY

The close consultation with Charter groups recommended by Cairns in relation to the amending process only worsens the situation of Birch's "ordinary unorganized citizen," that is, the citizen who identifies with no particular interest group, Charter-related or otherwise, or the citizen who rejects outright the logic of mirror representation. A fairer course would be to utilize an electoral mechanism that tempers the influence of organized groups and is more consistent with general as opposed to particular claims. The referendum is a ratifying mechanism. The elected constitutional convention, on the other hand, fits the proposal phase of the amending process. Both mechanisms raise the issue of sovereignty, while the convention raises the additional issue of the bounds of an amendment proper.

In his discussion of sovereignty and the Meech Lake Accord, Robert Vipond accepts Cairns's argument that there is a fundamental inconsistency between the amending formula (an affair of governments) and the Charter (an affair of citizens). Using the language of sovereignty, Vipond states that the rights theory of the Charter implies that the people are sovereign, in which case they ought to be involved in the process of constitutional change. [26] He defines sovereignty as the idea of ultimate political authority, or as a statement of a claim about political legitimacy: "If, as Blackstone said, every political system must have some final, supreme, irresistible power that is accountable to no one, then constitution-making is the quintessential sovereign act; to make a constitution is to make a claim about the source, exercise, and end of legitimate political power." [27]

As a matter of fact, nothing could be less applicable to the problem of amending a written constitution than Blackstone's theory of sovereign power, which he defined as the law-making power. Certainly he wrote that in any of the three forms of government—monarchy, aristocracy, democracy—there is "a supreme, irresistible, absolute, uncontrolled authority, in which the *jura summa imperii*, or the rights of sovereignty reside." [28] In Britain's mixed government, that authority was the King-in-Parliament, or the King, Lords, and Commons, the three elements of the supreme legislature, exquisitely balanced: "there can no inconvenience be

77

attempted by either of the three branches, but will be withstood by one of the other two; each branch being armed with a negative power, sufficient to repel any innovation, which it shall think inexpedient or dangerous."[29] But this is a description of the law-making power, and it is part of Blackstone's ode to British government as it had developed in the 18th century. Since there was no written constitution, the King-in-Parliament was both the government and the constituting power, a state of affairs that bears no resemblance to that of a government established under a written constitution. This is absolutely clear when Blackstone contemplates the end of his beloved constitution, that is, the corruption of the legislative power. Following Locke, he argues that this violates the implied or actual social contract on which the government is presumed to have been based. Since there is no formal way to rearrange things, society is thrown into anarchy, and the people are free to constitute a new legislative power. This could happen in Canada only if the written constitution itself were ignored, which means anarchy or civil war.

It is also important to note that Blackstone's account of *de facto* sovereignty in the British constitution contains no real theory of consent and therefore no concept of legitimacy arising out of consent. Of course, on Blackstone's definition, sovereignty is not necessarily bound up with legitimacy at all, which is why Vipond is wrong to suppose that sovereignty is a "shorthand way of expressing a claim about political legitimacy." Blackstone defends the British arrangement on several grounds, of which consent is probably the least important, and attaches only to the election of members of the Commons. The only other mention of consent is in connection with the social contract, and it amounts to nothing more than a convenient presumption of a general consent to the existing order of things that was given long ago.

In my view, Vipond confuses the real issue here, which is legitimacy, with an outdated and inapplicable notion of sovereignty. In a discussion of the founding of the American republic, Judith Shklar argues that popular sovereignty, or the sovereignty of the people, "implies nothing more than the primacy of recognized procedures in lawmaking, even in the sovereign act of amendment."[30] It is the rule-governed political process, not an irresistible power accountable to no one, that yields decisions. Process—not any process, but one that embodies consent requirements—replaces sovereignty. Therefore the will of the people is an appeal to legitimacy, not sovereignty.

Applying Shklar's point to the Canadian case, and in the full realization that Canada is a constitutional monarchy rather than a republic, I would argue that there are two possible crises of legitimacy, only one of which is relevant to the debate about the amending procedure. Violation of the rules can provoke a crisis, but no amending procedures were violated in the Meech Lake round. Something akin to alienation or exclusion also can provoke a crisis, and this involves the extent of the consent requirements embodied in the amendment rules. But how is it possible to determine a sufficient standard of consent, or to know when an old standard will no longer do? It is not enough to point to widespread criticism of existing rules, because that might have died down if the Meech Lake Accord had passed the legislative consent requirements—early. However, surely one guide is the content of an amendment proposal.

CONCLUSION

As Cairns points out, the Meech Lake Accord would have added the "second most significant series of constitutional amendments" to the constitution since Confederation.[31] The Constitution Act, 1982, added the most significant amendments. They are so significant, in fact, that many people persist in thinking that the 1982 act *is* the constitution. The reason lies not so much in the quantity as in the significance of the amendments. Prior to 1982, the British North America Act, 1867, was amended 22 times, and some of the amendments have great practical significance.[32] But they are more or less consistent with the design of the act; they elaborate on the pattern. If the Constitution Act contained only the new amending formula, it would fall into this category. However it contains the Charter as well, and the Charter is not an extension of any theme in the 1867 act. It is an altogether new departure.

Although the Meech Lake Accord was not a new departure, it took sides in a controversy as old as the 1867 act itself. As critics of the Accord pointed out, it pursued or strengthened the decentralist over the centralist impulse of the act. If it had been adopted, it would have set Canada firmly on a decentralist course. The question, then, is whether the new amending formula can bear the weight of such "amendments," because the new formula, like its conventional predecessor, utilizes the services of ordinary, elected officials only. In her discussion of the problems besetting those who found constitutions, Hannah Arendt exposes the argument against proceeding in this fashion, an argument based on the thought that it is unwise of politicians to make their own rules.[33] Certainly political activists see the point. During the Confederation debate itself, the Nova Scotian anti-Confederate, William Annand, argued that Nova Scotians had no objection to sending delegates from the province to a constitutional conference, provided that the resolutions agreed to were sent back to them for ratification. He cited the authority of Locke on the limits of ordinary legislative power: " 'The Legislative cannot transfer the power of making laws to any other hands. For it being only delegated power from the people, they who have it cannot pass it over to others. The *people alone* can appoint the form of the commonwealth, which is by constituting the Legislative and appointing in whose hands it shall be.' "[34]

The need to distinguish between the constituting power (pouvoir constituant) and the constituted power (pouvoir constitue) was summed up neatly by Tom Paine: "The constitution of a country is not the act of its government, but of the people constituting its government."[35] The problem is how to generate a legitimate constitution-making power, and the lesson of the failed Accord is that existing governments will not necessarily do. Following Annand and Locke, there are two ways to go, one of which is to take the proposal stage out of the hands of governments and instead proceed by way of a popularly elected convention, an idea that gained currency during the Meech Lake travails.[36] But the convention concept is fraught with difficulties, not the least being the selection process that is employed. Ideally, such a process would return intelligent, public-spirited and independent-minded citizens. In fact, a selection process designed to keep the political parties at bay would only wind up being taken over by special interests.

The alternate route is to require that constitutional amendment proposals put together by governments be subjected to a popular ratification process. The ratification vote can be adapted to the regionalism of Canadian political life by the requirement of regional majorities as opposed to a national majority. So qualified, this referendum-style vote is still a general one, and in my view this is a major advantage of it. A general vote encourages contending parties to cast their claims in terms of the general interest. It certainly gives citizens an opportunity to vote in the light of their view of that interest. However, populist procedures of this kind are contrary to the Canadian political tradition, and for that reason alone seem to be impracticable. Beset by criticism of the constitutional process, federal and provincial political elites are more likely to find ways of adapting executive federalism to include those who felt left out of the Meech Lake round. But this might not solve the legitimacy problem, especially if the next constitutional round is a major one.

The awful legacy of the Constitution Act, 1982, is the problem of Québec. Although the Québec government objected to the act, it was imposed on the province anyway. Obviously this situation is unstable and casts doubt on the legitimacy of the constitutional order generally, if the term, "legitimacy," is understood in a broad, political sense rather than a narrow, legal one. Certainly the Québec government continues to pursue constitutional change, and whatever the arrangements it eventually proposes, it is inconceivable that they will be minor. For this reason alone the country will face proposals that add up to a new constitutional order. My argument is that unless Canadians embark on constitutional change with the idea of making a democratic beginning, they will not get a beginning at all. If they revert to their habit of elite accommodation, then they are doomed to pursue their own peculiar style of constitutional politics that began with the Royal Proclamation, 1763. It is a style of treating constitutional matters as if they were ordinary political matters and it means unending constitutional restlessness.

NOTES

1. All references are to the Schedule, *Constitution Amendment, 1987* in *A Guide to the Constitutional Accord*, (Ottawa: Government of Canada, 3 June 1987).
2. Alan Cairns, "Citizens (Outsiders) and Governments (Insiders) in Constitution-Making: The Case of Meech Lake," *Canadian Public Policy*, XIV supplement (September 1988); and Robert C. Vipond, "Whatever Became of the Compact Theory? Meech Lake and the New Politics of Constitutional Amendment in Canada," *Queen's Quarterly* 96/4 (Winter 1989).

3. *The Globe and Mail*, 4 July 1990, A16.
4. "Meech and After," in vol. LXVIV, number 791 (July/August 1990), 2.
5. *The Globe and Mail*, 20 July 1990, A16.
6. Ibid., 20 June 1990, A18.
7. Ibid., 11 June 1990, A7.
8. All references to constitutional provisions are in Peter W. Hogg, *Constitutional Law of Canada*, 2nd ed. (Toronto: The Carswell Company Ltd., 1985). Section 49, the last provision of the formula as set out in the Constitution Act, 1982, does require that a First Ministers Conference to review the amending formula be convened within 15 years of the formula's life. See Appendix III, 885.
9. Ibid., section 46, 884–5.
10. C. Herman Pritchett, *The American Constitution*, 2nd ed. (New York: McGraw-Hill, 1968), 36–7.
11. See P. Gerin-Lajoie, *Constitutional Amendment in Canada* (Toronto: University of Toronto Press, 1950), 107, 182–4.
12. Cairns, "Citizens (Outsiders) and Governments (Insiders) in Constitution-Making," S123–4.
13. See Chaviva Hosek, "Women and the Constitutional Process," in K. Banting and R. Simeon, eds., *And No One Cheered* (Toronto: Methuen, 1983), 292–5.
14. Donald Smiley, *Canada in Question: Federalism in the Eighties*, 3rd ed. (Toronto: McGraw-Hill Ryerson, 1980), 98–9.
15. "An Outsider's Observations of Federal-Provincial Relations Among Consenting Adults," in R.D. Olling and M.W. Westmacott, eds., *Perspectives on Canadian Federalism* (Scarborough: Prentice-Hall, 1988), 281.
16. Ibid., 280–1.
17. Cairns, "Citizens (Outsiders) and Governments (Insiders) in Constitution-Making," S143.
18. Stefan Dupré, "Canadian Constitutionalism and the Sequel to the Meech Lake/Langevin Accord," in D.P. Shugarman and R. Whitaker, eds, *Federalism and Political Community* (Peterborough: Broadview Press, 1989), 245.
19. A.H. Birch, *Representative and Responsible Government* (Toronto: University of Toronto Press, 1964), 17–21.
20. Ibid., 15.
21. Alan Cairns, "Constitutional Minoritarianism in Canada," The J.A. Corry Lecture delivered at Queen's University, 6 March 1990, 2.
22. Ibid., 26.
23. Cairns, "Citizens (Outsiders) and Governments (Insiders)," S125.
24. Bernard Crick, "Republicanism, liberalism and capitalism: a defence of parliamentarianism," in Graeme Duncan, ed., *Democracy and the Capitalist State* (Cambridge: Cambridge University Press, 1989), 76, 79.
25. Birch, *Representative and Responsible Government*, 236.
26. Vipond, "Whatever Became of the Compact Theory," 806.
27. Ibid., 794.
28. Sir William Blackstone, *Commentaries on the Laws of England*, 16th ed., vol. 1 (London: T. Cadell and J. Butterworth and Son, 1825), 48.
29. Ibid., 50.
30. Judith Shklar, "The Federalist as Myth," *The Yale Law Journal* (90 (1981): 949.
31. Cairns, "Citizens (Outsiders) and Governments (Insiders)," S142.
32. See the Supreme Court of Canada's decision in *Reference Re Legislative Authority of Parliament to Alter or Replace the Senate* (1980) in P. Russell, R. Knopff, T. Morton, eds., *Federalism and the Charter* (Ottawa: Carleton University Press, 1989), 697–8.
33. Hannah Arendt, *On Revolution* (New York: The Viking Press, 1965). See chapter four, "Foundation I: *Constitutio Libertatis*," 139–78.
34. *A Letter to the Right Honourable The Earl of Carnarvon, Principal Secretary of State for the Colonies* (London, 1866), published in the *Morning Chronicle*, Halifax, 24 November 1866.

35. Thomas Paine, *Rights of man: being an answer to Mr. Burke's attack on the French Revolution,* excerpts in Robert Eccleshall, ed., *British Liberalism: Liberal Thought from the 1640s to 1980s* (London: Longman, 1986), 112.
36. Michael Bliss, "Has time come to let Meech die?" *The Globe and Mail,* 29 May 90, A7.

Constitution and Regional Cleavages: A View from Québec

EDMOND ORBAN

UNIVERSITÉ DE MONTRÉAL

For an author like Carl Friedrich, federalism is a process by which distinct political communities use common institutions for joint decision making on matters of common interest.[1] This definition applies as much to Canadian federalism as, for instance, to the European Community. It suggests a shifting equilibrium between common values and interests, on the one hand, and divergent "regional" values and interests on the other hand.

But if the interests and/or the values of one or several important regions are too distinct, or even of a clearly conflictive nature when compared to those of the national majority, this phenomenon could lead to a rather serious disequilibrium. It all depends on the importance of these differences and on their temporal and spatial dimensions.

Some authors describe this phenomenon as a disintegrative process because political integration requires, according to their view, a clearly established national identity or, if one prefers, a higher allegiance (Canadian, for example) prevailing over all others. Rosenbaum, in his study *Political Culture*, speaks of a stable hierarchy of political identification, or of primary loyalty, and he cites as an example the French Canadians who resist this type of integration (which is indispensable, according to him). "Pockets of resistance to national identification may remain, as with the French Canadians. Still, for most of the people the order of political allegiance is congruent with the hierarchy of government units."[2]

Thus from this perspective, the divisions between a region and the rest of the country or its majority have much more serious disintegrative effects when the principal allegiance is so clearly dysfunctional for the whole of the political system.

For Karl Deutsch, however, the minimum threshold of integration appears to be the establishment of a "security community."[3] Such a community implies that the principal political values (above all, democracy) be compatible and that at the same time the various governments be capable of responding to common problems without recourse to violence. In other words, it implies a mutual expectation that a minimum of (democratic) rules will be respected by both sides. These are the characteristics of a "pluralistic security community." As an example of this, he points to the friendly relations of two Scandinavian countries (Norway and Sweden) that now form an "unamalgamated security community."

Such a level and degree of integration are however too weak to justify the existence of a federal state, such as the United States, which he considers to be an "amalgamated security community." On the other hand, as in the case of contemporary Canada, the requirements of this model of integration are too numerous and demanding. Conversely, among the causes that lead to the disintegration of the "amalgamated" countries, the author underscores a rapid and strong increase in regional divisions of an economic, social, cultural, linguistic, and ethnic nature, and the incapacity of governments (and elites) to deal effectively with the demands of certain segments of the society. If we follow this reasoning to its logical conclusion, this obviously means that there exist other models of integrated communities than that of the classical federal state, as it presently operates in the modern world.

It is always difficult to insert the reality of complex phenomena into abstract categories, even if they are defined in relatively open terms. If we must, however, make a choice among the concepts and categories already mentioned, we could posit the hypothesis that Canadian federation is a border-line case. On the one hand, it is supposed to be a pluralist security community having reached the threshold of real integration, since there exists a minimal consensus concerning certain fundamental democratic values. On the other hand, considering the regional differences, it is not an amalgamated society. For Quebeckers in particular, it is the category of federalism itself that is put into question. The concrete manifestations of this federation are characterized by three fundamental facts, common to many modern federal states:[4]

1) centralization of national and international political decision making
2) administrative decentralization
3) cooperation among the various levels of government.

In the Canadian case, we observe that one of the member states increasingly rejects the Canadian federal state as it presently functions, but not necessarily federalism as such. Contrary to what is often asserted, it is not a movement running against the evolution toward larger integrated units. It is above all a search for solutions and a new framework that could, in the words of Gino Germani, permit notably the province of Québec to pass through a disintegrative phase before proceeding to a more adequate and innovative form of integration.[5]

This search in Québec is certainly not new, but over the last 20 years we have witnessed an escalation in the nature of the expressed demands. They extend from special status to full sovereignty, and include demands for associated status, distinct society (a step forward or backward?) and sovereignty-association. At the same time, there is a slow but increasing erosion of Québec's support for

84

present-day Canadian federalism, leading to the tensions that we are now experiencing and that are highlighted by the present constitutional crisis.

For foreign observers and somewhat superficial comparativists, the Canadian situation is all the more inexplicable in that, compared to the other federal states (notably those of the advanced industrialized world), political and economic centralization appear to be much less advanced. Furthermore, Canadian provinces have increased their powers and have notably improved and modernized their civil services. [6]

This is equally disconcerting for functionalists for whom federalism should constitute a solution for regional conflicts by managing and integrating the various regional diversities that are present, but not by directly acting against centrifugal forces (that underscore regional divisions) nor by homogenizing the society (amalgamation process).

In David Easton's systems analysis, divisions are considered to be dangerous only when they lead to disintegration, or in other words, when a group (or region) offers emotional (sic) ties that seriously compete with the fundamental political objectives of the whole of the country. [7] But at the heart of these matters, [8] we are confronted with the question of cleavages and their relationship with the main goal of the "national" society: integration—whatever its nature, degree, means, and institutions.

WHAT CLEAVAGES?

If we compare the economic situation of Québec to that of the other provinces, our perceptions may vary considerably from province to province. The comparison is relatively less favourable, at least in certain areas, if we take Ontario as the reference point. But in most other countries, we observe a much greater degree of regional disparities. In the United States, for example, some states are now experiencing a new decline, and this is also the case with several Swiss cantons and German länder in spite of such measures as redistribution and equalization payments.

Paradoxically, at the very moment that Québec appears to be reinforcing and diversifying its economy, we observe a worsening of the perception of cleavages within Canada, extending over all the principal areas of social, economic, political, linguistic, and cultural life.

This is a phenomenon all the more surprising if we consider that religion, which was once a very strong cultural factor, no longer plays an important role in regional identification, as it did in the age of *cujus regio illius religio*. The Protestant-Catholic conflict that in West Germany, for example, reinforced the Bavarian and Rhenish identities, has been reduced to similar levels as those observed in Canada and thus gives way to forms of ecumenism or simply to an indifference that renders religion impotent as a divisive factor.

On the other hand, the linguistic division in Canada takes on a greater importance since the francophone community finds itself in an increasingly minority position in Canada and in North America. Language thus plays the role of a catalyst

85

in exacerbating the relatively smaller conflicts that we observe in this country. Consider, for instance, the emotional impact of the Québec language laws 101 and 178, which in many respects simply represent legitimate attempts at self-defense. [9]

But it is not only language that serves as an identification factor, for we must add historical division and the collective consciousness, reinforced by the educational system and the mass media, that Québec has of its own history and of itself as a nation *per se* (which corresponds, in any case, to an objective reality). This history tends to dramatize the conflicts with the anglophone community on many issues vital to the survival of the francophone community. As well, English Canada is too often perceived as forming a quasi-monolithic society in spite of the many differences existing among the anglophone provinces. [10]

All in all, the conflicts of the last several years are less serious than those of the past (conscription, October Crisis, etc.) but the Québec national consciousness has never been more in evidence. It is not the object of this paper to analyse the foundation, form, and new structure of Québec's national identity, [11] since we wish only to underscore that it represents, for many partisans of Canadian unity, the principal cleavage within Canada. These people thus find it difficult, if not impossible, to accept the concept of two nations and, to a lesser degree, the idea of a distinct society.

This nationalism corresponds however to a strong desire to belong to an organic and distinct community such as those observed in many other regions of the world. It is expressed in many shapes and forms while remaining largely open to democratic ideals. At the same time, it is characterized by an ever stronger (and organized) desire to control the manoeuvring room that the international system leaves to modern states, whatever their level and degree of interdependence.

It is essentially in this area that conflict becomes inevitable, not only between provinces but also between a federal state possessing the full attributes of a sovereign state (and controlled by an anglophone majority) and an embryo of a modern state (the provincial and francophone state of Québec) wanting to increase its legislative powers. In this conflictive approach (excluding all other approaches), we have in effect a zero-sum game where what one player wins, the other loses. Thus, the so-called cooperative federalism is considered by the weaker of the two sides as another form of gradual assimilation, or as the Trojan Horse of centralization.

Be that as it may, the conflicts confronting Canadians over the Meech Lake Accord, and those conflicts of previous years, illustrate well this opposition between two visions of the respective roles of the integrative (and unifying) federal state and of the Québec provincial state. The latter is pushed forward by autonomist dynamics based on distinct historical roots, a perception of external threats to its own survival, and on a growing need to control a maximum number of tools required for its own economic and social development.

REDUCTION OR INCREASE OF CLEAVAGES: A FEW INSTITUTIONAL INDICATORS

Our analysis is restricted to those cleavages present over the last 20 years in the Canadian political institutions that are supposed to encourage integration and thus moderate such divisions. Ronald Watts, for instance, considers that the failure of federal institutions to encourage federal cohesion would be one of the causes of a disintegrative process; another would be the polarization of regional divisions. [12]

POLITICAL PARTIES

William Riker attributes considerable importance to national (federal) political parties in their integrative function, and above all when they are sufficiently decentralized as is true of the United States. "This decentralized party system is the main protector of the integrity of states in our federalism." [13]

In Canada, Alan Cairns considers that the present electoral system does not permit the two major federal parties to play such a role. "The capacity of the party system to act as an integrating agency for the sectional communities of Canada is detrimentally affected by the electoral system." [14] He presents as a principal example that of Alberta, consistently the victim of underrepresentation in federal institutions and particularly in the House of Commons.

Robert Boily also recognizes the failure of the federal political parties in this process of Canadian integration. But instead of attributing this to technical causes (the electoral system), he blames it on the fact that the so-called national parties have been unable to reflect Canada's national duality and regional diversity. He also writes of electoral balkanization and the incapacity of these parties to play an arbitral and integrative role. [15]

Donald Smiley, on the other hand, did not worry about this. He considered that this phenomenon is common to most Western countries and that in any case this function, which he described as one of aggregation and articulation, is ever more frequently taken over by other institutions, including governmental departments, pressure groups, task forces, royal commissions of inquiry, quasi-independent agencies, and other organizations active in the federal capital. [16]

Another indicator that follows from the preceding discussion needs to be mentioned: the growing independence of Québec political parties from the federal ones. In Québec's National Assembly, the Liberal Party of Québec is continually distancing itself from the Liberal Party of Canada [17] with which it collided during the constitutional "repatriation" process and the debate on the merits of the Meech Lake Accord. Furthermore, there is now an important Québec opposition party that is committed to Québec's political sovereignty. Its primary objectives are obviously incompatible with those of national parties. Donald Smiley underlines this phenomenon when he states that the Parti Québécois has succeeded in polarizing Québec society on nationalist lines, transforming the French Canadian identity into a Québécois identity. This is more than a symbolic transformation, since it leads to crucial and irreversible consequences: "there is here a crucial and no doubt irreversible development in the circumstances of French-English relations in Canada." [18]

This is a development that is not found in other industrialized federal states where the "provincial" parties are very often linked to the major federal parties, at least during national and regional elections. In the case of West Germany, with only a few exceptions, the provincial parties are essentially branches or relays for the national parties, with all the mutual interferences that this implies in federal as well as in länder elections.

Only those elements concerning political parties that are directly related to our investigation have been mentioned here, and we leave it to others to analyse them in greater detail and with other preoccupations.[19]

While discussing the federal political parties, we also could mention in detail the case of the Canadian Senate which was intended from the beginning, according to some "Founding Fathers," to play an important role in the defence of regional interests, and thus preserve federalism. "The Senate would be an important guardian of sectional and provincial rights and interests."[20] In fact, during the last 20 years, the partisan dimension has continued to assert itself, a phenomenon that is clearly illustrated by the recent behaviour of the Liberal Opposition in the Senate during debates on Conservative bills. As Robert MacKay wrote several decades ago, it is not, or it is no longer, the Senate that constitutes the ultimate political defence of the provinces, but rather the previous or the next general election.[21]

This weakness stems in part from the fact that senators are nominated by the federal prime minister largely from members of his own political party. Indeed, the vast majority of present senators are members of a federal party and act as such. This does not entirely exclude notable individual actions that sometimes influence the decision-making process, but such actions are limited to the personal rather than institutional level.

In conclusion, if at certain times the Senate has been able to integrate regional concerns, or even exceptionally to defend the regions, such a role essentially remains the purview of the federal political parties in the House of Commons. A regional role for the Senate is all the more surprising when we consider the inherent weaknesses and systematic risks of this nonelected institution, which in any case is condemned to disappear or to undergo a radical reform. Senate reform is also one of the major issues of constitutional negotiations where discussions often appear to repeat the historic confrontation between the small and big American colonies of 200 years ago. As reported in *The Federalist Papers*, "the equal vote allowed to each state is at once a constitutional recognition of the portion of sovereignty remaining in the individual States and an instrument for preserving that residuary sovereignty."[22] But this was at a time of dual federalism where state law was the rule and federal law the exception, to use an expression of the last century.

THE CONSTITUTION

For those countries that are truly concerned with the respect of basic democratic principles, the constitution is a symbol of great importance. In Aristotle's *politeia*, the concept refers to the global ordering of things in the City.[23] This concept is relatively close to the *Weltanschauung* of the German constitutionalists. As well, the constitution of West Germany is called the Fundamental Law (*Grundgesetz*). In the United States, it takes on an even stronger significance because of its history and becomes, as it were, an almost sacred symbol of national unity.

Any substantial constitutional revision thus represents a historic moment in the political system's evolution and a major indicator of its fundamental character. In Canada, it has served to reveal competing conceptions of federalism, notably one promoting a stronger central government (the Trudeau thesis) and one put forward by advocates of provincial autonomy. This last conception has been vigorously defended by successive Québec governments, and other provinces (such as Alberta) were also opposed to federal government encroachments, but not necessarily for the same reasons.

From a global perspective, however, clearly there exists a division between the anglophone majority and the francophone community on the issue of the federal division of powers. Prodded on by the Parti Québécois, the traditional policies of the provincial parties have generally become more radical in their demands. But as formulated in the rather moderate Meech Lake Accord, such demands seem very difficult if not impossible to accept for many adherents of classical federalism. It seems that for most anglophones, recognition of Québec's distinct society and above all the devolution of some important legislative powers contribute to the disintegration of the Canadian political system as they conceive it. It logically follows that this Canadian majority would insist on a fundamental agreement favourable to a process of pan-Canadian nationalization and to the consolidation of national institutions (government, administration, parliament, courts of law, etc.).

The addition to the constitution of a charter of individual rights and liberties is equally revealing in this respect, because when we observe what has occurred in other federal states, it appears that such a charter may well strongly increase federal powers in the name of democracy and thus set limits on provincial autonomy. In the United States, however, we should note that the first nine constitutional amendments (civil rights) did not apply, at least for a long time, to the states. Their subsequent application to the states by the federal courts (and especially by the Supreme Court), however, rapidly led to the nationalization and centralization of individual rights and freedoms. Whatever the advantages of such transformations, and especially for the minorities in certain southern states, they have had a considerable impact on state autonomy, even in the area of public finance. [24] In Switzerland as well, and even earlier in the United States, the area of rights and liberties has been practically "nationalized." The same is true in West Germany where the 1949 constitution, after a short preamble, lists several fundamental rights that bind all levels of government.

In a comparative perspective, the foreign observer has some difficulty to understand Québec's reluctance when confronted with a controversial Canadian charter of rights, especially if the observer is unaware of the major elements of the political context and does not consider the linguistic and economic consequences of such constitutional amendments. In fact, these consequences influence, at least indirectly, the question of the division of powers and the preservation of Québec's distinct society.

Whatever the ins and outs of the constitutional crisis, it has been aggravated (rather than resolved) by the adoption of the Canada Act in 1982. It indicates

89

the existence of a clear division in Canada, since all the anglophone provinces and the central government ratified the amendments in spite of the unanimous opposition of the two major provincial parties of Québec.[25] This situation is, as we have stated, one of the most revealing and serious indicators of a profound dissension, capable of leading to the disintegration of the political system, at least as it presently functions. This does not, of course, exclude other forms of reintegration based on some other completely different principles.

This constitutional reform[26] is all the more surprising and unacceptable for Quebeckers since it was supposed to symbolize that a renewed federalism, after the failure of the referendum on sovereignty-association, could henceforth respond to their most vital needs. It was however quite the opposite result that emerged. Ronald Landes concluded, as did many other authors, that "in many ways, the Canada Act illustrates a reassertion of Ottawa's influence and power in the federal system—an outgrowth, no doubt, of Trudeau's view that the political system had become too decentralized."[27] Further on, this author underlines the dangers of Québec's isolation and the failure of the reform that was supposed to have reinforced national unity.[28]

The Meech Lake Accord, in turn, was supposed to repair the damage caused by the passing of the Canada Act without Québec's participation. Not wishing to enter into the detail of this event, it is sufficient to mention that the rejection of this last constitutional agreement, once again at the expense of an isolated but united Québec, constitutes yet another indicator of a worsening situation in a process that may culminate, in the absence of spectacular reversal, in a "constitutional disintegration."

But whatever the efforts that are brought to bear in order to counter this destructive chain-reaction, these failures will have consequences that are all the more serious since they have contributed to awakening and above all aggravating the divisions separating the various actors involved at all levels. The most negative aspect results from the fact that the polarization has finally aligned itself on an English Canada—French Québec axis. This has the result of accelerating the cumulative effect of divisions, while the primary objective of federalism in all its forms is to reduce divisions to a degree acceptable to all of its member states or at least to the more important among them.

THE SUPREME COURT

The Supreme Court of Canada, a most important institution in this respect, is the interpreter of the constitution. Its behaviour interests us particularly with regard to the way in which it resolves conflicts between Québec and the federal government.

We notice that over the last 20 years, the Supreme Court has rendered about 100 relevant decisions. Some observers consider that in general the court has succeeded in notably reducing some divisions and the severity of political conflicts that accompany them. Guy Tremblay, in a study on the Supreme Court of Canada as a final arbiter of political conflicts, considers that it has "made a considerable contribution to the resolution of political tensions that had the potential to become more pronounced . . . By encouraging intergovernmental co-operation, it further increased the possibilities of adaptation within the status quo, which it seemed determined to maintain."[29]

Numerous Supreme Court decisions affect indirectly the economic powers of the provinces and the federal government. Consider for example the decisions on federal anti-inflation measures, taxation of energy resources, agricultural marketing boards, transport regulation, cable-TV communications,[30] incorporation of companies, etc. With fewer direct effects, at least at first sight, we also should mention decisions relating to labour relations, bankruptcy, criminal law, and increasingly individual rights and freedoms[31] (with the possibility of them being extended, as mentioned in a preceding paragraph on the Charter). Among the decisions of an economic nature concerning the maritime provinces of the east and west, there is the 1967 case on off-shore mineral rights that established federal jurisdiction on the Canadian continental shelf. This decision also has consequences for the province of Québec, especially regarding the granting of permits for mineral exploration in the Gulf of Saint Lawrence.[32]

In a study of Supreme Court decisions from 1949 to 1978, Gilbert L'Écuyer concludes that they were on the whole more favourable to claims of federal jurisdiction than were the previous decisions on the Judicial Committee of the Privy Council, but they appeared to respect rigorously, with a few rare exceptions (the study dates from 1978), the terms of the British North America Act and especially the original intent of the "Founding Fathers" concerning sections 91 and 92 that divide power between the two levels of government.[33] In other words, L'Écuyer supports Brossard's thesis when he states that if these decisions demonstrate a centralist bias it is because they simply give effect to a constitution that was from the start centralist, and we thus must change the constitution rather than accuse the Supreme Court. These two authors start from the principle that, in the long run, the Supreme Court naturally participates in a process of Canadian nationalization but that, because of their essentially judicial approach, the judges do not discuss in depth the integrative or disintegrative effects.

In a supplement to Brossard's study of the Supreme Court, James Leavy considers that the decisions for this post-1949 period are largely of a technical nature. All in all the court has rendered only a few noteworthy decisions on general constitutional principles, even when we include the division of powers cases concerning the patriation of the constitution. Until now, the Supreme Court's constitutional jurisprudence has been characterized by a technical approach typical of normal statutory interpretation and consequently by a kind of benevolent neutrality.[34]

This viewpoint is certainly not shared by Andrée Lajoie and her two coauthors in the section of their study on the Supreme Court entitled "Standardizing federalism (1976–1985)":

Even the Supreme Court, which had demonstrated a consistent centralist tendency since World War II but had recently grown less rigid, reversed the position it had taken in favour of provincial interests in the cases originating in Québec during the preceding period [1960–1975].[35]

These authors place the court's decisions in their political context[36] of political polarization and domestic conflicts. When evaluating the overall effect of such decisions, they consider that the court's jurisprudence has undermined Québec's constitutional demands, notably by denying the existence of Québec's right to veto constitutional amendments. According to their analysis, the lack of congruence between the political demands of Québec and the evolution of Canadian constitutional law (and of the Supreme Court's jurisprudence) over the last decade has increased even further.[37]

We should add that such conflicts have a tendency to polarize tensions on a Québec-Ottawa axis while the majority of other conflicts brought before the Supreme Court generally create multiple and scattered divisions within or among provinces, and thus have a more fragmented impact.

From this perspective, the Supreme Court decision on the patriation of the constitution (Québec's veto) has recently contributed, with other decisions on linguistic matters, in encouraging a sense of insecurity in Québec and at the same time reinforcing both material and psychological divisions that have long been dormant.

If we consider generally the Canadian political system and federalism, it becomes obvious that the Supreme Court cannot be considered as the principal factor of centralization and, at least with respect to Québec, of increasingly important divisions. The court is above all a reflection, or an indicator, of the recognized evolution of Western federations.[38] In these federations, a political centralization, in conjunction with a strong administrative decentralization, should be able to achieve the goal of national integration while at the same time decreasing regional divisions. Whether they achieve this is another question, but it appears that in any case Québec no longer desires this form of federalism.

CONCLUDING REMARKS ON THE DYSFUNCTIONALITY OF MODERN FEDERALISM

When we consider the nature of some of the cleavages and divisions already discussed, and above all the escalation in demands expressed by important segments of the Québec population, we can conclude that federalism as practised in the Western federations hardly offers us concrete solutions, and even less a universal model. Canadian federalism, in spite of some positive achievements to its credit, is characterized by an asymmetry between demands for autonomy (discussed in a previous section) and the relatively weak constitutional and institutional responses. It has not succeeded, especially over the last 20 years, in reducing the divisions opposing, on the one hand, the federal government and sometimes the anglophone provinces, and on the other hand, Québec. More important, this last province, far from being a province like the others (one among 10), tends to behave and develop like a separate state. And this occurs within the framework of a society that is not only distinct in many regards, but one that also manifests a more or less organized consciousness of forming, as it were, a nation. [39]

Not wishing to dwell on this point, we should however take notice of its importance. We also can understand the desire of former prime minister Trudeau and of many anglophones to reject the concept of "Two Nations," for it could have profound implications for any fundamental reform of the political system. But at the same time, such a position ignores an obvious reality, that of a people's deeply felt need to preserve its own heritage and personality.

While having common interests with the rest of the country and in particular with certain neighbouring provinces, Québec is distinguished more and more by its national character and its need to translate this into appropriate political structures. The north-south orientation of its economy, at the expense of Canadian east-west trade and which is confirmed and reinforced by its clear endorsement of free trade with the United States, is yet another cause of discord with many English-Canadians in the "centre" of the country. [40]

All this is occurring at a time when "profitable federalism" appears out-dated [41] because of the size of the federal public debt. Under other circumstances and in another political and economic context, this phenomenon would not be any more worrisome than in any other federation. The United States federal budget deficit and public debt have also taken on alarming proportions, undermining future financial aid for the states. But in Canada, much hope was placed on cost-shared programmes (with clearly fewer conditions attached than in the United States) to reduce some of the regional disparities and divisions while preserving a minimal degree of financial and political autonomy for Québec.

In conclusion, we have perhaps exaggerated some of the divisions already mentioned, especially if we accent their conflictive nature. Taken together, however, they are sufficiently important to reveal the fundamentally dysfunctional aspects of a federal system that is no longer able to insure a minimal output in response to the demands of one of its most dynamic member states. These demands are part of a movement putting into question the very foundations of the decision-making apparatus, but they do not necessarily affect—far from it—the foundations of common values concerning the democratic process of the entire country.

We thus can remain hopeful that the ineluctable transformations that we will eventually experience will at least occur within a framework of a pluralist security community (as previously defined). This concept leaves the road open to an entire range of possible solutions that need not be considered here.

As well, no lasting solution will be possible without a wide consensus [42] within the population of Québec (and between its two main political parties) on the optimal degree of sovereignty and on the institutions that this will imply in an interdependent world.

Québec itself has too often been divided at certain moments of its history, starting with Antoine-Aimé Dorion's opposition to George Cartier over the centralist federation project and on to the referendum of 1980. However, a new cohesion appears to be steadily emerging in Québec; eventually, the two major political parties must, one way or another, come together in spite of their present differences.

NOTES

1. Carl Friedrich, *Tendances du fédéralisme en théorie et en pratique* (Bruxelles: Institut belge de science politique, 1971), 19.
2. Walter A. Rosenbaum, *Political Culture* (New York: Praeger Publishers, 1975), 53.
3. Karl Deutsch, et al., *Political Community in the North Atlantic Area: International Organization in the Light of Historical Experience* (Princeton: Princeton University Press, 1957), 194–196.
4. For a more detailed analysis of these issues, see for example our book: *La dynamique de la centralisation dans l'État fédéral moderne: un processus irréversible?* (Montréal: Québec-Amérique, 1984). Four countries are considered: Canada, United States, Switzerland, and the Federal Republic of Germany.
5. Gino Germani, *Politique, société et modernisation* (Gembloux: Duculot, 1971), 143–146. (disintegration and reintegration in the process of social modernization)
6. This is a matter that merits a much longer discussion. We have previously addressed this issue, using a theoretical framework (integrating several different perspectives) that allows for some comparisons between modern federal states. See our *La dynamique de la centralisation*, part II.
7. David Easton, *Analyse du système politique* (Paris: Colin, 1974), 228.
8. In order to agree on a minimum of common concepts, I have used texts of known authors that have become so-called classics, without feeling obliged to follow the use that they make of these concepts nor the conclusions that they draw from factual analysis.
9. The principle of linguistic territoriality, applied to the francophones of Belgium and Switzerland, allows for protective measures for the French language in all areas of social activity, measures that are clearly more extensive than those adopted by Québec. On this subject, consult J.A. Laponce, "Protecting the French Language in Canada: From Neurophysiology to Geography to Politics, the Regional Imperative," *Journal of Commonwealth and Comparative Politics* 22 (July 1985): 169. "Assuming the policy of a state to be the survival of a minority language, territorial solutions ... appear functional while, by contrast, the Canadian solution that denies the possibility of permanent linguistic borders appears dysfunctional."
10. Consider the resentment of the western provinces toward the central provinces of Ontario and Québec in Larry Pratt and Garth Stevenson, eds., *Western Separatism: Myths, Realities and Dangers*, (Edmonton: Hurtig, 1981).
11. See notably Alain Gagnon, ed., *Québec: State and Society* (Toronto, New York: Methuen, 1984), Part I, "Québec Nationalism" and the chapters by F.P. Gingras, N. Nevitte, A. Gagnon, M.B. Montcalm and S. Ryerson. See also the bibliography included in these chapters, and the recent writings of Louis Balthazar.
12. Ronald Watts, "Survival or Disintegration," in Richard Simeon, ed., *Must Canada Fail?* (Montréal: McGill-Queen's University Press, 1977), 53.
13. William Riker, *Federalism: Origin, Operation, Significance* (Boston: Little Brown and Company, 1964), 101. Among the other federal institutions capable of playing a national integrative role, he also mentions the Senate and the Supreme Court.
14. Douglas E. Williams, ed., *Constitution, Government and Society in Canada: Selected Essays by Alan C. Cairns* (Toronto: McClelland and Stewart, 1988), 137.
15. Robert Boily, "Un fédéralisme en éclatement," in *Québec, un pays incertain* (Montréal; Québec-Amérique, 1980), 32.
16. Donald Smiley, *Canada in Question: Federalism in the Eighties*, 3rd edition (Toronto: McGraw-Hill Ryerson, 1980), 146.
17. Even to the degree of favouring the principal political adversary of the Liberal Party of Canada during the federal elections of 1988, namely the Progressive Conservative Party. This federal party elected its candidates in 63 of the 75 Québec seats in the House of Commons, while in 1980 it had been reduced to a single member.
18. Smiley, *Canada in Question*, 246.

19. See, for example, Raymond Hudon, "Polarization and Depolarization of Québec Political Parties," in Alain Gagnon, ed., *Québec: State and Society*, and Réjean Pelletier, "Political Parties in the State since 1960" in the same volume.
20. Robert MacKay, *The Unreformed Senate* (Toronto: McClelland and Stewart, 1963), 112.
21. This observation by MacKay (*The Unreformed Senate*, 121) is confirmed by a Université de Montréal's master's thesis written by Luc Lalongé, "Le Sénat canadien et la défense de l'autonomie provinciale," which clearly shows how this federalist concern was rapidly eclipsed by others.
22. *The Federalist Papers* (New York: Doubleday, 1961), 182–3.
23. The concept is used here in its widest sense. In Aristotle's "Politics," it corresponds more to the present-day concept of the state, rather than the city. See Marcel Prélot, *Politique d'Aristote* (Paris: Presses universitaires de France, 1950), 7.
24. Edmond Orban, "Droits de la personne et processus de centralisation: rôle de la Cour suprême des États-Unis," *Canadian Journal of Political Science*, 20 (December 1987): 4, 724–729.
25. It should be noted that the Liberal Party of Québec, which supported the "No" side during the Québec referendum on sovereignty-association, stood united with the Parti Québécois in its rejection of the Canada Act of 1982.
26. For a study of the history of the "patriation" of the constitution and its effects on Canadian federalism, Gil Rémillard, *Le fédéralisme canadien* (Montréal: Québec-Amérique, 1985), tome 2. For a detailed analysis of the various clauses of the Canada Act of 1982, Gérald Beaudoin, *Le partage des pouvoirs* (Ottawa: Éditions de l'Université d'Ottawa, 1983). See also Edward McWhinney, *Canada and the Constitution 1979–1982* (Toronto: University of Toronto Press, 1982).
27. Ronald Landes, *The Canadian Polity* (Scarborough: Prentice-Hall, 1983), 398. For a more critical and detailed analysis, see notably Gérard Boismenu, "Le Québec et la centralisation politique au Canada, le 'beau risque' du Canada Bill," *Cahiers de recherche sociologique*, 1985, 119–138.
28. Ronald Landes, *The Canadian Polity*, 399.
29. Guy Tremblay, "La Cour suprême du Canada, dernier arbitre des conflits d'ordre politique," dans Ivan Bernier and Andrée Lajoie (sous la direction de), *La Cour suprême du Canada comme agent de changement politique* (Ottawa, Ministre des Approvisionnements et Services, 1986), 216 (our translation). Concerning more directly Québec, consider the Cable-TV case.
30. *Régie des services publics contre Dionne*, 1978, upholding federal authority.
31. Among these cases are found several concerning linguistic rights and the restrictions imposed by two Québec laws (Bills 101 and 178).
32. We should mention Jacques Brossard's study *Le territoire québécois* (Montréal: Presses de l'Université de Montréal, 1968), 190–219. On the interpretation of the Supreme Court of Canada, the author underlines the irreversibly centralizing tendencies of the court that result from the strongly centralized nature of the constitution itself. For the more recent period, see Brossard and Leavy, below.
33. Gilbert L'Écuyer, *La Cour suprême du Canada et le partage des compétences 1949–1978* (Québec: Éditeur officiel du Québec, 1978). The study considers four areas of Supreme Court impact: economic, social, cultural, and institutional. See also Peter H. Russell, *Leading Constitutional Decisions*, 3rd edition (Ottawa: Carleton University Press, 1982).
34. James Leavy, *Mise à jour, 1967–1982, de la Cour suprême et la constitution de Jacques Brossard* (Montréal: Presses de l'Université de Montréal, 1983), 46.
35. Andrée Lajoie, Pierette Mulazzi, and Michèle Gamache, "Les idées politiques au Québec et le droit constitutionnel canadien," dans Ivan Bernier and Andrée Lajoie (sous la direction de), *La Cour suprême du Canada comme agent de changement politique*, 55.
36. On the importance of the political context in order to appreciate the relative impact of a Supreme Court decision, see Edmond Orban, "La Cour constitutionnelle fédérale et l'autonomie des Länder en République fédérale d'Allemagne," *Revue jurdique Thémis*, 22 (1988). For a general analytical framework see *A Framework for Studying the Controversy Concerning the Federal Courts and Federalism*, Washington, Advisory Commission on Intergovernmental Relations, April 1986, M–149.

37. Andrée Lajoie et al., "Les idées politiques au Québec," 79.
38. Consider particularly the Western federations that are analysed in our study *La dynamique de la centralisation dans l'État fédéral*.
39. For a recent example, consider the U.S. Department of State's evaluation: "Québec satisfies generally admitted criteria for national self-determination, namely a distinct ethnic character, a clearly defined geographical space, with a separate legal system and government." Quoted by Jean-François Lisée, "La crise canadienne, la solution de Washington," *L'Actualité*, 15 (April 1990), 33.
40. But less monolithically than is generally thought. See, for example, Robert Young, "L'Ontario et la fédération libre-échangiste," dans *Un marché, deux sociétés, libre-échange et autonomie politique* (Montréal: ACFAS, 1987), 141–150.
41. For example, the editorial of Alain Dubuc, "La fin du fédéralisme rentable," in *La Presse*, 22 February 1990. This author remarks that the "centralizing federalism of Trudeau was based not only on principle but also on the power of the public purse. It was Ottawa's riches that allowed it to promote *unifying* programs." (Emphasis and translation are ours.)
42. Already in 1979 Edward McWhinney, a Canadian observer of Québec politics, appeared to believe that Québec would achieve a certain level of constitutional consensus thanks to a polarization with the rest of the country that would eliminate all intermediary solutions. This is of course open to question. *Québec and the Constitution, 1960–1978* (Toronto: University of Toronto Press, 1979), 14.

Bibliography Concerning Constitutional Questions as seen Mainly by French Canadian Authors During the Last Twenty Years

Ares, R. *Nos grandes options politiques et constitutionnelles*. Montréal: Éditions Bellarmin, 1972.

Banting, K., and R. Simeon, eds. *And No One Cheered: Federalism, Democracy and the Constitution Act*. Toronto: Methuen, 1983.

Bastien, R. *La solution canadienne*. Montréal: Éditions La Presse, 1979.

Beaudoin, G.A. *La constitution du Canada: institutions, partage des pouvoirs, droits et libertés*. Montréal: Wilson et Lafleur, 1990.

_____ . *Essais sur la Constitution*. Ottawa: Éditions de l'Université d'Ottawa, 1979.

Beaudoin, G.A., and Y. Renaud. *La constitution canadienne*. Montréal: Guérin, 1977.

Beck, S.M., and I. Bernier, eds. *Canada and the New Constitution*. Montréal: Institut de recherches politiques, 1983.

Bergeron, G. *Incertitudes d'un certain pays*. Québec: Presses de l'Université Laval, 1979.

Bergeron, G., and R. Pelletier, eds. *L'État du Québec et devenir*. Montréal: Boréal Express, 1980.

Bernard, A. *La politique au Canada et au Québec*. Québec: Presses de l'Université du Québec, 1979.

Black, E. *Divided Loyalties: Canadian Concepts of Federalism*. Montréal: McGill-Queen's University Press, 1975.

Blanche, P., and J. Woehrling. *L'Accord Meech-Langevin et les compétences linguistiques du Québec: opinions juridiques*. Québec: Éditeur officiel du Québec, 1988.

Boismenu, G., and F. Rocher. «L'Accord du lac Meech et le système politique canadien,» *Politique*, 16 (1989), 59–86.

_____ . «Une réforme constitutionnelle qui s'impose ...,» in Y. Bélanger and D. Brunelle, eds. *L'ère des libéraux: le pouvoir fédéral de 1963 à 1984*. Montréal: Presses de l'Université du Québec, 1988.

Brossard, J. *L'accession à la souveraineté du Québec: modalités politico-juridiques*. Montréal: Presses de l'Université de Montréal, 1976.

Brunelle, D., «Les rapports des sages et la loi constitutionnelle de 1982: une analyse régressive,» dans R.D. Bureau and P. MacKay, eds. *Le droit dans tous ses états*. Montréal: Wilson et Lafleur, 1987.

Cahiers de Droit (Les). *La réforme des institutions fédérales canadiennes* (numéro spécial), 26 (March 1985).

Croisat, M. *Le fédéralisme canadien et la question du Québec*. Paris: Anthropos, 1979.

Décary, R. «Langue et société ... distincte,» *Langue et société* 20 (Fall 1987), 11–12.

Devoir (Le). *Le Québec et le lac Meech* (dossier). Montréal: Guérin, 1987.

Dion, L. *Le Québec et le Canada, les voies de l'avenir*. Montréal: Québecor, Montréal, 1980.

Dufour, C. *Le défi québécois*. Montréal: L'Hexagone, 1989.

Faribault, M. *La révision constitutionnelle*. Montréal: Fides, 1970.

Forest, R.A., ed. *L'adhésion du Québec à l'Accord du lac Meech*. Montréal: Éditions Thémis, 1988.

Grenier, B. *La déclaration canadienne des droits, une loi bien ordinaire?* Québec: Presses de l'Université Laval, 1979.

Johnston, R., and A. Blais. "Meech Lake and Mass Politics: The Distinct Society Clause," *Canadian Public Policy* 14 (special issue September 1988), S25–S42.

Lalande, G. *In Defense of Federalism: A View From Québec*. Toronto: McClelland and Stewart, 1978.

Lalonde, M., and R. Basford. *The Canadian Constitution and Constitutional Amendment*. Ottawa: Office des relations fédérales-provinciales, 1978.

Latouche, D. *Le Canada et le Québec: un essai rétrospectif et prospectif*. Ottawa: Ministère des Approvisionnements et Services, 1986.

Mackay, J. *Le courage de se choisir: essai*. Montréal: L'Hexagone, 1983.

Malone, M. *Une place pour le Québec au Canada*. Montréal: Institut de recherches politiques, 1986.

Mathews, G. *L'Accord, Comment Robert Bourassa fera l'indépendance*. Montréal: Le Jour, 1990.

McRoberts, K., and D. Postgate. *Développement et modernisation du Québec*. Montréal: Boréal Express, 1983.

McWhinney, E. *Québec and the Constitution: 1960–1978*. Toronto: University of Toronto Press, 1979.

Moniere, D. *Les enjeux du référendum*. Montréal: Québec-Amérique, 1979.

Moniere, D., and Coll. *Québec: un pays incertain*. Montréal: Québec-Amérique, 1980.

Morin, C. *Lendemains piégés: du référendum à la nuit des longs couteaux*. Montréal: Boréal Express, 1988.

––––––. *Le combat québécois*. Montréal: Boréal Express, 1973.

––––––. *Le pouvoir québécois ... en négociation*. Montréal: Boréal Express, 1972.

Orban, E. *La dynamique de la centralisation dans l'État fédéral: un processus irréversible?* Montréal: Québec-Amérique, 1984.

Parti Libéral du Québec (Commission constitutionnelle). *Une nouvelle confédération canadienne*. Montréal: Parti libéral du Québec, 1980.

Rémillard, G. *Le fédéralisme canadien*, vol. 1, 2nd edition. Montréal: Québec-Amérique, 1983.

Revue Juridique Thémis (La). *La Charte des droits et libertés: concepts et impacts* (numéro spécial), 18 (1984).

Robert, D. «La signification de l'Accord du lac Meech au Canada anglais et au Québec francophone: un tour d'horizon du débat public,» in P.M. Leslie and R.L. Watts, eds. *Canada: The State of the Federation, 1987–1988*. Kingston, Ont., Institute of Intergovernmental Relations, 1988, 117–156.

Roy, J.L. *Le choix d'un pays: le débat constitutionnel Québec-Canada, 1960–1976*. Montréal: Léméac, 1978.

Simeon, R., ed., *Le Canada face à son destin*. Québec: Presses de l'Université Laval, 1978.

Valieres, P. *Les héritiers de Papineau, itinéraire d'un "nègre blanc"* (1960–1985). Montréal: Québec-Amérique, 1986.

Woehrling, J. «La reconnaissance du Québec comme société distincte et la dualité linguistique du Canada: conséquences juridiques et constitutionnelles,» *Canadian Public Policy*, 14 (special issue, September 1988), S43–S62.

Interpreting the Political Heritage of André Laurendeau

GUY LAFOREST

UNIVERSITÉ LAVAL

For the current Canadian federal regime to have any chance to maintain itself in Québec, it had to find within its means the strength to provide adequate, significant space for political duality. Throughout the history of Québec and of Canada in the 20th century, André Laurendeau has been one of the most effective and passionate spokespersons for duality. He fought hard and sometimes despaired for a way to reconcile his primary allegiance to Québec and his loyalty to Canada. The dilemmas of Laurendeau symbolize those of a good number of people in contemporary Québec. I still believe that the majority of the population does not want to choose between Québec and Canada. Following the example of Laurendeau, the majority would prefer dual allegiances and complex federalism. To interpret the political heritage of André Laurendeau in 1990, one has to formulate the most difficult of questions: what should be done when complex federalism and dual allegiances are being expelled from the logic of the Canadian federal system?

The first part of this paper will be devoted to a brief presentation of Laurendeau and of political duality. This will be followed by an analysis of the Meech Lake Accord, a document crafted to some extent in the spirit of political duality. The consequences of the failure of the Accord will be examined. The third section will study the demise of duality through the workings of the 1981–1982 constitutional package. In conclusion, I will look at the prospects for the restructuring of Québec and Canada.

ANDRÉ LAURENDEAU AND POLITICAL DUALITY

A major Laurendeau revival is currently underway in Québec. Twenty years after his untimely death in 1968, a couple of major conferences were held in Montréal to honour his memory. [1] More recently in the spring of 1990, Laurendeau's diary during his years as cochairman of the Royal Commission on Bilingualism and Biculturalism was published. The diary is a fascinating document. It offers glimpses into the life of the commission as well as into the complex mind of Laurendeau. Since the present conference is held in Saskatchewan I should start with a question Laurendeau asked himself in Regina, in 1964:

> How would it be possible to make our interlocutors understand that an "ethnic group," even relatively strong within its own province, but representing merely 3% of the total Canadian population, is not at all the same thing as an organized entity like Québec society, numerous, possessing its own institutions, as well as a specific and ancient history?[2]

Laurendeau's interrogation was the question concerning duality, or the impossibility to fit Québec within a single Canadian mould. Later on, in Saskatoon, Laurendeau was told by a member of the Doukhobor community that the French should be dispersed across Canada. An Irish Protestant pastor told him that the problem stemmed from the fact that French Canadians had not accepted the consequences of the Conquest. They reorganized themselves in Québec, licked their wounds, and were now (1964) ready to take action. As long as they will not accept Canadian and North American realities, the lament went on, problems will perpetually recur.[3] André Laurendeau was quite ready to accept many of the realities of modern life in Canada and North America. He strove with his friends to bring Québec nationalism in line with the modern world. However, until the end of his life, he clung to the dream of preserving and promoting Québec as a distinct society in Canada and North America.

André Laurendeau was undeniably one of the leading intellectuals of Québec in the 20th century. He had several different and equally distinguished careers. In the thirties, he contributed to the foundation of Jeune-Canada, a youth movement seeking to give new life to French Canadian nationalism. Later, he became editor of an important journal, *L'Action nationale*. In the forties, he led the struggle against conscription in Québec. This period witnessed the highest level of his political engagement. For a time, he worked as provincial leader for a new party, the Bloc populaire. He even was elected to the National Assembly. Dissatisfied with his experience, Laurendeau moved on to the confines of *Le Devoir*, where he stood up in the 1950s against the authoritarian regime of Duplessis. His career undoubtedly culminated with his nomination by Lester B. Pearson as cochairman of the inquiry studying the state of bilingualism and biculturalism.

At one of the major conferences held in 1988 to commemorate the spirit of Laurendeau, both Fernand Dumont and Charles Taylor agreed on the essence of his message. What made Laurendeau so unique, according to these scholars, was his attempt to find a synthesis between universalism and particularism. Laurendeau, it was argued, resisted the temptation to apply blindly to his own society the pronouncements of foreign intellectual discourses and masters.[4] In other words, he did not abdicate the necessity of political judgement.

Fully aware of the situation of the French as a minority in Canada and North

America, Laurendeau tried to coin a kind of federalism and liberalism that would allow French people to flourish on this continent. His solution was a dualistic political regime, granting Québec special status in Canada. Laurendeau did not live long enough to formulate his blueprint in a comprehensive and specific fashion. The closest approximation to such a blueprint can be found today in the anonymous pages of the general introduction to the first volume of the report of the B&B Commission, published in December 1967. We know that Laurendeau was the author of these famous "blue pages." In these paragraphs, he clearly states that official bilingualism will not be sufficient to guarantee the integral preservation of the French culture.[5] Full equality of opportunity between the two dominant cultures requires the recognition of the existence of two distinct societies. The unmistakable fact that Québec is the heartland of French Canada will have to be politically acknowledged. This should be translated into more powers and greater constitutional autonomy for Québec; Laurendeau's implicit message was obvious: the survival of a Canada in crisis depended upon its ability to integrate political duality.

THE MEECH LAKE SAGA AND ITS CONSEQUENCES

The Meech Lake Accord, despite all its real and imagined flaws, provided significant space for duality. Its most important section was an interpretive clause that stated, first of all, that linguistic duality was a fundamental characteristic of Canada. This opened room undeniably for a major aspect of André Laurendeau's vision. However, the clause in question reduced duality to its linguistic dimension. Moreover, in its last formulation, it was couched in strictly individualistic terms. Twenty-five years ago, as we just saw, Laurendeau had other things in mind when he referred to duality. He also included within this concept the communitarian aspects of culture and the political requirements of Québec as the heartland of French Canada.

Alongside linguistic duality, the Meech Lake Accord's second clause contained a section affirming that the whole constitution of Canada, thus including the Charter of Rights and Freedoms, would have to be interpreted with the knowledge that Québec was recognized as a distinct society within Canada. The distinct society clause, as it has become known, was the greatest political victory in 20 years for the heirs of André Laurendeau. The clause symbolically granted a form of special status to Québec. It would have somewhat broadened the range of reasonable limitations to rights and liberties in a free and democratic society, as in the first section of the Charter. It also could have been used by the court system to clarify uncertainties in the division of powers between the federal government and its counterpart in Québec. It would nevertheless be wrong to believe that the distinct society clause had enshrined duality as the paramount principle of constitutional interpretation.

Within the Meech Lake Accord itself, the distinct society clause was carefully surrounded by a battery of other devices. The preamble mentioned provincial equality. Whereas only the Québec government and the National Assembly benefited from the stronger language of promotion, thus advantaging the distinctiveness of Québec, all governments and legislatures had the obligation to preserve linguistic duality, which was the only dimension of Canadian reality within the Accord to be considered as a fundamental characteristic. The courts would have prudently scrutinized these three principles—provincial equality, the distinctiveness of Québec, and linguistic duality—in all the cases in front of them. Québec had no guarantees whatsoever that the distinct society clause—the flag-bearer of political duality—would have carried the day in any particular occasion. The victory of duality was also circumscribed by two additional sections affirming that the division of powers between governments remained unaffected and that the aboriginal and multicultural rights in the Charter (sections 26 and 27) could not be reduced by the operation of the distinct society clause.

Had the Meech Lake Accord been accepted, the constitution of Canada would have remained faithful to what was, according to Ramsay Cook writing 20 years ago, the meaning of Confederation. In 1867, the founders of Confederation, in Cook's opinion, had been wise enough to produce a constitution in which an equilibrium between principles, a tension between visions, had been devised.[6] As we shall see in a moment, the constitutional operation of 1981–1982 tried to substantially reduce this ambiguity, in favour of a centralist nation-building project. Considered from this angle, the Meech Lake Accord had only restored the tensions, ambiguities, and misunderstandings that have been there all along between 1867 and 1982. Some, following Jean-Charles Bonenfant, will say that Cook overstated the case with regard to the intentions of the Fathers of Confederation.[7] They will argue that the tensions and ambiguities were produced more by history than by intent. This debate will never be concluded. My point here, simply put, is that these checks, ambiguities, and blurred sovereignties between visions were necessary to the flourishing of complex federalism in Canada. When all this is discarded in favour of a constitution with crystal-clear principles, as Michael Behiels calls them, the very nature of our federalism becomes threatened and so does Canada.[8] If Canada as it stands disappears, it will have been fatally wounded by people who loved her too much.

Why was an agreement resembling the Meech Lake Accord required in the first place? A significant number of politicians and intellectuals from Québec and English-speaking Canada, including among them Gil Rémillard and Donald Smiley, had been arguing all along that the constitutional package of 1982 had serious problems of legitimacy in Québec. The Constitution Act, 1982, was adopted without the prior or subsequent consent of either the government of Québec, the National Assembly, or the people—who are the ultimate possessors of sovereignty. The new constitution reduced the powers of Québec in two sectors, education and language, that are considered of paramount importance in the province. No government of Québec would sign these documents in their present form. The Meech Lake Accord addressed this problem head-on. From the perspective of this legitimacy crisis weakening the fundamental institutions of Canada, the Meech Lake saga is endowed with two layers of meaning.

First, all the efforts put into this new constitutional round since 1984 by the federal government and all its provincial counterparts amount to a pragmatic confirmation of the existence of the problem. All major actors, all governments, and all parties have indirectly recognized, through their behaviour, that the absence of Québec's signature was indeed a major problem. Despite the failure of the Meech Lake Accord, this tacit admission should provide a form of consolation for Québec.

The second layer of meaning brings no consolation whatsoever to the partisans of political duality in Québec. The political context that led to the initial formulation of the Meech Lake Accord was extremely propitious. A strong Tory government was in place in Ottawa, with a clear mandate for "national reconciliation." Some of the new prime minister's key advisers, such as Senator Arthur Tremblay, were well-known supporters of the dualistic vision. In Québec, the Liberals led by Robert Bourassa formed a majority government in December 1985. The PQ and radical nationalism appeared to be in disarray. Seemingly, the road was open to a moderate solution. A good relationship had developed between Mulroney and Bourassa. Conservatives were in power in a majority of the provincial capitals. In principle, they would not be inimical to the initiatives of the federal government. David Peterson and the Liberals ruled in mighty Ontario. From the start, they indicated their desire to develop good relations with Québec. To complement these favourable political conditions, the country was going through a period of sustained economic growth. These circumstances were more than propitious. They provided the Canadian federal regime with a unique opportunity to solve once and for all its legitimacy problem in Québec. The opportunity was lost. It is unlikely ever to emerge again, for reasons I will now consider.

THE 1982 CONSTITUTIONAL PACKAGE AND THE DEMISE OF DUALITY

In the wake of the failure of the Meech Lake Accord, the premier of Québec, Robert Bourassa, said that from now on his government would seek bilateral arrangements with its federal counterpart. Many things have been said and written since. We shall hear more precisely in the near future from the Special Parliamentary Commission of the National Assembly inquiring into the political and constitutional future of Québec. Until then, it should be clear to all interested observers in Canada that Bourassa's initial statement stands unaltered. Québec will never again submit itself to the kind of negotiations among federal and provincial governments that led to the formulation and ultimate demise of the Meech Lake Accord. Sometime before agreement was reached at Meech Lake in April 1987, Eugene Forsey wrote that it would be extremely difficult to put anything of consequence into the constitution or to take anything of consequence from it. He was fatefully right.[9]

The amending formula that flows from the 1982 constitutional package is quite rigid in itself. This is only the first formidable obstacle to substantial change. If, somewhat miraculously, an agreement is reached between the 11 first ministers, as occurred with the Meech Lake Accord, another major hurdle emerges: the three-year deadline for ratification in Parliament and all legislatures. Such a length of time is the equivalent to a political eternity. The fortunes of governments are bound to change within such a period. At some point, the delicate federal and provincial balances that led to a fragile agreement will evaporate, forcing all players into the starting blocks one more time. Despite these terrible odds, unanimous agreement among the 11 first ministers was reached on two occasions during the Meech Lake saga, with a third consensus one millimetre away from the light of day. And all this, as I showed earlier, in generally favourable political and economic circumstances. As if these obstacles were not impressive enough, a third one was cleverly put right at the heart of the Constitution Act, 1982. The first two obstacles are devilish and tricky to overcome. One cannot fault Robert Bourassa and his government for spending so much energy in that endeavour. They almost made it. But the third obstacle is the most dangerous one. It convinces the partisans of political duality in Québec that success for them is impossible within the present rules.

Patriating the constitution and law-making were not the only objectives contemplated by those who produced the 1982 documents. As with Jean-Jacques Rousseau's legislator in *The Social Contract*, the founders of 1982, led by Pierre Elliott Trudeau, had an ontological preoccupation. It is not an exaggeration to say that they wanted literally to transform Canadians, to refashion the identities of ordinary citizens all over the country. The major instrument of this monumental task was the Charter of Rights and Freedoms. The Charter was, and continues to be, the key weapon in the nation-building offensive launched in the early 1980s by the last Trudeau government.

The Charter invites more and more Canadians every day, individuals and groups alike, to give their primary allegiance to the institutions of the level of government that defends and promotes their rights and liberties. The Charter is animated by a drive toward homogeneity. As Mr. Trudeau told the Special Joint Committee of Parliament inquiring into the Meech Lake Accord in August 1987, the Charter creates an understanding among Canadians that all citizens of the whole country share an identical group of fundamental values.[10] Federalism is weakened by the Charter. The latter is animated by a quasi-unitary vision of Canada, one in which, according to Kenneth McRoberts, "only the federal state is the legitimate expression of a national will."[11] Mr. Trudeau spoke eloquently about his intentions when he addressed the Senate in March 1988, during the debate on the Meech Lake Accord:

It had been a struggle to establish the sovereignty of the people over all levels of government, and, by the proclamation of the Constitution Act, 1982, the battle for the people's rights was won. The war was not over, the Charter was not perfect, and we still have no referendum process in the amending formula. But the legal community was seeing to it that the Charter was having a real meaning, and the media were reporting the rights of the people over the rights of government, and people began to discover that they had a community of values, that the bonds of Canadian nationhood existed, and so on.

But that process of constitutionalizing the people of Canada, which had begun in 1982, was stopped in its tracks by the 1987 accord. [12]

Thus, the objectives were clear: to create a community of values, to constitutionalize the people of Canada. Something in the Meech Lake Accord, Mr. Trudeau contended, went against all this. The campaign against the Accord led by Mr. Trudeau played a decisive role in its ultimate demise. Despite all the talk surrounding the flawed process, the opposition to the Accord was driven by people who wanted to establish the supremacy of the Charter over and against the distinct society clause. It is very important to note that liberal philosophy was not the major impetus of this opposition. The battle between the Charter and the distinct society clause did not amount to a struggle between liberal individualism and communitarianism. As David Elkins has brilliantly argued, there is a verdant variety of community rights in the Charter. [13] A complex equilibrium is at work in the Charter between the rights of individuals and those of communities. Canadian nationalism and the longing for a homogeneous community of values among individuals and groups across this land were the real opponents of the distinct society clause. With the failure of the Meech Lake Accord, the citizens of Québec were not told that they should not have collective rights. Rather, they were warned that their collective rights should be no different from those of Canadians living outside Québec.

There is no room in the constitutional package of 1982 for Québec nationalism, for the collective dimension in the identity of Québec's citizens. The Charter-led nation-building policy of the early 1980s is the most formidable obstacle against any attempt on the part of Québec to initiate reforms to the Canadian federation along dualistic and asymmetrical lines. The amending formula, the political process for ratification, and the nation-building policy transform the constitutional package into an impregnable fortress. Moreover, from the perspective of Québec, time does not help matters. Dualism and asymmetrical federalism— special status for Québec—will become less and less attainable with the ability of the Charter to refashion the political culture of English-speaking Canada. More and more people will see themselves as "First and Foremost Canadians," to use an expression made popular by Clyde Wells after the failed attempt to rescue Meech Lake, with equal rights for individuals and provinces, and they will demand the same commitment from the inhabitants of Québec. Within the current institutional framework, the dualistic dream cherished by André Laurendeau and his political heirs is dead.

CONCLUSION

The Spicer Commission, launched in early November 1990 by the Mulroney government, sets up a new process of dialogue involving all Canadians, including the people of Québec. If ever there has been a champion of meaningful dialogue in 20th-century Canada, it had to be André Laurendeau. He worked and died while cochairing the greatest experiment at meaningful dialogue in the history of the country, the Royal Commission on Bilingualism and Biculturalism. If, as I believe, it has become practically impossible to create significant space for the dualistic vision within the current constitutional framework, the ability of the Spicer Commission to produce meaningful results must be put in doubt. Laurendeau was right about the need for generous, open dialogue between Québécois and Canadians. His message is still valid in 1990. However, for those who continue to believe in political duality, as Laurendeau so eloquently did, the lessons of the 1980s must be lucidly understood. Meaningful dialogue can only occur in a new institutional framework. More people every day are coming to this conclusion in Québec City and Montréal, but also in Calgary, Saskatoon, and Toronto.

The current impasse, despite all its stress, provides us with a wonderful opportunity for meaningful dialogue. Québécois and Canadians must accelerate the process of hard thinking concerning a variety of options. We have started to hear a lot about a new Canada-Québec union, taking the form of bi-national federation or confederation, or even a multiregional arrangement involving significant recognition and powers for the First Nations. This is all very good. It is indeed possible that the best interests of Québec and Canada would be served if the citizens of both societies could find a way to be compatriots in a substantial sense, still to be defined. However, sharing a higher-level *patria* will remain impossible without a mutual recognition by the two nationalisms, the one prevailing in Québec and the other asserting itself in the rest of Canada. The logic at work in the Constitution Act, 1982, and in the Charter of Rights and Freedoms, is profoundly dominated by the attempt to create and foster a new Canadian nationalism. In such an institutional context, meaningful dialogue with Québec nationalism is, in realistic terms, impossible. I take this to be the single most important lesson of the failure of the Meech Lake Accord.

Restructuring in the hope of eventually making real compatriots of Québécois and Canadians, in a clear acceptance of the distinctiveness of both societies and of their specific conditions in North America will have to start by a rupture. In some quarters, this will be seen as the return of the state of siege mentality that characterizes parochial nationalism in Québec. Such a pathological obsession will forever be with us. This time, however, at such a crucial juncture in our history, I am reasonably optimistic that a different kind of wisdom will prevail. I consider a rupture, a breakup of the current federal system, simply as a prudent updating of André Laurendeau's political heritage. If Québec and Canada are to find a way of going on together without much disruption, the present impasse must be rapidly overcome. Such an initiative will inevitably come from Québec. Strange as this may sound, compared to the negative warnings of the 1980 referendum campaign, I think that the best interests of Canada would be served by sending encouraging signals to Québec, inviting as it were the kind of clear-headed and careful boldness that we all need.

There are no guarantees for success in the perilous enterprise that we have in front of us. We have learnt from Machiavelli that in such circumstances, we must carry on no matter what the odds are, in the hope that fortune may smile on us this time around. When the moment of truth comes in Québec, I am convinced that such key figures as Claude Ryan and Gil Rémillard will base their decisions in part on their desire to honour the memory of André Laurendeau and his valiant struggle for political duality. Québec will always remain in an uncomfortable position in America. But its will to carry on as a distinct entity is as indomitable as ever.

NOTES

1. See Nadine Pirotte, ed., *Penser l'education, Nouveaux dialogues avec André Laurendeau* (Montréal: Boréal, 1989), and Robert Comeau and Lucille Beaudry, *André Laurendeau. Un intellectuel d'ici* (Sillery: Presses de l'Université du Québec, 1990).
2. André Laurendeau, *Journal tenu pendant la Commission royale d'enquête sur le bilinguisme et le biculturalisme* (Montréal: VLB éditeur/Le septentrion, 1990), 55.
3. Ibid., 237.
4. Fernand Dumont, "Y a-t-il une tradition intellectuelle au Québec," in Pirotte, ed., *Pense l'education*, 68; Charles Taylor, "La tradition d'une situation" in Pirotte, ed., 90–91.
5. *Rapport de la Commission royale d'enquête sur le bilinguisme et le biculturalisme*, "Introduction générale," (Ottawa: Imprimeur de la Reine, 1967), vol. I, paragraph 33, XX, paragraph 83, XXXVI.
6. Ramsay Cook, *Canada and the French Canadian Question* (Toronto: Macmillan of Canada, 1966), 178–179.
7. Jean-Charles Bonenfant, "L'Esprit de 1867," *Revue d'histoire de l'Amérique française*, XVII(I), (1963), 36–37.
8. Michael Behiels, "Introduction," in Behiels, *The Meech Lake Primer: Conflicting Views of the 1987 Constitutional Accord*, XXIV.
9. Eugene Forsey, "Changes Québec wants should get a careful look," *The Globe and Mail*, 17 March 1987, A–7.
10. Pierre Elliott Trudeau, "Il doit y avoir un sens d'appartenance," in Donald Johnston and Pierre Elliott Trudeau, *Lac Meech Trudeau parle* (Montréal: Hurtubise HMH, 1989), 41.
11. Kenneth McRoberts, *Québec: Social Change and Political Crisis*, 3rd edition (Toronto: McClelland and Stewart, 1988), 400.
12. Pierre Elliott Trudeau, "Who speaks for Canada? Defining and Sustaining a National Vision," in Michael Behiels, ed., *The Meech Lake Primer: Conflicting Views of the 1987 Constitutional Accord* (Ottawa: University of Ottawa Press, 1989), 93.
13. David Elkins, "Facing our Destiny: Rights and Canadian Distinctiveness," *Canadian Journal of Political Science*, XXII, (December 1989), 699–716.

COMMENTARY

GARTH STEVENSON

BROCK UNIVERSITY

I disagree with the statement in Professor Orban's paper that our present problems are less serious than those that we surmounted in the past. The old Canada of 1867 was based on two ideas: a preference for what the BNA Act termed "a constitution similar in principle to that of the United Kingdom" and the desire to build a transcontinental east-west economy distinct from, and in competition with, the United States. These ideas were shared not only by most anglophones but by francophone elites such as Sir George-Étienne Cartier. They formed the basis for an association between Québec and anglophone Canada that perhaps left Québec in a somewhat subordinate position, but was broadly acceptable to both partners for almost a century.

The significance of the National Policy was gradually lessened after 1935, although much of it remained in place. Furthermore, Québec after the Quiet Revolution began to challenge its position within Confederation and to demand a renegotiation of its terms. Nonetheless, our traditions of consociational elite accommodation seemed to make this possible and thus to preserve Confederation through incremental changes. The Meech Lake Accord was the culmination of this approach, and its failure is thus highly significant.

Anglophone Canada, or "everything but Québec," has changed dramatically over the last decade. Instead of duality we have multiculturalism. Instead of Peace, Order, and Good Government we have what I would call charterism: an increasing tendency to assert individual rights and certain group rights against the state. These developments are creating a Canada within which Québec cannot be accommodated easily, and perhaps not at all. Furthermore, the Canada-United States Free Trade Agreement has undermined the last vestiges of the National Policy and removed the economic underpinnings of Confederation.

On the other hand, Québec, as Professor Orban and Professor Laforest have suggested, displays a growing consensus around the need for more powers: the product of its economic maturity, social peace, and the reorientation of its external economic ties on a north-south rather that east-west basis. In these respects it has changed significantly since the referendum of 1980.

In these circumstances I find it difficult to disagree with Professor Orban's bleak view of the prospects for Canadian federalism. Canada seems to lack the necessary degree of social, economic, or political integration to support the institutions of a federal state. Indeed there no longer seems to be any logical basis, either cultural or economic, for a "Canada" with its present political boundaries. Even politically, it is no longer easy to say what we have in common with one another that distinguishes us from the United States.

Thus I share some of Peter Russell's fear that the Spicer inquiry will reveal very dangerous divisions, but I am not sure that we could conceal them in any event. My sense of opinion in anglophone Canada is that it is somewhat confused but that there is less and less commitment or high priority attached to keeping Québec within Confederation. Special status for Québec is much less popular than outright independence. Both Québec and anglophone Canada share one characteristic: each thinks it could live without the other while each thinks that the other depends upon it. Moreover, anglophone Canada's regionalism is still powerful. The recent proposal by some Québec Conservatives for a five-region Canada, presuming that the Prairie and Atlantic provinces could give up their separate identities, shows incredible ignorance. Also the fiscal crisis of the federal state, as Professor Orban notes in his paper, is extremely serious.

Turning to Jennifer Smith's paper, I largely agree with her comments on representation and her rejection of what she calls the "mirror" concept. I also think it is valuable to note the difference between the devising of amendments and their ratification, and to suggest as she does that the procedural requirements for the two stages need not be the same.

At the same time I believe that our present amending formula is part of the problem. Few people took much notice of it when it was adopted, but its unworkability has now been demonstrated. It is incredible that it was so poorly drafted that we do not even know whether the three-year deadline really applied to the Meech Lake Accord or not. Furthermore we do not know the meaning of key phrases in this complex formula such as "reasonable compensation" or "relating to education or other cultural matters" or "the composition of the Supreme Court."

Professor Smith says that a constituent assembly would be impossible and that ratification by referendum is too contrary to our political tradition to be considered. I disagree. Our political tradition includes the Dunkin Act, which provided for referenda even before Confederation, the better-known Canada Temperance Act, the two-stage referendum that brought Newfoundland into Confederation, and the Québec referendum of 1980. Even if it did not, traditions can be abandoned. The Charter of Rights and Freedoms, as she points out, was a break with our traditions, but it has rapidly become a cherished symbol in anglophone Canada. There are precedents for referenda in both anglophone Canada and Québec, and I suggest that no constitutional settlement that is not ratified by referendum will be legitimate in the future.

COMMENTARY

REG WHITAKER

YORK UNIVERSITY

We should be grateful to Jennifer Smith for her very careful and well-considered analysis of the process of Meech Lake. This is particularly valuable as she places the process in the context of elite-mass dichotomy, which must lie at the heart of any attempt to explain the failure. She somewhat tentatively suggests the referendum option as an alternative. This raises the very pertinent issue of the limits and contradictions of popular participation in constitution making.

Alan Cairns has pointed to the "mobilization of bias" outside the state. Professor Smith correctly questions the "mirror representation" theory when these societal forces try to participate in the constitutional process. There are indeed serious objections to the notion that self-appointed spokespersons of groups can always appropriately "speak" for their members. There is even a new kind of elitism masquerading under the name of democracy. This may involve little more than the extension of the number of elite players, each allegedly wielding blocs of influence.

The referendum may be a device for tactically evading this mobilization of bias. A referendum represents the "people" as a whole embodying them as a collective presence. The rights discourse engendered by the Charter encourages a serialized, fragmented concept of the people, the people sliced into individual and group instances. In 1981 there was strong support for the Charter; each group saw advantages in defining rights in its own particular image. Yet Trudeau's proposal for the referendum as a way of breaking amendment impasses (even based on concurrent regional majorities as it was), gathered virtually no spontaneous popular support. In short, it seems that people recognized themselves more readily in their particularity than in their universality. During the Meech Lake fiasco, expressions of democratic or populist resentment of the closed process were rampant, but it was unclear whether these were voiced in the name of the people as a whole or people in particular.

This is one current dilemma of community. Another is the question of the legitimacy crisis of politicians and political institutions evident from current opinion polls. Elite accommodation and the political culture of deference to authority have been in sharp decline for some years. We may have reached a point of no return, when it is no longer possible to reclaim these older values and habits. These two problems are interrelated and both have to do with the question of the forms which democracy is taking, as the older constitutional and political values deteriorate. This is a real constitutional conundrum: how, in a society like that of Canada, is a majority, and thus an effective notion of political community, validly constituted? That Canadian society is in the process of democratization is not in question.

111

But as Tocqueville told us long ago when studying the first democratic state, others "would not be led necessarily to draw the same political consequences that the Americans have derived from a similar social organization." What is very much in question is whether democratization, in the process of corroding old forms, will simply play a negative and disintegrative role, or whether it will point toward newer, and possibly stronger, forms of community. Pollsters tell us that the sense of personal efficacy on the part of individual Canadians is strengthening, while there is a perceived decline in the efficacy of public institutions: this is a challenge which would-be constitution-makers and those of us who write and speak about such things need to keep at the centre of our attention.

This leads me to Edmond Orban's paper, which poses the problem of Québec to the rest of Canada—a problem that must be situated firmly in the context of the crisis of democratic community. As the "people" have come more and more into play, the effect at the level of Québec-Canada relations has been divisive. It could not have been otherwise, because as the concept of the "people" becomes clarified, so it becomes clear that there are two types of peoples in Canada (two at least, not forgetting the First Nations).

Canadian political scientists have not generally recognized that since the 1960s political development has moved on two quite divergent tracks. First is the growing democratization of both Canadian and Québec societies. Second, successive attempts to find a new accommodation between Québec and the rest of Canada have been at the expense of the first. The perverse, and unintended, consequence of Québec's democratic national aspirations to self-determination upon the rest of Canada has been to constantly displace politics away from greater popular participation onto the old and increasingly discredited plane of elite accommodation. Since Québec's demands were invariably for more powers to Québec this reinforced the tendency of Canadian federalism to be understood as the government of governments, rather than the government of people. Meech was the final *reductio ad absurdum* of this tendency.

I am not suggesting any blame or pointing to any villains. Rather I am suggesting that this is a structural impasse. Here Professor Orban makes a mistake that is not unusual for Quebeckers looking at Canada. He writes that it is "logical that the Canadian majority would insist on a fundamental agreement favourable to a process of pan-Canadian nationalism." There are some people in Canada—perhaps with Cairns we might refer to them as the Charter Canadians—who do look to the national state as the guarantor of their rights and liberties. There is also a good deal of Canadian nationalism (the free trade election proved that). But there are also extremely important forces, especially in western Canada, that demand greater regional recognition and decentralization.

A considerable part of the legitimacy crisis today is based upon genuine regional grievances. These might well lead to more than one separatist movement. On the other hand, if Ontarians would listen carefully and respectfully to the voice of the West being articulated by the Reform Party, they would discover that many Westerners are asking to be let in, not out. But getting in will require massive restructuring of the institutions of national government to better reflect regional perspectives.

The Québec-driven agenda for constitutional reform is the problem here, not the solution. Québec, for instance, has consistently blocked Senate reform, and will continue to do so as long as it is a partner to Confederation. This is hardly surprising, since Québec will view an equal, elected, and effective Senate as undermining its position. This is only one example. From the point of view of the rest of Canada, Québec is a blockage in the ability of the system to respond to the legitimacy crisis.

The precondition for a solution to Canada's problem, the necessary if not sufficient condition, may well be that Canada and Québec should go their separate ways. We might begin by looking into the terms and conditions of a mutually advantageous divorce, with negotiations over post-separation economic association to be decided by two sets of negotiators, each representing their own (enlightened) national interests. I have come very reluctantly to this position, but I am persuaded that this may be the only way to open up the necessary constitutional agenda for a democratic Canada.

CONSTITUTIONAL REFORM: CHARTER RIGHTS AND FREEDOMS

Charter Influences on Future Constitutional Reform

W.R. LEDERMAN
QUEEN'S UNIVERSITY

The constitution of Canada must be considered as a whole with interacting and interdependent parts, one of which is the Charter of Rights and Freedoms of 1982. As section one of the Charter states, Canada is "a free and democratic society." More specifically we have a federal division of ordinary legislative powers, provincial and federal executives that embody the English cabinet system, and an independent judiciary on the Act of Settlement model from England. In addition, since 1982, we have a specifically entrenched Charter of Rights and Freedoms that sets standards for ordinary statutes, both provincial and federal. I consider these institutions, and the processes they follow, to be essentially sound. We should then continue to base ourselves on them in making a fresh effort to seek needed constitutional changes for Canada.

I concern myself in what follows with constitutional changes that would not involve the secession of Québec from the Canadian federal union. I do not regard such separation as inevitable and believe that we should be prepared to go a long way to avoid it. The Canadian Charter of Rights and Freedoms, 1982, might help very significantly in the task of saving the Canadian federal union, as I shall suggest later. But first, a brief look is needed at the way to negotiate legitimate constitutional change.

THE CONSTITUTIONAL REFORM PROCESS

There should be a consultative period at both federal and provincial levels addressed to the public under the auspices of the federal and provincial parliaments. This would take the form of public hearings by official committees or commissions reporting back to the parliamentary body or bodies that established them. This would match in English-speaking Canada what is already under way in Québec.

I envisage some joint action of this sort, for example: a joint consultative commission for the four Atlantic provinces and one also for the four western provinces. The Yukon and Northwest Territories should be included in the western group. There also would be an Ontario commission, and we already have a Québec commission reporting to the National Assembly there. Finally, there would be an over-all commission set up by the Parliament of Canada. The aboriginal peoples of Canada should be represented on every one of these commissions. To repeat, these commissions should conduct public hearings and make reports and recommendations to the parliamentary bodies that established them.

The foregoing consultative stage would only be the start of the process of constitutional change. Thereafter, there must be a political stage of selecting and particularizing proposals for change, and of taking responsibility for promoting them by attempting to invoke the relevant constitutional amending procedures in Part V of the Constitution Act, 1982. Conferences of first ministers would still be necessary, unless we propose to abolish responsible government under the cabinet system, and to replace it with something else. But, if we do not, then such conferences are necessary and logical as the final stage of negotiations. At these conferences, under the auspices of the elected and responsible first ministers, amendments in final form can be drafted and referred back to the Parliament of Canada and the respective provincial legislatures for the final legislative approval required under Part V of the Constitution Act, 1982. Perhaps the consultative stage was too much neglected in the Meech Lake period from 1987 to 1990, but, even if true, that does not mean that the "conference of first ministers" stage could be or should be dispensed with in a new round of negotiations.

But, at this point in time (late 1990) one major difficulty arises. The logic of Québec nationalism dictates that Québec should negotiate only with English-speaking Canada as a whole, and should not sit in a federal-provincial conference where the province of Québec would have just one voice among 11. This need not be the nature of the conference. The negotiating rules could be somewhat rearranged under the leadership of the federal government to give the Québec government as much one-on-one negotiating status as needed. There would in effect have to be a conference within a conference, or a two-tier conference. There would be a sub-conference of the nine English-speaking provinces and the federal government to prepare a single position to be negotiated as such with the Québec government. The latter negotiations would take place in a plenary session of the conference. This two-stage treatment could be used for all agenda items deemed by Québec to be vital to her as a distinct society. Sophisticated leadership by the federal government would be essential to the success of such a negotiating arrangement, but it could well be workable. If the result were agreement on certain revisions of the terms of the Canadian federal union sufficient to keep Québec in the union, then the amending procedures of Part V of the Constitution Act, 1982, could be followed to implement the new terms. Thereafter, Québec would continue in Canada with its status as a province defined by the new arrangements.

The revisions of the basic terms of the Canadian federal union that I have in mind would occur primarily in the present constitutional division of the subjects of legislative powers between Canada and the provinces. Québec would end up with more autonomy in certain areas of legislative jurisdiction deemed vital by French Quebeckers than other provinces would need or want. Many problems arise about such asymmetry of course, but they are not insurmountable. We won't know what could be accomplished unless and until we try. I have just suggested procedures for negotiation through the medium of our existing governmental institutions and practices. However, after 1982 a relatively new factor entered the picture. I refer to the Canadian Charter of Rights and Freedoms, which could have a benign effect on efforts to accomplish basic constitutional change. The remainder of my comments will have this focus.

CHARTER RIGHTS AND FREEDOMS AND BASIC CONSTITUTIONAL CHANGE

Many people complain that we do not know what Canada stands for or where our society is headed. My advice to them is to read the Charter and some of the leading judicial decisions on its interpretation since 1982. Perhaps they would feel better about our country. In my opinion, the Charter has been a resounding success since it came into force in April 1982. Most of the ideals and principles it contains have wide acceptance in all parts of Canada, including Québec. The Charter itself does not need much in the way of change; indeed, the only change I would like to see is the elimination of Charter section 33, the notorious override clause. Except for that, the Charter should, for the most part, stand as it is and thereby provide some guidelines for reforms in other parts of the constitution yet to come. This is the first decade in Canada when we have faced a coming period of major constitutional change with such a Charter in place as superior constitutional law. Moreover, the authoritative interpretation of the Charter is in the hands of the judges of our long-standing single national superior court system, which culminates in the Supreme Court of Canada.

It is important nevertheless to appreciate that the judges and elected members of our parliamentary bodies, federal and provincial, are not rivals but partners in giving effect to the requirements of the Charter. One example of this partnership is visible in the *Reference re Education Act of Ontario and Minority Language Education Rights* (1984). This was a single unanimous judgment of the Ontario Court of Appeal, the court consisting of the maximum panel of five judges. It was handed down on 26 June 1984, and takes up 70 pages in the law reports. This Ontario judgment is parallel to the *Protestant School Board Case* in Québec.

I can only indicate very briefly why I think the Ontario case is of great importance. The court interpreted section 23 of the Charter to mean, by necessary implication, that, where numbers warrant, quite separate school buildings were required in the school districts, in which not only the language of instruction, but the language of the library, the playground, and the luncheon room would be French. Further, these distinct schools were to be controlled by trustees elected

117

by the section 23 minority parents, Franco-Ontarian parents, their control extending to the buildings, hiring of teachers, budgeting, and curriculum.

In its reference questions to the court, the Ontario government essentially asked two things: Did the present Ontario Education Act comply with section 23 of the Charter? In any event, would the plans of the Ontario government for future statutory changes in the Ontario school legislation comply with the Charter? The plans had been set forth in great detail in an official White Paper of the Ontario government published in 1983. The government submitted this document to the court. In answer to the first question, the court said that the present Education Act infringed section 23 of the Charter because it left too much discretion with district school boards dominated by majority language trustees. Then the court assessed the plans for the future in the Government White Paper. They ruled that, if the government and legislature carried out those plans and enacted the proposed legislation, they would be in compliance with section 23 of the Charter. It was submitted to the court that the judges could not assess the Government White Paper because it was hypothetical and was not expressed in legislative form. The reply of the judges was:

> The argument that the question is abstract and hypothetical, however, has no validity in this case. The proposal for minority language education is described in such detail in the White Paper that an opinion can be expressed on it and no legislative draft is required. Moreover, the Court has been provided with a plethora of factual information which enables it to assess the impact of the proposal.

The court concluded its judgment with these words:

> The judiciary is not the sole guardian of the constitutional rights of Canadians. Parliament and the provincial Legislatures are equally responsible to ensure that the rights conferred by the Charter are upheld. Legislative action in the important and complex field of education is much to be preferred to judicial intervention. Minority linguistic rights should be established by general legislation assuring equal and just treatment to all rather than by litigation.
>
> For these reasons, we are of the opinion that the proposals contained in the White Paper are within the legislative authority of the Legislative Assembly of Ontario.

The proposals in the White Paper are not free of political controversy in Ontario, but, under the parliamentary system, government-sponsored legislation is usually enacted. (The appropriate legislation was introduced in the Ontario legislature in December 1984.) I would suggest that those who now propose basic constitutional changes in Canada should keep one eye on the Charter of Rights and Freedoms. Those people should ensure that their proposals, if relevant to Charter provisions, are in harmony with them.

Finally, there is something else typical of many Charter cases. The general standards of an entrenched Charter of Rights and Freedoms are frequently heavily

118

dependent on detailed implementation by ordinary statutes and regulations, and, at this latter ordinary level, legitimate alternatives and exceptions may appear and require dealing with. Often, the specific reforms people want are available by ordinary statutory action at either the provincial or federal level and are not basic constitutional issues at all, or at least should not be. The point is that if we characterize too many things as constitutional, we put too much of potential legal change to meet societal needs beyond the reach of the flexible statutory means of change. It is at times difficult enough to get an ordinary statute through in response to some urgent need for new legal measures. For those who would change or add to superior constitutional law, the problem of limiting what is to be considered "constitutional" in this sense is very real. The limits have to be severe. You cannot constitutionalize the whole legal system. One cannot turn every legal issue into a specially entrenched Charter issue or a specially entrenched issue of the federal division of legislative powers.

For the most part, in the total of legal changes needed to maintain and advance our society as a going concern, the chief instruments of such changes must be ordinary statutes passed by a simple majority in one or the other of our parliamentary legislative bodies, federal or provincial. The flexibility in lawmaking that this affords is essential. Nevertheless, whenever the statute in question, federal or provincial, is relevant to a Charter standard, judicial review of it can compel compliance with that standard. This facilitates the vindication of basic individual and group rights which all Canadians have in common by virtue of the Charter as superior constitutional law. Remember though that the Charter standards are highly selective. They are by no means relevant to everything one finds in the thousands of volumes of statutes, and regulations authorized by statutes, that crowd the shelves in Canadian law libraries. Most of this material is simply irrelevant to anything in the Charter. Moreover, of the few parts that are relevant, some are positively so. That is, they are ordinary statutes and regulations that are harmonious with the Charter and are facilitative respecting this or that Charter provision.

So, I say: Read the nine printed pages of the Canadian Charter of Rights and Freedoms in the Constitution Act, 1982. There you will find much of what should be constant in the legal and constitutional reforms that lie ahead.

The Charter and
the Crisis in Canada

ROBERT MARTIN

UNIVERSITY OF WESTERN ONTARIO

To say that Canada faces a crisis today is to state the obvious. Even journalists are telling us as much, so it must be true.[1] Public opinion polls released at the end of 1990 confirm that a majority of Canadians are seriously concerned about the survival of our country.

· The crisis has manifested itself in a number of ways, but the two most obvious and most pressing are that our federal union may disintegrate and we are rapidly being absorbed, economically and culturally, into the United States. The roots of the crisis lie in corporate power and, more particularly, in the fact that as corporate power becomes more international, it does not see an autonomous, unified Canadian state as useful.

Recent Canadian political leaders, especially Brian Mulroney, have seen their first duty as responding to the needs of corporate power. This has been evident in the ongoing process of constitutional reform with which we have been mesmerized for the past three decades.[2] The major result of that process has been a progressive weakening of the ability of the Canadian state to respond to corporate power. The adoption of the Canadian Charter of Rights and Freedoms in 1982 led to institutional and ideological changes which significantly furthered the process.

There are two issues about corporate power. The first arises in all states. To what extent can representative institutions confront corporate power and seek to subordinate it to the needs and interests of the people? This is, in the late 20th century world, the democratic question.

The other issue is experienced more acutely in smaller states like Canada. To what extent can national culture and national identity be maintained in the face of the homogenizing effects of corporate power? This is the national question.

The Charter has provided encouragement to a process which has seen the ability of Canadian institutions to address the democratic question and the national

121

question severely limited. The Charter has achieved this by making our political system and our thought processes less democratic and more American. The result is that our political and social agendas will be determined more and more by corporations, largely foreign, and less and less by representative Canadian institutions.

THE ANTIDEMOCRATIC EFFECTS OF THE CHARTER

Many commentators have identified the antidemocratic tendencies which have been strengthened by the Charter.[3] I will highlight some of the ways in which these tendencies have manifested themselves. Concretely, what we are talking about is judicial review of legislation.

The first requirement in understanding this phenomenon is that we be honest about it. American commentators have often tried to obfuscate the antidemocratic character of judicial review by describing it as "counter-majoritarian," which certainly sounds less ominous. We should not obscure reality through the use of convoluted language. Antidemocratic is the proper phrase.

In what ways has the Charter had antidemocratic effects? An answer to this question requires a brief investigation of what exactly is meant by "democratic." Democracy has to do with rule by the *demos,* by the people. A polity is democratic to the extent its institutions respond to and reflect the needs, interests, priorities, and values of the mass of the people. This is all, I would have thought, self-evident. It needs to be emphasized, however, because our notion of the meaning of democracy has become confused in recent years. We have come to imagine that democracy has more to do with the protection of individual rights than with rule by the people. This perception, widespread as it may be, is inaccurate. A concern for the individual is the defining characteristic of liberalism, not of democracy.

We like to call our political system liberal-democracy. The very term implies at least a distinction between the two notions, a clear sense that they are not synonymous. I would go further and argue that liberal-democracy is, by its nature, contradictory, that there is an inherent tension between liberalism and democracy.[4] Our democratic institutions have been able to impose limits on the freedom of individuals in order to protect or benefit the mass of Canadians. But the effect of the Charter, as interpreted by our courts, has been to render our politics more liberal and, inevitably, less democratic. As a result, collective gains made by Canadians through the political process have been swept away in the name of individual rights.

The Charter, more precisely, has been the means whereby parliamentary government has been undermined, corporations have acquired unprecedented legal rights, and popular organisations, particularly the trade unions, have been attacked.

Perhaps more important than these substantive effects of Charter litigation have been its ideological and cultural effects. The Charter has served to reinforce antidemocratic ways of thinking.

PARLIAMENTARY GOVERNMENT

It is not my purpose to argue that parliamentary government in Canada, or elsewhere, is perfect. There are flaws and these are well known: the role which

122

money can play in elections; the stifling effects of party discipline; the ways a single-member constituency, first-past-the-post electoral system can distort the reality of popular feelings. Indeed, our current national government is a product of all these flaws. None of them, however, justifies the degree to which our courts have subverted parliamentary government.

Parliamentary government was the democratic heart of our political system. To subvert parliamentary government in Canada is, then, to subvert democracy.

In a formal sense, we have moved from a constitutional system based on parliamentary supremacy, divided as it was between the federal and provincial legislatures, to one based on constitutional supremacy. This, Charter apologists argue, means simply what it says, *constitutional* supremacy, not *judicial* supremacy. But, and this is something we need to keep reminding ourselves of, constitutions are not self-executing. The principle of constitutional supremacy must be made immanent through the acts of some group of human beings. Since the adoption of the Charter that group of human beings has been the judges, particularly the judges of the Supreme Court of Canada. Thus, in a practical sense, constitutional supremacy has come to mean, and it is difficult to imagine what else it could mean, judicial supremacy. [5]

The Supreme Court of Canada has supplanted Parliament and the provincial legislatures as the final institutional arbiter of what is socially and politically permissible in Canada. The judges gave express recognition to this fact when they conferred upon themselves the distinction "guardian of the constitution." [6] That this is, in a formal sense, antidemocratic should be obvious. The authority of elected, accountable representatives of the people has been superseded by the authority of appointed, nonaccountable lawyers. We have, in less than a decade, become accustomed to the notion that the final word on social and political policy no longer belongs to the legislatures. Whatever decisions may be reached by legislators, these decisions must eventually receive the approval of the judges.

This change in the role of the Supreme Court of Canada has also manifested itself in the court's style, in the way it does its work. It is evident that the judges no longer regard themselves as members of a mere court, which seeks only to resolve legal issues between parties. Their method of work is now that of a legislative committee. Thus, the Supreme Court is prepared to receive argument from a wide array of intervenants, [7] both public and private, and to consider evidence of a social, political, or economic nature. [8] And in writing their judgments the judges appear to feel obliged to produce essays in philosophy or political theory. These are invariably lengthy, seldom illuminating, occasionally laughable, and definitely not a pleasure to read.

The courts have not been content merely to subvert parliamentary democracy, they have also seen fit to attack the fundamental role and privileges of legislative institutions. In *Schachter* v. *The Queen* [9] the Federal Court of Appeal had no compunction about arrogating to itself the performance of an expressly legislative function. The court held that a federal statute had denied a social benefit to a defined group in a way which violated the equality guarantee in the Charter. The question was, what should the court do, what remedy should it grant? There was no doubt the offending statutory provision could have been declared to be of no force or effect. The court chose not to do this, but rather to order that the benefit be paid to the group to which it had been denied, even though no funds had been appropriated for that purpose by Parliament.

The privileges of Parliament have been grandly swept aside, the courts in one instance ordering a provincial legislature to permit its proceedings to be televised[10] and, in another, directing that a Senate committee hold its proceedings in public.[11]

Indeed, the courts have gone to the point of accepting that even noncurial bodies may review the constitutionality of legislation. In *Cuddy Chicks Ltd.* v. *Ontario Labour Relations Board*[12] the Ontario Court of Appeal upheld the authority of an administrative tribunal to declare legislation invalid on the basis of conflict with the Charter. One judge said:

> even a private individual may determine in his or her own mind whether a law is inconsistent with the provisions of the Constitution, and act accordingly.[13]

What these last few examples suggest is a judiciary convinced of its own supremacy and increasingly contemptuous of legislative, that is to say, democratic, institutions.

CORPORATE POWER

I suggested earlier that there is an inevitable antithesis between corporations and democratic institutions, between popular power and corporate power. Corporations have been able to use the Charter to enhance their own power at the expense of democratic institutions.

The courts early on decided that corporations, as well as ordinary human beings, could claim the various rights set out in the Charter. In *Hunter* v. *Southam Inc.*[14] the Supreme Court of Canada accepted that a corporation could enjoy protection from unreasonable search and seizure. In *A.G. Québec* v. *Irwin Toy Ltd.*[15] the ability of a corporation to claim free expression was upheld. Most astounding, to me at any rate, was the court's decision in *R.* v. *Big M Drug Mart Ltd.*[16] that a corporation was entitled to freedom of religion. The court did not trouble to inquire which faith Big M Drug Mart subscribed to or how exactly the company manifested that faith. That is to say, there was no concrete analysis of how the freedom of religion of the litigant actually before the court was being interfered with. The court simply dealt with freedom of religion in the air.

This points to a consistent feature of Charter litigation: its abstractness. In Charter cases the Supreme Court of Canada avoids the concrete and embraces the abstract. The result is that the abstractions which the judges prefer to use in writing their judgments consistently obscure the concreteness of what they are deciding. Concretely, *Hunter* v. *Southam* is not about search and seizure, *Irwin Toy* is not about free expression, and *Big M Drug Mart* is not about freedom of religion. Each is about corporate freedom and, more particularly, about the desire of corporations to do business as they wish free from the troublesome burden of state regulation.

The abstractness of Charter decisions is obfuscating in another sense. The typical Charter case does not, as some might imagine, involve a clash between right and wrong. More commonly a Charter case involves a clash between a collective right, usually one created through legislation, and an individual right, often claimed by a corporation. Thus, from another perspective, *Hunter* v. *Southam* concerns the collective right to control monopolies versus the individual right to the unrestricted accumulation of wealth; *Irwin Toy* pits the collective right to protect children from manipulative advertising against the individual right to flog one's wares; *Big M Drug Mart* counterposes the collective right to a common day of rest and the individual right to do business whenever one wishes.

The most useful Charter guarantee for corporations may turn out to be section 7. The Supreme Court of Canada decided in *Reference re Section 94(2) of the B.C. Motor Vehicle Act*[17] that the section created substantive as well as procedural rights. The judges stated a willingness to strike down laws which they regarded as "unfair," regardless of whether any specific Charter guarantees were violated.

We have, or once had, in this country what is known as a mixed economy. The ownership of the means of production is primarily in private hands. But the state, largely in response to popular grievances and demands, has, as a matter of fundamental social policy, decided that the owners of the means of production should not be permitted to act entirely at their discretion; that they can, and should, be regulated. The means by which such regulation is usually imposed is legislation.[18]

The Charter has placed a weapon to fight regulation by the state in the hands of corporations. Or, to suggest a different metaphor, the Charter allows corporations to go to the courts in an attempt to make an end-run around the legislatures. This has become a major growth area in Canadian law. Some practitioners now describe themselves as specialists in constitutional law. This means they assist corporations in fighting restrictions on Sunday shopping,[19] or tobacco advertising,[20] or monopolies.[21]

TRADE UNIONS

While corporations have been the big winners in Charter litigation, trade unions have gained the least. This should hardly be a surprise given the unmistakable class position of the judges.[22]

The fact that many people have been surprised by this result or have actually argued that the Charter might be used to the benefit of the labour movement, illustrates again how the Charter tends to promote the abstract at the expense of the concrete. The abstract question—Are rights a good thing for the labour movement?—suggests an affirmative answer. The response to the concrete question—In the struggle between capital and workers, which side will the judges prefer?—is less clouded by ideology.

Some, at least, of the Charter cases involving labour have been antidemocratic in the sense already noted. That is, they have involved an attack on legislation which recognizes the special role of unions. The legal position of unions in Canada is not the result of the common law, which was always hostile, but of popularly inspired reforms brought about through legislative action. Some unions had hoped to win constitutional recognition of a right to strike and a right to bargain collectively. Not only have these not been achieved,[23] there is real concern that the once-secure legislative shelter from which the labour movement operated may be dismantled.[24]

Attacks on the trade union movement are antidemocratic in an additional sense. Democracy, as it has been discussed in this paper, does not just happen. It requires that certain institutions exist and flourish. I believe one such institution is the trade union. A lively, independent trade union movement is essential in a democratic society. To the extent the Charter has served as a means whereby the labour movement has been weakened, it has also been a means for weakening democracy in Canada.

THE WAY WE THINK

The Charter has had an incalculable effect on the way Canadians think. I suspect the most significant effect of the Charter has been in promoting the Americanization of our thought processes. This will be discussed in more detail below. For now I want to highlight the role the Charter has played in promoting antidemocratic ways of thinking.

The Charter has done a great deal to undermine the legitimacy of the political process. It promotes the quick judicial fix over the arduous and unpredictable demands of politics. To put the same point slightly differently, the courtroom is being accepted as a proper forum for the resolution of political disputes. The authority of judges to act as guardians of the constitution and of politics and of morality and of just about everything else is seldom challenged. A recent book about the Charter was titled *Litigating the Values of a Nation*.[25] It does not seem to have occurred to the editors that in a democracy values are not resolved through litigation.

Certainly the Charter has made Canadians more litigious. It has encouraged the spread of the idea that social issues can be disposed of in the courtroom. Many people have come to believe that for every social ill there must be a legal remedy and, more important, that they can find a just resolution of their claims in the courtroom. A major result has been that people have transferred the responsibility for prosecuting their political battles from themselves and their friends and associates to their lawyers. Rather than doing the difficult political work of organizing and fighting, many seem to prefer to hand the struggle over to lawyers. As this trend continues it must reinforce habits of passivity and docility amongst the people.

This is also an approach to political and social struggle which is doubly self-defeating. Political victories are not, cannot be, won in the courtroom for the simple reason that courts, whatever contrary pretensions may have developed, can only resolve the specific legal issues actually being litigated. Judges cannot will the material conflicts which gave rise to those issues out of existence. People seeking social justice in the courtroom become frustrated and dispirited. They also become broke as all the money they worked so hard to raise goes to pay lawyers.

The Charter has also given a great boost to another profoundly antidemocratic tendency: interest-group politics. Democratic politics is predicated on the notion of the citizen. The citizen is the subject of democratic politics.

A citizen is an informed, active, multifaceted man or woman. The citizen acts simultaneously on a host of social issues. The member of an interest group is, in contrast, one dimensional. He or she has one social goal, one social interest. Everything else is inconsequential.

By its nature interest-group politics contradicts the ideal of citizenship. More to the point, interest-group politics and judicial review seem to have been made for each other. The interest group is impelled into the courtroom at least in part by the knowledge that it will not be able to achieve its goals in the broader political arena. Like corporations, interest groups seek to circumvent the democratic process. And it seems to be more than simply fortuitous that a substantial amount of the money interest groups spend in trying to further their aims through Charter litigation comes from the government of Canada.

HOW THE CHARTER IS MAKING US MORE AMERICAN

The U.S. political scientist Seymour Martin Lipset observed in *Continental Divide*[26] that

> perhaps the most important step that Canada has taken to Americanize itself—far greater in its implications than the signing of the free trade treaty— has been the incorporation into its constitution of a bill of rights, the Charter of Rights and Freedoms.

I believe Lipset is correct. But what exactly is meant by "Americanizing" and how has the Charter contributed to it?

We must always be conscious of certain fundamental differences between Canada and the United States. These can be seen by looking at the founding documents of the two countries, documents which set out the basic ideas which were to inform their development. The Declaration of Independence speaks of "life, liberty, and the pursuit of happiness." This says to me that at the centre of the U.S. project is the individual and at the centre of the individual's existence is the pursuit of material wealth. The British North America Act of 1867, in decidedly less ringing terms, talks of "peace, order, and good government." These words speak to me of a society which has a sense of its own organic nature and of the mutual rights and obligations of its members. The U.S. was born out of the revolutionary liberalism of the 18th century. Its political, intellectual, and cultural history have been defined by that liberalism. The Canadian tradition is different. It is a fundamentally Tory tradition.[27]

Before looking in more detail at the ways in which the Charter has assisted in the process of our Americanization, we must remind ourselves of one fundamental

127

and inescapable fact: the Charter is, culturally and historically, an American document. It is true that the Charter was drafted by Canadian lawyers, but that drafting was a technical rather than a cultural exercise. It is, I would think, undeniable that the idea of creating a constitutional guarantee of rights is an American idea and that the basic model for all such documents is the U.S. Bill of Rights. Furthermore, both the idea and the practice of judicial review of legislation are American inventions.

It is also true that the direct textual sources of the Charter are found, not in the U.S. Bill of Rights, but in the Universal Declaration of Human Rights (1948), the European Convention on Human Rights (1960), and the International Covenant on Civil and Political Rights (1966). But there are two qualifications which must be noted. First, the U.S. Bill of Rights is the inspiration and, in some cases, the source for these texts. Second, and more important, the international documents noted are steps in a process which has seen thinking about human rights progress far beyond its 18th century origins. The legal and political rights of the U.S. Bill of Rights, now referred to as First Generation rights, have in recent years been supplemented and substantially transformed by the addition of Second—social, economic and cultural—and Third—self-determination, development, peace, a clean environment—Generation rights. Apart from its linguistic guarantees, the Charter deals only with First Generation rights. It is an 18th century document.

We have already noted some of the obvious ways in which the Charter has promoted the Americanization of Canada. It has transformed our system of parliamentary government. It has led to a redefinition of what Canadian judges do and the way they do it. When it heard its first appeal involving the Canadian Bill of Rights in 1963, the Supreme Court of Canada stated clearly it was not interested in looking at U.S. case law.[28] But with its first major Charter decision in 1984[29] the court made it equally clear that it was open to argument based on U.S. cases. Today our courts are awash with American jurisprudence. American decisions, American monographs, American journal articles are cited in profusion and discussed at agonizing length.

One begins to wonder whether the judges of the Supreme Court of Canada still realize they live in a different country. At the least a Canadian might be forgiven for imagining that the judges now feel it to be their responsibility to promote the Americanization of our legal system. Mr. Justice Gérard LaForest has been quoted as boasting, "We have accomplished in five years what it took the Americans 50 to do."[30]

I want to turn now to three ways in which the Charter has been used in our ongoing Americanization. These are: abolishing our history; exalting individualism; and delegitimating politics and the state.

ABOLISHING OUR HISTORY

We are very quickly forgetting that we once had our own values, our own institutions, and our own ways of doing things. We have largely lost the sense of our own uniqueness. Clearly the Charter has not been the most significant factor in this process. That distinction must go to television. But the Charter has done a great deal to persuade us that American ways are best and that where there is a social problem in Canada the proper approach to it will be found in the application of American law.[31] The whole mindset was well summed up for me when a leading Charter practitioner observed at a conference, "The Charter is the best thing to happen to this country since professional baseball."

More concretely, and I get this largely from students, serious misconceptions about pre-Charter Canada are beginning to take root. There is an idea about that prior to the Charter Canadians had no rights. We had, presumably, slumbered on for decades through a dark night of oppression only to be awakened on that glorious day in April 1982 by the brilliant sun of constitutional rights. I sense that students really don't believe me when I tell them there was nothing new about the rights in the Charter and that Canadians had enjoyed most, if not quite all, of them for a long time. At a deeper level, the impression seems to be growing that Canada was not a proper country until the Charter.

EXALTING INDIVIDUALISM

Our judges, who seem to have even less knowledge of Canadian history than law students, are now proclaiming the social and political primacy of the individual. We once respected freedom of expression because we saw it as the indispensable precondition for parliamentary government.[32] Now we are told by our judges that free expression is important because we value something called "individual self-fulfillment."[33]

For Madame Justice Bertha Wilson, the most expressly ideological of our judges, the Charter created a broad constitutional guarantee of individual autonomy. In *Morgentaler*[34] she set out her personal understanding of the Charter. "The Charter is predicated," she said, "on a particular conception of the place of the individual in society." That place was clearly at the centre. "The rights guaranteed in the Charter erect around each individual, metaphorically speaking, an invisible fence over which the state will not be allowed to trespass." From this perspective she had no difficulty in finding a "right to individual liberty" in the Charter. But she went further. In matters of conscience, in what she called "fundamental personal decisions," the wishes of the individual were to be accorded precedence over the priorities of the state.

Madame Justice Wilson has adopted a highly personal and idiosyncratic approach to judging. She has taken the view that few, if any, social issues should be regarded as beyond the purview of the courts.[35] She has also shattered the traditional Canadian perception of judicial neutrality, by arguing that all judges, like all human beings, are biased[36] and by stating that, not only does she have political and social ideas, but these ideas inform her judging.[37] More important, for present purposes, is the fact that Wilson has been the most American of our judges, both in her enthusiasm for an activist approach and in the preconceptions which she has imposed through her judgments.

Wilson's justification for her individualism derives from the historical conflation

129

I discussed earlier. She observed in *Morgentaler* that "an emphasis on individual conscience and individual judgment lies at the heart of our democratic political tradition." This is, again, to confuse liberalism and democracy. Far more important, while some might see the statement as a reasonable summary of the history of the U.S., it is a grossly distorted reading of our history.

It would be quite wrong to imagine that Wilson has been the only judge to espouse these individualistic ways of thinking. She has simply been the most forthright. The point is, however, that the courts are playing a significant role in reshaping and redirecting our thinking. Canadians are being taught to see ourselves first and foremost as individuals. We are being taught to align our thinking more and more with that of Americans.

The Charter has given encouragement to rights-thinking which has, in its turn, both complemented and reinforced individualism. Rights-thinking is an essential element in American culture. Each individual is fitted out with rights. These are seen as weapons, a quiver filled with jurisprudential arrows, to be used in prosecuting the ceaseless war of each against all. By its nature, rights-thinking separates human beings from each other and encourages them to see themselves as disconnected individuals.

We have come to conceptualize our needs as human beings and our desires and our whims as rights. As we perceive the demands which we make on other people in the language of rights, we become more alienated and more individualistic. And having defined our social relations in rights terms, it only makes sense that every social conflict should eventually be susceptible to judicial resolution.

DELEGITIMATING POLITICS AND THE STATE

Again, one must not place all the blame on the Charter. In a practical sense, the contemporary process of delegitimating the political and worshipping the economic, of celebrating the wonders of the "free market," begins with the Reagan-Thatcher counterrevolution. The result has been that the state, "the government," has come to be seen as inherently evil and oppressive. As the state loses its legitimacy, politics become suspect, since the object of politics is the state. And, finally, the very notion of democracy is open to question.

The delegitimation of the state has been especially insidious in Canada. The most superficial acquaintance with our history shows that Canada has been, and continues to be, very much a creation of the state. The first major initiative of the new Canadian state, and a basic consideration in the formation of that state, was the construction of a transcontinental railway. Canada, as a physical entity, was built by the state. Likewise the development of a Canadian identity, of a sense of ourselves as Canadians, was very much the work of the state, primarily through the agency of the CBC. In more recent times, the entire range of state-sponsored social programmes and economic enterprises was seen as a central element in shaping our perception of being Canadian. To put the legitimacy of the state in doubt is to put the legitimacy of Canada in doubt.

The Charter has, once again, given great encouragement to this process.

Charter cases are typically seen as involving an individual seeking to uphold a right in the face of the implacable hostility of the state. If rights are perceived as "good," which clearly is the way they are, then the state must be seen as "bad."

I believe that the Americanization of Canada is undesirable. It is undesirable because as we lose our sense of ourselves and of our history we lose the ability, and what is more serious, the reason, to preserve Canada as an independent and autonomous state.

We also weaken the ability of our popular institutions to respond to corporate power. We run the risk of our politics turning into the same trivial sideshow as American politics, where the important decisions, the ones which determine the social and economic agenda, are not made in the Congress or the state legislatures, but in corporate boardrooms.

THE REASON WHY

Why did all this happen? Why is a democratic, independent Canada in a crisis? Clearly, a complete answer cannot be provided in a brief essay like this. There is a host of factors—economic, cultural, geopolitical—which have impelled us into our current condition. The more pertinent question for present purposes is why did our legal system respond to the adoption of the Charter in the way it has? Why was our pre-Charter legal culture jettisoned so quickly and enthusiastically? To be more precise, I do not believe anyone in Canada foresaw that the judges would use the Charter in the way they have? How do we explain this behaviour?

The usual explanation is found in the Charter itself. Once we adopted a constitutional guarantee of rights, so the stock answer goes, the judges were forced, like it or not, to take on an activist role. In 1983 a colleague and I wrote:

> There is nothing in the language or structure of the Charter which will require the Supreme Court of Canada to renounce the restraint which characterized its approach to the Canadian Bill of Rights. [38]

I still believe this to be true. To explain why the Charter has transformed our legal culture we have to look outside the Charter.

First, judges and lawyers, like all other Canadians, have spent their lives being subjected to American television, American movies, American music, American sports, American books, American everything. If ordinary Canadians sometimes forget they don't live in the U.S. or occasionally imagine American ways are better than ours, why shouldn't judges and lawyers?

Second, the Charter has inspired vastly increased interest in constitutional law, lawyers, and judges on the part of the mass media. I would guess that prior to its decision in *Drybones* [39] in 1969 most Canadians probably didn't know there was a Supreme Court of Canada. Equally, I would suspect few wasted their time reflecting on the constitution. This has changed.

The Charter now looms large in all public debates. During the summer of 1989 Canada was briefly transformed into a gigantic constitutional law seminar

131

as the media focused attention on the attempts of two women to litigate their way to abortions. And the judges of the Supreme Court have become public figures. We see their faces regularly on television. They, or most of them, now give interviews[40] and feel free to express themselves publicly on a range of issues.[41] And since the judges are involved in upholding rights, which every journalist in Canada agrees are wonderful things, reporting about the Supreme Court and its judges tends to be favourable. Might I suggest the judges like this favourable reporting and even respond to it and welcome it?

A third reason must surely lie in the scathing criticism that was heaped on the court by legal commentators throughout the 1970s, particularly in relation to its decisions on the Canadian Bill of Rights. I assume judges read legal periodicals and I would also assume some of them must have been stung by the often unpleasant opinions they read there. I cannot avoid believing that at least some of the persons now on the court determined they would never be the objects of such criticism.

Finally, and most important in a cultural sense, we must look at the effects of legal education. There is no full-scale study of the historical development of legal education in Canada. A recent report on the subject, *Law and Learning: Report to the Social Sciences and Humanities Research Council of Canada by the Consultative (sic) Group on Research and Education in Law* (the Arthurs Report),[42] disclaims any attempt at being a historical analysis. Indeed, the Arthurs Report tells us very little about Canadian legal education in a cultural or ideological sense.

The Arthurs Report fails, and this is a serious failure, to come to grips with the role university legal education has played in Americanizing our legal culture. The report does note the growing number of law teachers who have done graduate legal study in the U.S.,[43] but generally sees this as a good thing. It does not seem to have occurred to the report's authors that many of the debates which took place in the 1940s, 50s, and 60s between practitioners and academics—positivism versus realism, the use of casebooks—were, in fact, debates over the Americanization of legal education.

The most important year in the history of Canadian legal education was undoubtedly 1949, when Cecil Wright, John Willis, and Bora Laskin resigned from the profession's law school at Osgoode Hall and revived the Faculty of Law at the University of Toronto. The significance of that event lies in the fact that the U of T law school was created in conscious imitation of an American model. The goal was to create another Harvard Law School.

The founders at Toronto introduced the techniques and the values of Harvard. Most significant of these was the belief, born out of legal realism and brought to full flower by the lawyers of the New Deal, that the law could and should be used as a means of creating a better society. Judges shouldn't just decide cases, they should become social engineers. At the heart of this conception of law, then, was a belief in judicial activism, a belief that "good" judges, who had been properly schooled could use the law to achieve social betterment.

I would argue that the most influential article ever to appear in a Canadian

132

legal periodical was Laskin's "The Supreme Court of Canada: A Final Court of Appeal of and for Canadians," published in the *Canadian Bar Review* in 1951.[44] An unmistakable message conveyed by this article, its central message in my opinion, is that the Supreme Court of Canada, newly freed from stultifying subservience to the Judicial Committee of the Privy Council, should begin to pattern itself after the Supreme Court of the United States.

It is interesting, to put the Americanization of Canadian legal education in perspective, to note that, from the late 1950s to the mid-1970s, legal education played a role in American foreign policy. U.S. foreign policy during this period was largely defined by the Cold War, by the need to everywhere and always oppose the U.S.S.R. This objective dictated that the Soviets be challenged in the third world. The primary tactic was to win hearts and minds. American ideas and American values were to be used to persuade people to accept capitalism domestically and to adhere to American goals internationally. Legal educators, as a matter of deliberate policy, played a role in this process. They attempted to bring to Asian, African, and Latin American universities precisely the approach to legal education favoured by the Arthurs Report.[45]

The Harvard model has long since become the accepted, and the only acceptable, approach at the common law faculties in Canada. Everything about Canadian law schools—teaching methods, law reviews, deans' lists, even academic fashions (Critical Legal Studies is simply the most recent)—apes American models. The point is that the overwhelming majority of anglophone lawyers in Canada have been professionally socialized into an American tradition which celebrates the values and goals of the American legal system. This tradition has taught Canadian lawyers that constitutional rights are wonderful and should be enforced by activist judges.

This is the setting into which the Charter was introduced. How could its reception have been anything but what I have described?

WHAT IS TO BE DONE?

The situation is not hopeless. Canada still exists and we still have democratic institutions. It is a matter of gaining back what we have lost. There are various political possibilities. I intend only to discuss those which exist at the level of the legal system. What is required is a conscious, systematic effort to undermine the legitimacy of Charter-based judicial review. This effort would manifest itself in three ways.

The first thing that can be done would not only assist in breaking the ideological grip of the Charter, but would contribute to improving our national intellectual health. We should seek in our thinking to eschew the abstract and embrace the concrete. This could have a number of useful results. The Charter would cease to inhibit our ability to see what is happening to Canadian society. We might become less inclined to believe that since our rights are being protected, everything must be all right. Then, we might go to the next stage and inquire

133

about the effects of actual Charter decisions on our lives. Thus we would ask concrete questions such as, "Has Sunday shopping made our lives better?" And finally we might begin to ask ourselves whether we really want to create in Canada a replica of U.S. society. Is it our collective wish to exist only as isolated individuals, all our economic relations mediated through money and our social relations mediated through the law?

Second, we should be much more critical of the judges and what they are doing. If the judges are going to perform the tasks once reserved to politicians, then they must be subjected to the same critical scrutiny as politicians. Fortunately, the judges have removed a judge-made obstacle to this sort of activity. It is no longer a crime in Canada to be publicly critical of judges.[46] We should speak out against the judges for subverting democracy and trying to turn us into Americans. We should also be critical of the sanctimonious twaddle which is emanating from the Supreme Court of Canada. Consider the following:

> The diversity in forms of individual self-fulfilment and human flourishing ought to be cultivated in an essentially tolerant, indeed welcoming, environment not only for the sake of those who convey a meaning, but also for the sake of those to whom it is conveyed.[47]

The author of those words is now Chief Justice of Canada. The subject of his rhapsody was communications on the street between a prostitute and potential clients.

Third, and finally, we should seek the rehabilitation of section 33 of the Charter, the "override" provision. Section 33 has been much criticized by those who think the Charter is marvellous. It has been portrayed as a monstrous contradiction of the whole objective of guaranteeing rights, a standing invitation to oppressive governments to impose their evil goals on an innocent and unsuspecting citizenry. I don't see it that way. Section 33 could be the means of resuscitating parliamentary democracy in Canada. It could be used to reassert the popular will against judges who attempt to frustrate that will, especially since the judges themselves have not been prepared to invent substantive limits on the use of section 33.[48]

There are two obvious examples of legislation which could be insulated against judicial review. Both cases involve socially desirable policies which were frustrated by the courts. In both the policies in question had clear popular support and their reintroduction would, I believe, be well received. One example is federal and the other is provincial.

The first is found in the Canada Elections Act.[49] Beginning in 1974, Parliament placed limitations on election-campaign spending by both political parties and interest groups. In 1983 these restrictions were tightened up and the tightening was supported by all three parties in the House of Commons. In 1984 a single judge of the Alberta Court of Queen's Bench invalidated, on the basis of the Charter, these restrictions on spending.[50] One result was that corporations were able to spend tens of millions of dollars during the 1988 federal election to persuade

Canadians that free trade with the U.S. would be good for them. A Royal Commission on Electoral Reform and Party Financing is now completing its work. It may recommend the reintroduction of spending limits. This would be an obvious and, I believe, desirable and popular occasion for Parliament to exercise its authority under section 33.

The second example is from Ontario. It is clear that a strong majority of people in the province favour what is now called a "common pause day" or, in more direct language, are opposed to Sunday shopping. The wishes of the majority have been circumvented by the courts.[51] The new government of Ontario is formally committed to the reintroduction of a common pause day. This would be another excellent opportunity to use section 33.

It is still possible for the people of Canada to fight back against corporate power. The damage wrought through the Charter can be reversed.

NOTES

* I wish to thank Adelso Mancia Carpio for his research assistance. I also would like to thank my colleague, Berend Hovius for his comments.
1. See, as one example, the editorial pages of *The Globe and Mail*, 12 October 1990.
2. Anne F. Bayefsky, *Canada's Constitution Act, 1982 and Amendments: A Documentary History*, 2 vols. (Toronto, 1989) is a compendious collection of official documents.
3. The fullest statement, and one with which I generally agree, is found in Michael Mandel, *The Charter of Rights and the Legalization of Politics in Canada* (Toronto, 1989).
4. The point is developed at length in C.B. Macpherson's classic primer on political theory, *The Real World of Democracy* (Toronto, 1966). See also his *The Life and Times of Liberal Democracy* (Oxford, 1977).
5. See Jamie Cameron, "Liberty, Authority, and the State in American Constitutionalism," *Osgoode Hall Law Journal* 25 (1987): 257, and R.I. Cheffins and Patricia Johnson, *The Revised Canadian Constitution: Politics as Law* (Toronto, 1986), especially chapter XI.
6. *Hunter v. Southam Inc.*, [1984] 2 S.C.R. 145, at 155.
7. See John Sopinka, "Intervention," *The Advocate* 46 (1988): 883.
8. As an illustrative decision, see *Ford v. A.G. Québec* (1988), 54 D.L.R. (4th) 577 (S.C.C.).
9. (1990), 66 D.L.R. (4th) 635.
10. *New Brunswick Broadcasting Co. Ltd. v. Donahoe* (1990), 71 D.L.R. (4th) 23 (N.S.S.C.).
11. *Southam Inc. v. A.G. Canada* (1989), 27 F.T.R. 139. This decision was overruled by the Federal Court of Appeal on 23 August 1990.
12. (1989), 70 O.R. (2d) 179 (C.A.).
13. Ibid., 209, per McKinlay, J.A.
14. See note 6.
15. (1989), 58 D.L.R. (4th) 577.
16. [1985] 1 S.C.R. 295. It may not be strictly accurate to say of these cases that they involved corporations *claiming*, in a positive sense, Charter rights. What the corporations were allowed to do by the court was to rely on Charter guarantees as defences against state acts authorized by legislation. I would argue the practical result of these decisions is that corporations can claim Charter rights.

17. [1985] 2 S.C.R. 486.
18. A discussion, especially useful since it was written before Ronald Reagan and Margaret Thatcher came to power, of the legal issues involved can be found in W. Friedmann, *The State and the Rule of Law in a Mixed Economy* (London, 1971).
19. *R.* v. *Edwards Books and Art Ltd.*, [1986] 2 S.C.R. 713; *R.* v. *Paul Magder Furs Ltd.* (1989), 49 C.C.C. (3d) 267 (Ont. C.A.); *R.* v. *Canada Safeway Ltd.*, [1989] 5 W.W.R. 122 (B.C.C.A.); *Regional Municipality of Peel* v. *A and P Canada Ltd.* (1990), 71 D.L.R. (4th) 293 (Ont. H.C.J.); *R.* v. *Westfair Foods Ltd.* (1990), 65 D.L.R. (4th) 56 (Sask. C.A.).
20. The Tobacco Products Control Act, S.C. 1988, c. 20 promises to spawn a vast amount of jurisprudence.
21. The Competition Act, S.C. 1986, c. 26 has been much assaulted under the Charter. See *Alex Couture Inc. et al.* v. *A.G. Canada* (1990), 69 D.L.R. (4th) 635 (Qué. S.C.); *R.* v. *Wholesale Travel Group Inc.* (1990), 63 D.L.R. (4th) 325 (Ont. C.A.); and *R.* v. *Nova Scotia Pharmaceutical Society*, unreported, Nova Scotia Supreme Court, Trial Division, September 1990.
22. See Martin, "Ideology and Judging in the Supreme Court of Canada," *Osgoode Hall Law Journal* 26 (1988): 797.
23. See *Re Public Service Employee Relations Act* (1987), 38 D.L.R. (4th) 161 (S.C.C.) and *Professional Institute of the Public Service of Canada* v. *Commissioner of the N.W.T.* (1990), 72 D.L.R. (4th) 1 (S.C.C.).
24. *Lavigne* v. *Ontario Public Service Employees Union* (1989), 31 O.A.C. 40 (Ont. C.A.).
25. J.M. Weiler and R.M. Elliott, eds., *Litigating the Values of a Nation: The Canadian Charter of Rights and Freedoms* (Toronto, 1986).
26. *Continental Divide: The Values and Institutions of the United States and Canada* (New York, 1990), 225. It is a discouraging comment on the Canadian psyche that we tend to believe these sorts of things about ourselves only when we are told them by Americans.
27. The classic statement of this perspective is found in George Grant, *Lament for a Nation* (Toronto, 1965). See also Charles Taylor, *Six Journeys: A Canadian Pattern* (Toronto, 1977) and *Radical Tories: The Conservative Tradition in Canada* (Toronto, 1982).
28. *Robertson and Rosetanni* v. *R.*, [1963] S.C.R. 651.
29. *Hunter* v. *Southam Inc.*, see note 6.
30. Quoted in Claire Bernstein, "Supreme Court Catching up on Charter-judging," *The London Free Press*, 21 April 1990. Canadian judges like to absolve themselves from any responsibility in all this by writing speeches and articles in which they argue that while U.S. jurisprudence may be "helpful" or "instructive," it should not be followed "blindly." See, as an example, Madame Justice Beverley McLachlin, "The Charter of Rights and Freedoms: A Judicial Perspective," *University of British Columbia Law Review* 23 (1989): 579. Former Chief Justice Brian Dickson recently observed, "Canada and the United States are not alike in every way"; see *R.* v. *Keegstra*, Supreme Court of Canada, 1990, unreported.
31. There has, for example, recently been some concern that libel law has a "chilling effect" on the mass media. The solution which many are advocating is that we simply follow the U.S. law. See the discussion in Martin, "Does Libel Have a 'Chilling Effect' in Canada?," *Studies in Communications* 4 (1990): 143.
32. *Re Alberta Statutes*, [1938] S.C.R. 100.
33. *A.G. Québec* v. *Irwin Toy Ltd.* (1989), 58 D.L.R. (4th) 577 (S.C.C.). We also, apparently, now believe in a "market-place of ideas." *Keegstra* v. *R.*, [1988] 5 W.W.R. 221 (Alta. C.A.).
34. *Morgentaler, Smolling and Scott* v. *The Queen*, [1988] 1 S.C.R. 30.
35. *Operation Dismantle* v. *The Queen*, [1985] 1 S.C.R. 441.
36. "Will Women Judges Really Make A Difference?", *Osgoode Hall Law Journal* 28 (1990): 507.
37. Madame Justice Bertha Wilson, "Decision-making in the Supreme Court," *University of Toronto Law Journal* 36 (1986): 227.
38. B. Hovius and R. Martin, "The Canadian Charter of Rights and Freedoms in the Supreme Court of Canada," *Canadian Bar Review* 61 (1983): 354.

39. [1970] S.C.R. 282.
40. See Bernstein, note 30.
41. See the speech by Madame Justice Wilson, note 36.
42. Ottawa, 1983.
43. Ibid., 18.
44. *The Canadian Bar Review* 29 (1951): 1038.
45. See James Gardner, *Legal Imperialism: American Lawyers and Foreign Aid in Latin America* (Madison, 1980). A blueprint for Americanizing legal education in the third world is found in International Legal Center, *Legal Education in a Changing World: Report of the Committee on Legal Education in the Developing Countries* (Uppsala, 1975). The similarities between this report and the Arthurs Report are striking.
46. *Kopyto v. R.* (1988), 24 O.A.C. 81 (Ont. C.A.).
47. *Reference re Sections 193 and 195.1(1)(c) of the Criminal Code*, [1990] 1 S.C.R. 1123. The Chief Justice was quoting words first used by Dickson in his Irwin Toy judgment, see note 15.
48. See *Ford v. A.G. Québec*, note 8.
49. R.S.C. 1985, c E-2.
50. *National Citizens' Coalition Inc. v. A.G. Canada* (1984), 11 D.L.R. (4th) 481 (Alta. Q.B.).
51. The Ontario Retail Business Holidays Act, R.S.O. 1980, c. 453 provided, with some exemptions, for Sunday closing in Ontario. The act was held to be valid by the Supreme Court of Canada in *R. v. Edwards Books and Art Ltd.*, see note 19. The act was amended in 1989 (S.O. 1989, c. 3) to allow municipalities to determine whether they would permit Sunday opening or not. The amended act was then held to be invalid. *Regional Municipality of Peel v. A and P Canada Ltd.*, see note 19.

COMMENTARY

DEBORAH COYNE

GOVERNMENT OF NEWFOUNDLAND

It is now widely agreed that the Charter of Rights and Freedoms is transforming the general conduct of politics and our language of political discourse. Equally, at least since the Meech Lake debacle, it is now widely agreed that the Charter has in particular transformed the dynamics of constitutional reform.

As Alan Cairns and others have observed, with the implementation of the Charter in 1982 and the entrenchment of basic rights and freedoms against all levels of governments, Canadians now have a very real sense that the constitution belongs to the people. It is not something that can be tinkered with by the pre-1982 methods of elitist executive federalism. The Charter has bolstered Canadians' firm belief in the equality of all citizens in Canada. This translates into an insistence on the uniform application of the Charter across Canada so that all Canadians have the same rights and freedoms wherever they live.

These two principles as I would call them—that the constitution belongs to the *people* and that all Canadians should have the same rights and freedoms— emerge as perhaps the most significant lesson we have learned from the Meech Lake debacle. And I am confident that the *people* of Canada want the country to hold together. So to ensure this result we need to let the people into the process in a meaningful way.

I will address two topics. First, I will argue that the Charter is unique to Canada and will not have an inevitably "Americanizing" impact on us, as some observers rather simplistically assert. Second, I will comment on the specific Charter issues during the debate over the Meech Lake Accord in the hope that we can draw some lessons for the future.

The Charter has profoundly altered the relationship between the individual and the state, and the political and socioeconomic fabric of the country. It is now the key component of our constitution that articulates the fundamental values that are common to all of us and that define ourselves, our concept of the Canadian federation, and our commitment to a fairer, more compassionate society.

As a uniquely Canadian document, the Charter must be interpreted in light of Canadian political traditions. It is a late 20th century document—one that is not preoccupied, for example, with how to limit government as was the case 200 years ago when the American constitution emerged. In sharp contrast to the American Bill of Rights, the Charter reflects a belief that there need not be any contradiction between state regulation and individual liberty, and that freedom where appropriate is enhanced by our public institutions and state action.

The Charter also blends an emphasis on individual freedom with respect for community values. For example, it requires us to take into account cultural,

139

religious, linguistic, and aboriginal communities in interpreting the rights guaranteed to individuals. These unique aspects of the Charter are most obvious in the broad guarantees of equality, minority language and education rights, mobility rights, and our commitment to multiculturalism, all of which are subject "only to such reasonable limits prescribed by law as can be demonstrably justified in a free and democratic society."

This formula for reasonable limits is a critical element of the Charter. It is set out explicitly in the first section of the Charter, and is just one of many specific contrasts to the American Bill of Rights. Nothing specific was set out in the American document and it took years for the judiciary to develop the concept of judge-made limits on rights and freedoms that provided governments with the needed flexibility to implement, among other things, progressive social legislation.

In the view of many constitutional experts, the balancing performed to date by our courts pursuant to section 1 of the Charter accommodates well the Canadian tradition of greater public action, as well as our federal diversity. For example, in the Bill 101 sign law case, although the Supreme Court of Canada found that banning English on outdoor signs was a breach of freedom of expression, it also held that it would nevertheless be permissible, under section 1, for the Québec government to mandate greater predominance for the French language vis-à-vis any other. As we all know, the Québec government rejected this option and took the regrettable step of invoking the notwithstanding clause to sustain the complete ban on English. But I am confident, having read a great deal of commentary on the subject particularly by francophones in Québec, that a significant number of thoughtful moderate Quebeckers could have accepted the Supreme Court option, which was indeed the original position of the Québec Liberal Party.

(I should just note here that I have always believed, and do even more so now, that the notwithstanding clause must be removed at the earliest opportunity. It was an unfortunate concession to some of the premiers in 1981 and is most certainly an alien feature in any Charter. Moreover, for those sincerely concerned about preserving the necessary scope for state action, the reasonable limits clause of the Charter is proving very satisfactory, and there is no need, if there ever was, for the notwithstanding clause.)

Some months after the Bill 101 decision, I recall a conversation I had with Claude Morin, a former Parti Québécois minister of intergovernmental affairs. It was on the eve of the release of another Supreme Court decision on the validity of certain stringent Québec regulations of commercial advertising aimed at children. Morin, like so many in the nationalist-dominated elite and media in Québec, was lamenting the expected result that the court would knock down the regulations on the grounds of a breach of freedom of expression, something that would provide yet another allegedly iniquitous example of the operation of the Canadian Charter against the interests of Québec. Needless to say, these were crocodile tears since Québec nationalists preferred precisely such a result in order to use it to further their own interests.

I replied to Morin that, in my view, he was wrong and that he was forgetting the balancing of interests that the court was required to perform under section 1 of the Charter. I thought it was highly likely that the court would consider the regulations to be "reasonable limits prescribed by law as can be demonstrably justified in a free and democratic society." My prediction proved true much to the disgruntlement I am sure of Morin and other nationalists.

To demonstrate further the unique features and impact of the Charter, it should be noted that its focus on rights and fundamental values clearly shapes the public policy agenda through legal challenges to legislative and administrative action. It also shapes the agenda through the increased sensitivity of policy makers who are determined to "Charter-proof" any proposed legislation or other government action in order to preempt such legal action, through the activities of groups and individuals, who use the Charter as a symbolic document in their lobbying efforts with governments.

The Charter influence is perhaps most obvious with respect to our approaches to dealing with the inequality and inequities in society, notably our employment and social assistance policies. For example, we are increasingly conscious of the needs of disadvantaged groups such as women, visible minorities, Native Canadians, the disabled, and are taking steps through affirmative action and pay equity initiatives to improve their well-being. We also more frequently speak of a person's right to a decent minimum standard of living, a decent quality of life, as something that is as worthy of protection as traditional property rights and contractual rights.

More broadly, the Charter is having a subtle nationalizing effect as it gives expression to a national citizenship that is independent of territorial/regional location and that transcends regional identities. This appeal to our nonterritorial identities (for example to ethnicity and gender) finds concrete expression in the new popular coalitions that are emerging.

In discussing the profound impact of the Charter, I want to single out the minority language and education rights. These illustrate not only the unique character of the Charter, but also the perennial debate over how best to protect minority rights in Canada that surfaced yet again with a vengeance during the Meech Lake debate.

Canadian history is littered with examples of the dangers of having to rely only on benevolent government action to protect minority rights. The decision in 1982 to vest minority language rights in individuals represented an important historical compromise. It provided members of minority language groups with legally enforceable rights that could be asserted against both levels of government.

The Charter guarantees of minority language and education rights are unique, however, because they reflect a blend of individual rights and group identities: individual rights are contingent on membership in the relevant community or collectivity. This is because language rights do not exist in a vacuum—to provide meaningful protection we also must ensure the preservation and promotion of linguistic communities. So the language guarantees, while accorded to individuals, reflect a positive obligation on the courts and legislatures to promote the opportunity to use and develop one's language.

141

We have seen several important court challenges, such as those instigated by members of francophone minorities outside Québec, that have successfully forced provincial governments to expand the availability of French-language services and French-language education. The important thing to note is that to the extent that francophone minorities outside Québec are able to galvanize governments into promoting their interests and the bilingual character of Canada, this sends positive signals to French-Canadians in Québec and helps to build up their confidence in both themselves and Canada. This is a critical component of any long-term reconciliation of Québec's position within Canada.

Of course what definitely does not help is the equal and opposite reaction created by the intolerant English-only resolutions in some Ontario municipalities and the stomping on the Québec flag by some APEC (Alliance for the Preservation of English Canada) extremists. Unfortunately this effect was even magnified irresponsibly by the media, which played the otherwise marginal flag scene over and over again on Québec television.

That brings me to the Meech Lake Accord. I do not have time to go into a detailed analysis of how the distinct society clause would have disrupted the linguistic equilibrium that has gradually emerged over the years and would potentially have halted future progress toward strengthening the bilingual character of Canada as a whole. By way of general observation, however, the distinct society clause undermined the idea that all Canadians have common rights and freedoms regardless of where they live because it directed that the entire constitution, including the Charter, would be interpreted in light of geographic and sociocultural considerations. In other words, the nature of our basic rights would henceforth vary depending on which province we live in, which linguistic group we belong to, and so forth. This is clearly not a desirable course for a democracy that has always prided itself on its ability to sustain a diverse yet tolerant society and to promote bilingualism and multiculturalism throughout Canada.

As was demonstrated clearly during the Meech debate, Canadians generally will not tolerate any uneven application of the Charter to Canadian citizens. A fortiori, they were outraged when this was accomplished in a secretive meeting of first ministers. I will turn briefly to this particular aspect of the Meech debate.

From my perspective, the widespread sense of outrage and concern with the process leading to, and the substance of, the Meech Lake Accord was apparent right from the beginning in 1987. But there was no outlet for the opposition given the total failure of the Liberal and NDP parliamentary opposition in Ottawa. Hence my efforts and those of many others to create the Canadian Coalition on the Constitution.

The concern about how the Accord undermined the Charter was probably the most common thread among opponents of the Accord. In addition, they were concerned with its excessive provincializing impact. The lack of sensitivity to the Charter or the concerns of what Alan Cairns calls "Charter Canadians" was all too obvious in the very text of the Accord.

For example, just before the Accord was signed at the Langevin Block meeting, a new clause was inserted (article 16) stipulating among other things that certain provisions in the Charter dealing with aboriginal rights and our multicultural heritage were not affected by the distinct society clause. Unfortunately, this had the effect of compounding the widespread concern, mentioned above, since it then explicitly exposed all other Charter rights to the distinct society clause. Most important, the last minute ad hoc decision to insert article 16 simply confirmed that at Meech Lake the first ministers had not been sensitive to Charter concerns. In retrospect, it definitively made the case for a radical opening-up of the process.

Few of the Accord supporters had yet realized the far-reaching impact of the entrenchment in 1982 of the Charter, and the subtle but powerful sense of attachment that most Canadians now had to their constitution. The Accord signatories and negotiators, perhaps epitomized by Senator Lowell Murray, still operated in the pre-1982 mode: constitutional change was only a matter for first ministers at the executive level who, after all, were elected to represent their respective electorates. This was captured succinctly in a response of Senator Murray to a question from a Special Committee member in 1987 who suggested that the two Territories should have been represented at the Meech negotiating table. Murray's reply was simply "but they are not provinces." It was as if he could not fathom the idea that there are people in the Territories whose interests were affected and who had been denied a voice.

Indeed, Meech supporters were fond of saying that the closed-in executive level process they followed was set out in the 1982 Constitution. This is wrong. Admittedly the 1982 Constitution provides for amendments by way of resolutions of the appropriate legislative assemblies and Parliament. But it does not say what process is to be pursued in arriving at those resolutions. Nothing precludes any first minister from deciding, for example, to hold a referendum in his or her province to determine which form the resolution should take. To argue that the First Ministers Conference is the required process is one of many fabrications and myths perpetrated by Accord supporters.

Another fabrication and myth that emerged during the hearings in the summer of 1987 and that was to play an important role throughout the debate was that to oppose the Accord was to be anti-Québec. Brian Mulroney strengthened national forces in Québec by constantly talking about the alleged "exclusion" of Québec from the 1982 Constitution. Equally serious was how he and other Accord supporters distorted the concern about the Charter. Because the basis for concern was the special role accorded to the Québec government, Quebeckers were irresponsibly encouraged to believe that opponents opposed the preservation and promotion of the French language and culture by the Québec government and were determined to erase Québec's distinctiveness in a bland sea of uniform lowest common denominator bilingualism from coast to coast.

This fabrication was strengthened by the apparent absence of any major group in Québec professing concern about the Charter. The reality was of course that, for example, the Fédération des femmes du Québec was funded by the Québec government and would hardly have challenged the hand that fed it. In contrast, the arms-length Québec Human Rights Commission did quietly join in a 1988 joint communiqué with other provincial commissions expressing concern for the impact of the Accord on the Charter.

The fabrication was also strengthened by the difficulty in getting any sort of balanced coverage in the nationalist-dominated, inward-looking Québec media. I am convinced that had Quebeckers been able to listen to and analyze the opposition objectively, it would have been possible to explain that the Charter issue would have arisen had it involved any other provincial government. The opposition to the Accord provisions stemmed from the outrage that, after finally entrenching our rights and freedoms in 1982, 11 first ministers would even attempt to tinker with them and, in a private meeting, purport to expand a government's ability to override these rights and freedoms. In the Canada of 1987, with half a decade of Charter experience, this kind of "reform" was simply unacceptable at the very least in the absence of significant further debate and careful analysis of all the implications.

In addition, virtually no one opposed to the Accord denied or challenged Québec's distinctiveness. On the contrary, they welcomed it and encouraged it. The Québec government already is using its substantial existing powers to preserve and promote the French language and culture and, in fact, has taken very effective action. Claude Ryan failed to reply to Marc Lalonde's challenge during a *Le Point/Journal* debate in the spring of 1990, to provide a single example of a Québec law or initiative that had been stymied by the 1982 Constitution. Even the sign law provisions of Bill 101 were struck down for infringing the Québec Charter as well as the Canadian Charter. The tremendous advances made to secure the French language and culture have been confirmed most recently by a study commissioned by Québec's Counseil du Patronat du Québec and submitted to the Bélanger-Campeau Commission.

Yet Quebeckers were constantly being told that somehow they had gained something specifically new and different in the Accord that was essential to the survival of their language and culture and that opponents were now trying to take away. Virtually never were they presented with any of the broader arguments about the impact of the Accord's provisions on Canada as a whole, and the long-term value to Québec of remaining within a viable Canadian federation committed to bilingualism.

I have set out the Charter aspect of the Meech Lake debate in some detail in the hope that this will contribute to greater understanding of the forces underlying the failure of the Accord. This, in turn, should ensure that as we undertake serious constitutional reforms, not only do we implement an entirely new and open participatory process of constitutional reform which will in particular ensure a meaningful dialogue with Quebeckers, but also that we recognize the strong commitment of all Canadians to the Charter of Rights and Freedoms.

It is my hope that all Canadians, including of course our leaders, will rise above the petty squabbles, intolerance, and misunderstandings that have so regrettably characterized our recent past. We must remember how we are regarded with envy and admiration in so many parts of the world and realize how bemused are those on the outside looking in to see us in our present state of disarray. There are so many urgent challenges facing Canada and the world right now that we must not, however inadvertently, hobble ourselves through constitutional discord and fail to set the examples that so many people expect of us.

THE MEDIA
AND CONSTITUTIONAL
REFORM IN CANADA

Mirror? Searchlight? Interloper?:
The Media and Meech

JOHN MEISEL

QUEEN'S UNIVERSITY

A realistic appraisal of the role of the media in constitutional reform requires that two related but nevertheless separate dimensions be explored: coverage of specific constitutional events as well as media impact on the prevailing sense of community, societal ties, and the way in which diverse individuals, groups, and regions react to, and value, one another. Although both these dimensions are touched upon in this paper, the former receives the major attention.

What follows is a somewhat impressionistic examination of a number of discrete aspects that together illumine the role played by Canadian media during the recent era of constitution making. The approach adopted is McLuhanesque in the sense that it is nonlinear; although the evidence gathered does not comprise a fully comprehensive, systematic survey of media coverage, it provides a sufficient base on which to rest several concluding observations and recommendations for the future.

Following are the features of media behaviour that struck one observer as particularly salient during the recent process of constitutional review.

THE MEECH LAKE EXPERIENCE AS A TURNING POINT

Neither the process of constitution making nor the coverage accorded it will ever be the same as before or during the Meech Lake episode. It became obvious, as the Accord was reached and then debated at length, that a significant number of Canadians found the method of escaping Canada's constitutional impasse, imposed by the incomplete arrangement of 1982, quite unacceptable. For some, the monopolization of the negotiations by governments was self-defeating; others concluded that the time imposed for ratification by the Canada Act was counterproductive. Several groups considered that their right to be directly involved, or at least viably consulted, had been ignominiously flouted. Many could not accept what they saw as the too-secretive character of much of what went on. Widespread head-shaking was also caused by what some considered the exclusive, or at least excessive, involvement of constitutional lawyers and politicians and consequent locking out of the ordinary citizens from efforts to find a new constitutional arrangement. These and other such reactions caused the Meech Lake experience to become totally discredited as a model for revising the ground rules guiding the country's governance. Next time, other means would have to be found.

One belief shared by almost all critics of the constitutional process from the late 1980s to the Meech Lake debacle is that future efforts will have to be much more open. A vital concomitant of this conclusion is that the media will have greater and probably different access to what will transpire. The opportunities for the media to influence how people see forthcoming efforts to adjust or replace Canada's constitution will therefore be even greater than they were in the past.

The full meaning of this conclusion can only be appreciated when it is realized that the 1990 coverage was much more massive than anything Canada had ever seen in this domain. Two developments in particular were responsible: one was the highly dramatic climax of the first ministers' Ottawa meetings in June and the aftermath in the Manitoba and Newfoundland legislatures; the other concerned the advent on the broadcasting scene of Newsworld, the CBC's 24-hours-a-day, seven-days-a-week, satellite-delivered television news channel. Although the service was available only in English and only on cable, it drew very large audiences to its nonstop programming which orginated in centres throughout the country. Quite apart from the attention paid the constitutional game by the other electronic and printed media, the regular CBC coverage, special newscasts, and background information, with Newsworld now on the scene the country was blanketed by journalistic reports originating with the CBC. It was estimated that on the final Saturday of the First Ministers Conference in June, almost 4 million Canadians watched the CBC at one time or another during the day.[1] This widespread attention indicates that there is considerable appetite among TV audiences for public affairs programmes when they are exciting and that in the future, more open and participatory constitution making is likely to offer broadcasters huge and rich markets.

HIGH EXPOSURE/LOW COMPREHENSION

The large audiences for the Meech Lake coverage present us with an intriguing paradox: despite what was clearly extensive exposure, a high proportion of Canadians believed that they were inadequately informed about the content of the Accord. A CBC News-*Globe and Mail* poll in early February 1990 reported that 71% of those interviewed said they knew little or nothing about the Accord, and only 28% said they knew a fair amount or more.[2] After the 1988 election, the Meech Lake Accord succeeded free trade as the most prominent domestic political concern. During the year starting in October 1988, it ranked fifth in network coverage of

148

national issues.[3] Nevertheless, two-thirds of Canadians told an earlier CBC News-*Globe and Mail* poll that they were slightly informed or not at all informed about the Accord.[4]

The media clearly had not succeeded in conveying the actual substance of the constitutional changes entertained by Canada's governments. It is, of course, a moot point whether the communication failure is to be ascribed to flawed media presentation or to the uninterested, inattentive character of the population.

An admittedly limited study (it focused only on the CBC) during the early stages of the Accord (30 April to 5 June 1987) found that the CBC's television coverage "was highly abbreviated, sensationalized and oriented to conflict and personalities ... As a consequence, some of the broader issues underlying the Accord were never fully explained to the audience ... The newsformat," the author concludes, "severely distorted the public's views of Meech Lake."[5] Studies cited later in this paper demonstrate that the CBC's record was no worse than that of other media. Lydia Miljan, who examined the performance of both English networks, concluded that

> it is not necessarily the time constraints which dictate coverage of issues; it is what television newscasters choose to emphasize in the time allotted and who they choose to interview that dictates coverage ... (N)ews personnel choose to emphasize trivial matters because those matters best adhere to the news personnel's definition of news. Many news reports went in detail about political maneuvering and as a result did not have the opportunity to discuss substantive points. This attitude was echoed by Peter Mansbridge, "News is news: it's what happens that day. It's what's different; it's what's changed. It is not a backgrounder on constitutional matters."[6]

In the light of the evidence at hand, we must, therefore conclude that the blanketing of the country with media reports does not necessarily ensure a high level of public understanding. Thus, thought should be given to what needs to be done to improve the quality of public affairs coverage, irrespective of its quantity. I shall return to this matter below.

THE MEDIA AS ACTORS

Communications theories assign a plethora of functions to the media, ranging from modest roles to extraordinarily intrusive effects on social and political life.[7] It is usually assumed that, at a minimum, they mirror events occurring in the world, and that they inform people of current developments. Some observers conclude, in addition, that they set the agenda of what will be discussed by the political class, of what will receive public attention. The constitutional developments in the period under review were thrust onto everyone's consciousness by governments and politicians, who, after the 1984 federal victory of the Conservatives, decided to revise the constitution. In this instance, the media covered events "created" by others, but they nevertheless had an immense political influence. They did not merely report on what was happening—their actions actually affected the political

149

process itself. The media were significant actors. Among the many instances illustrating this phenomenon, three stand out.

At the time of the 1990 First Ministers Conference, the Québec media, which have for a long time tended to be strongly independentist, made it quite impossible for Premier Bourassa to make any concessions, even in the unlikely event that he had wished to do so. It had been widely accepted in Québec that absolutely *no* changes could be made to the Accord and there was much fear in nationalist circles that in the pressure cooker that was the First Ministers Conference, Bourassa might be persuaded to yield ground on some points important to the other governments, particularly Manitoba and Newfoundland. According to one impeccable witness,

> from the sophisticated Radio-Canada noon-hour hotline to the private stations' inflammatory invitations to public comment, you would have believed that ... Bourassa had just given away the shop. He had begun to negotiate the "parameters" of future Senate reform—and that was proof enough that English Canada was ganging up on him and succeeding in breaking his spine. At worst, many were accusing him of not even having a spine; at best they were fed up and simply demanding that he call off the meeting.[8]

The pathological suspicion, exaggeration, and distortion exhibited toward Bourassa by much of the Québec media was so extreme that, at one point, Premier David Peterson of Ontario convened a group of French-speaking journalists to reassure them that his Québec counterpart had not failed to defend Québec's interests.[9] Brian Mulroney took similar steps on behalf of the Québec premier vis-à-vis the Québec press. At any event, since it seemed that whenever Bourassa appeared to so much as smile, an outcry from much of the Québec media accused him of betraying his pledge to preserve the terms of the original agreement. He had absolutely no room to manoeuvre. The slightest flicker of accommodation toward the rest of the country would have prompted a savage protest, seriously undermining his political position in Québec.

Quite a different example of the media becoming actors was evident in CBC radio's "Cross Country Check-up" on 5 February 1990. For this occasion, the corporation assembled quite a large group of francophones in a Montréal studio. French-English relations were the central theme of the discussion. A great many anglophone callers were clearly upset about language issues; bilingualism, Québec's Bill 178, and Ontario's French Language Services Act (Bill 8). Many were not only strongly anti-French but also woefully ignorant about the legislation and policies they were attacking. One got the impression that many were members of anti-French groups like the Alliance for the Preservation of English Canada (APEC) or the Confederation of Regions Party (COR). Whenever they delivered themselves of some misinformed statement, this was met by the derisive laughter of the franco-phones gathered in the Montréal studio. This, in turn, could not but have infuriated the callers. While the Montréal group attempted to counter the often-bigoted views expressed, they did so in a partisan, *engagé* manner certain to be met with suspicion by the other side. No moderator or otherwise clearly "neutral" expert ever corrected the errors made by the callers. The result was that the programme deeply exacerbated ethnic tensions, thereby influencing the context in which the Meech Lake Accord was evaluated by the listeners. In this instance, there was almost no intention to influence the political climate negatively, but this is what the CBC did.

Critics of the CBC's handling of the First Ministers Conference—and they were legion—accused the CBC of having become a major player in the Meech Lake drama by giving the impression that a serious crisis was threatening the country—a crisis which, they asserted, did not, in fact, exist.[10]

Whether one agrees with these charges depends on whether one believes that the Meech Lake chapter in Canada's history constituted a major national crisis. Opponents of the Accord saw the CBC's extended coverage, and the language of some of its journalists, as evidence that the corporation had been captured by the government of the day. Whatever conclusion one reaches on this matter (I return to it below), the fact remains that the coverage itself given the constitutional proposals became part of the main events and that the CBC did more than merely report on events, either willy-nilly or by design.

This active involvement was enhanced when many of the leading players (premiers and senior officials) used the opportunities provided by the CBC and the other media to make widely disseminated statements during the negotiations which, they hoped, would affect not only public opinion but also the other parties involved in the constitutional process.

THE MEDIA AND THE BROADER CONSTITUTIONAL CONTEXT

The press had an impact on the state of mind which people brought to the constitutional debate. One of the central features of any constitution is that it determines what will be the respective position of, and the relationships among, the people constituting the country. The attitudes one takes to these matters depend not only on one's views on where the individual stands vis-à-vis the whole community and the state, but also how one judges others: those of the opposite sex, a different class, various religions, diverse parts of the country, ethnic backgrounds, and diverse cultures. While it is difficult to specify exactly the role played by the media in shaping these attitudes, there is little doubt that they have some impact on them. This is particularly the case when an important medium tends to espouse a point of view on a relevant issue and then relentlessly flogs a particular line on it while giving less attention to contrary views.

One of the most contentious features of the Meech Lake Accord was the distinct society clause and the position of Québec in Canada. Language policies are extraordinarily pertinent to these issues and were, therefore, critical to much of what was thought and said about the 1987 agreement. The exposure given to the facts and viewpoints on these matters by the media over a long period of time consequently had considerable bearing on the position people took on the Accord. To generalize about the performance of Canadian media in this respect would

151

be foolhardy. The record of one, normally excellent newspaper, however, provides a useful case study. The Kingston *Whig-Standard* has, at least in the eyes of this reader, a truly sorry record of fanning animosity between English- and French-speaking Canadians. A telling instance of this paper's malevolence came to my attention as I was preparing this paper. The 12 October 1990 edition prominently carried one story on the front page, under a sensational red headline—a colour used only extremely rarely by *The Whig-Standard* for headlines. "Language Showdown" it screamed, over this subtitle: "Federally imposed bilingualism has northern natives upset." Under a Yellowknife dateline, the piece taken from *The Edmonton Journal* informs the reader that a member of the Northwest Territories Legislative Assembly argued during the opening day of the fall session that Ottawa had no right to impose French on the Native majority in the Territories. Quite apart from the question of whether Ottawa in fact had attempted to do this, one must wonder what editorial judgement led to this item being placed and displayed so prominently in the Kingston newspaper, which normally pays scant attention to the Northwest Territories and hardly ever places news about this part of the country on the front page, let alone under a red headline.

The seemingly bizarre major focus on a remote and relatively minor matter makes every sense, however, in the context of *The Whig-Standard's* posture toward bilingualism and relations between Canada's two dominant linguistic families. The editorial page, with a couple of notable exceptions, was relatively balanced in its treatment of language policy, perhaps because *The Whig-Standard* has a team of editorial writers (including some citizen representatives) each of whom signs his or her editorials, with the result that on some issues the editorial page plays host to diametrically opposed views. It is perhaps significant, however, that the editor himself had published some editorials displaying an anti-French bias. But if the editorial page was relatively benign, in the present context, the same cannot be said for the news coverage and for the letters-to-the-editor.

The Whig-Standard consistently and prominently reported events occurring in its readership area and elsewhere which either reflected anti-French sentiments or which could be expected to arouse them. Thus, for instance, meetings of groups like APEC received highly visible coverage, even when the number of people involved was exceedingly small. The placing of these reports, and their size, conveyed the impression that these gatherings attracted the same numbers and were as important in terms of their consequences as events organized by mainstream political formations—a treatment normally not accorded other fringe groups. This kind of coverage conveyed the impression that the anti-French sentiments were more widespread than they in fact were and endowed them with a cloak of respectability likely to have a band-wagon effect on the readers.[11]

A much more blatant and less insidious means of publicizing anti-French sentiments was evident in the letters-to-the-editor, which are very extensive in *The Whig-Standard*. A constant and massive francophobic outpouring focused on alleged threats to English-speakers because of official bilingualism, discriminatory language legislation in Québec, Ontario's Bill 8, alleged excessive concessions by Ottawa to Québec, the perils of inserting the distinct society clause in the constitution, and a wide range of topics reflecting unfavourably on Québec and French Canadians. Many of these letters came from the same individuals who, while they might not have had the mordant wit and terrifying memory of Eugene Forsey, far exceeded even his penchant for frequent epistolary disputation. It is almost certain that these effusions were in part orchestrated by organizations devoted to the preservation and strengthening of British elements in Canadian society and/or who opposed the equal status of French in our midst.

The result of this persistent presence in the correspondence columns of intolerant, bigoted and, more often than not, quite inaccurate material was to fan intergroup hatred. It is a moot point whether the newspaper intended to bring this about but it certainly did nothing to prevent it from happening. It would in no way have been inconsistent with the canons of freedom of the press to have taken at least two corrective measures: to have been more selective in the acceptance of letter after letter, often from the same individual, ad nauseam repeating the same fulminations, and to make some effort to set the record straight and to correct the constantly repeated misinformation spread by the correspondents on such things as the provisions of Canadian and Ontario language legislation.

By failing to do this, *The Whig-Standard*—and other similarly delinquent media—contributed to a climate of opinion prevailing in English Canada that encouraged some politicians to bury the Meech Lake Accord and hence, to my mind, the opportunity of building the foundation for a viable coexistence, in one federal union, of Québec and the rest of Canada. Thus the media affected not only the manner in which people perceived and responded to specific developments along the way to a constitutional solution but also the broader sociological and psychological context that provided the parameters within which solutions could be sought. The nature and frequency of the coverage by the Québec press of the burning of the Québec flag in Brockville is, of course, an equally telling example on the other side.

THE NEED TO DISTINGUISH BETWEEN DIVERSE MEDIA

It would be foolhardy, in considering media effects, to assume that the media are all alike. Important differences prevail between the daily press and periodicals, between printed and electronic services, between public and private broadcasters. In addition, the styles and consequently the effects of Canadian and foreign media vary considerably, notably in broadcasting where, despite the powerful influence of the American television networks, Canadian programming in many respects displays unique indigenous characteristics. And even when one and the same medium is under scrutiny, one must distinguish between its performance at various periods of time. All too little is known about most of these differences, but some intriguing straws in the wind are worth pursuing with respect to the media coverage of the Meech Lake era.

The CBC, as we noted above, came in for a good deal of criticism during the period under review. Some important aspects of its television coverage are discussed below, but first a comment on CBC radio is in order. Some programmes, with "Morningside" perhaps comprising the outstanding example, were thorough, eclectic, deeply probing, and eminently fair. Others, however, can only be described as tendentious. Thus an edition of "Sunday Morning," reporting in August 1987 on evidence presented to the Parliamentary Committee on the Accord, noted at the beginning of the broadcast that arguments both for and against the Accord were put to the committee and then, for the remainder of the programme, presented almost exclusively the voices of those opposed. But overall, CBC radio was pretty close to exemplary in its coverage of the constitutional review. The quality was, in fact, so high, that in some respects CBC radio can be perceived as an electronic equivalent of the traditional morning newspaper—that is, a paper devoted to the extensive and serious coverage of public affairs, but without the heavy coverage of business news. Public reactions to media coverage of the Meech Lake events produced an interesting insight into the manner in which people perceived television and the print press insofar as news reporting was concerned. An Angus Reid poll dated 11 June 1990 asked respondents whether they thought that the media "have generally provided balanced and responsible reporting on Meech Lake" or whether the latter was considered "biased and irresponsible." Overall, about 60% gave a favourable rating and 30% an unfavourable one. The CBC was seen to have provided balanced coverage of Meech Lake by almost two-thirds (64%) of the respondents, newspapers by a little over half (53%), and CTV by 55%. Among the many intriguing aspects of this poll is that the electronic media, and particularly the CBC, were seen as more trustworthy, and that the poll was given very little publicity by the print media. Furthermore, according to CBC sources, its findings were not mentioned by Angus Reid when, on "As It Happens," he accused the corporation of biased coverage of the Meech Lake situation.[12] A later poll by Reid, in which he sought to gauge opinion in the specially "sensitive" provinces of Manitoba and Newfoundland, revealed that while only 46% of Manitobans found CBC coverage balanced, 70% of Newfoundlanders thought it was. Only 54% of the latter group trusted the newspapers, and CTV was seen as having had balanced coverage by only half the Newfoundland respondents. While a high proportion of Manitobans found CBC news lacking in balance, as we just saw, only an infinitesimally smaller number found the newspapers more balanced, and the "score" for CTV was identical with that of the CBC.[13]

Many observers, as we have noted, particularly those opposed to the Accord, thought that the CBC was biased in the agreement's favour and that it therefore presented the pro-Meech forces in a better light than it did its enemies. Lydia Miljan, who we have cited earlier, and who writes and compiles *On Balance*, the Fraser Institute-linked organ that can by no stretch of the imagination be described as pro-CBC, examined the performance of the corporation in this context during the climactic week of 4 June to 10 June, when the first ministers held their fateful meeting in Ottawa.

Her findings are, to my mind, anything but conclusive and, in any event, are at least as damaging with respect to CTV as to CBC. The private network, however, was never attacked by anyone for being biased. While she found that on some dimensions she utilized to test the notion that the CBC was biased, the data back the charge, on others the supporting evidence is ambiguous. Her hypotheses are supported only in part. Furthermore, two of her four assumptions seem of questionable validity. The first, which she saw as confirmed, was that pro-Meech bias was deemed to be present if the situation was defined as comprising a crisis. The fourth, also supported in her view, assumed that emphasis was placed in the coverage on ways needed to ratify the Accord. Events, particularly in Québec after the final failure, seem to me to support eloquently those who insisted all along that nonratification would usher in a major constitutional crisis. To have seen this in the summer of 1990, as the CBC did, cannot be a valid basis for accusations of bias; the CBC merely had insight. To have emphasized the process required for the Accord's ratification seems to me to have been sensible and unbiased news judgement. After all, ratification or nonratification was the essential issue in the summer of 1990.

Miljan's second hypothesis, that premiers opposed to Meech Lake would be portrayed negatively, was only partially supported by the data. She notes that the critical opponent, Newfoundland, received balanced coverage. The third hypothesis, that the coverage would stress that the Accord's failure would cause disastrous political and economic consequences, was also supported only partially and was, in any event, a reasonable assumption to be made by a broadcaster. And here, as on several other dimensions, the performance of CTV came closer to the author's expectations than that of the corporation. "Only 3.6 per cent of CBC and 2.1 per cent of CTV coverage actually addressed the consequences of the success or failure of Meech." When the consequences of failure were discussed, "42 per cent of CBC and 14.3 per cent of CTV coverage was neutral."[14]

The fairly extensive literature on alleged CBC bias fails to take into account the possibility that the position of the corporation, to the extent that it can be said that it had one, underwent changes over time. It was my impression that when the Accord was first drafted and then revised in the Langevin text, the coverage by the CBC tended to be hostile but that this hostility dissipated as time went on. One possible explanation of this phenomenon is discussed in the next section.

CBC TELEVISION: GUILTY OR MALIGNED?

Because of its dominance of television coverage, the CBC was called by one observer "the medium of record" insofar as the Meech Lake Accord went. One reason for its preeminence resulted from the fact, noted above, that, during the June 1990 climactic days of negotiations among the first ministers, it had allocated to the coverage of the events an unprecedented and unrivalled number of operatives, drawn from all its services. The national news editor, John Owen, has estimated that the overtime and other expenses incurred by the CBC during the first ministers' meeting in June ran to well over $100,000.[15] Other insiders estimated that $350,000 may have been a more realistic figure.

The CBC was also exceptionally aggressive in canvassing all aspects of the process and in seeking out, and verifying, information available from the 11 delegations that converged at the Ottawa Conference Centre and their hotels in June. The scene, when the sessions adjourned each day, was extremely difficult for the electronic media. There was only one microphone for a mass of reporters, who took up about 18 metres of the pavement, and only those close to it had any chance of obtaining a usable television story. Because of its numerical strength, the corporation was able to occupy and so "hold" a place close to the microphone and then have its news stars, Wendy Mesley and Don Newman, step in when something was going on. Mesley and Newman's strategic location and powerful lungs, as well as their being easily recognized by the emerging premiers, enabled them to dominate the scrums. This often led to other networks, even CTV, carrying on their news programmes the questions to the principal players in the constitutional drama framed by the journalists of the crown corporation.

The CBC's high visibility and pivotal role in reporting Meech and other public affairs were enhanced by its collaboration with *The Globe and Mail*. The CBC News-*Globe and Mail* poll attracted considerable attention, partly because of its quality but also because it received dramatic and extended news coverage on "Sunday Report," as well as in Canada's national newspaper. Rick Salutin, a lively playwright and journalist, not known for a deep aversion to flamboyant exaggeration, went so far as to accuse the corporation and *The Globe and Mail* of jointly being an informal propaganda tool—"a remarkably effective ministry of propaganda"—serving the Mulroney government. Jeffrey Simpson's regular presence on "Sunday Report," and his eventual strong support for the Accord, as well as Newsworld's use of the *Globe*'s business reports, were seen by Salutin as further proof of this allegedly "common law merger" between the public broadcaster and Toronto's morning oracle.[16] I shall return to these charges below.

Throughout this paper we have encountered numerous critics of the CBC's handling of the Meech Lake Accord. A variety of reasons is no doubt responsible for this. Hostility against the biggest boy on the block, who may strike some as a bit of a bully, was probably part of it; traditional Canadian ambivalence about the CBC—national icon and national whipping boy—also played a part; genuine philosophical differences with the corporation over its reading of the importance and implications of the success or failure of the Accord undoubtedly prompted some attacks; and rivalry among diverse media and networks also was important. One CBC executive, whose consent for being quoted was not sought, suggested in an archaic and anatomical metaphor that some attacks on the corporation resulted from penis envy.

It is somewhat surprising that the CBC should have come under so much and so widespread attack for apparently aiding and abetting the federal government's cause in the constitutional debates since, at the beginning of the process, according to one of the corporation's strategically placed senior officers, some key people in the CBC tried to show that the agreement was a fraud and tried to ferret out and use people like Trudeau, who, they hoped, would attack and discredit it. This one case is so important, and sheds so much light on some fundamental issues involved in the role of media in the political crisis, that I dwell on it at some length.

First, the *dramatis persona*. Our witness is Mr. Elly Alboim, at the time (and still, while I write) national political editor of CBC Television and the Ottawa bureau chief. He is also an adjunct professor in the Carleton School of Journalism. Douglas Fisher portrayed him as "the reigning guru of our self-described 'investigative' journalists and the 'hands-on' boss in CBC-TV's presentation of big ticket politics. Alboim, not Mansbridge or Newman, supervised Meech coverage." [17]

At a conference, whose proceedings have happily been published, Mr. Alboim shed some startling and extraordinarily useful light on how he and his colleagues saw the Meech Lake Accord and how they approached the task of reporting it during its early formative phase in 1987. His comments were made against the backdrop of criticisms that the media failed to prevent what he called "the public's illiteracy" on the Meech Lake issue because they stressed the process used in fashioning an agreement, rather than its substance. Insofar as the CBC was concerned, at least according to its Ottawa bureau chief, this was done intentionally because Mr. Alboim, apparently knowing a great deal more than anyone else, was dead certain that the constitutional exercise was merely a personal ploy by Mulroney to make himself look better than Trudeau. The welfare of the country, in this view, was irrelevant and absent from the governments' minds. According to Alboim,

> this was a highly political and highly cynical exercise that had very, very little to do with the re-constitutionalizing of Canada. It had very, very little to do with the final content of the document. The motivations were clear from the outset. Brian Mulroney needed, for his own purposes, to establish that he could do in Québec what Pierre Trudeau could not. *That was, to my mind, the sole motivation for the federal initiative.* I have no illusion that there was any vision of Canada, or any deeply felt sense of loss about Québec not signing the constitutional agreement in '82. I think we were engaged in a highly political and partisan exercise by the Prime Minister. I think the motivations of many of the anglo-premiers were equally clear. They were dragged into a process that they did not want to participate in. They were blackmailed into a process they had difficulty staying out of and they were determined to capture as much as they could in exchange for their acceptance. There was no selflessness, the premiers walked in with an agenda, a very clear one and they knew what they could get and they got it. This wasn't a nation-building exercise. [18]

Having thus identified the situation, Alboim noted that "we ... were watching a naked exercise of power and were attracted to the reportage of the exercise of power more than we were attracted to covering some of the substance of the accord." (p. 236) All this was going on, according to Alboim's perception of events, while the federal government "was in free fall," (p. 237) having sunk to the lowest rating in the polls of any Canadian government so far, and having suffered a number of other set-backs. [19]

Media organizations in this country smelled blood in a way that we have never smelled blood before. Some thought that we were in a situation similar to the American press in the early days of Watergate. We were focused on the extraordinary story of what appeared to be the collapse of the government with the largest mandate in Canadian history. Meanwhile, what was going on was a fairly quiet and arcane discussion about constitutional renewal that, in our view, had no focus. (p. 237)

Among the reasons which drove the media, in the view of our participant observer, to the strong emphasis on process and to less stress on the ongoing "arcane discussion" about the constitution was, curiously, the conclusion that Brian Mulroney had, through Meech Lake, brought about a fundamental change in Canada's system of government—a change that was not noticed by the public. The old hands in the gallery, he observed, "suspected that we had a new national cabinet made up of First Ministers that had as much clout as the current cabinet ... the Prime Minister had created an alternate level of government." (p. 240)

The aforementioned aspects of the arrangement of 1987, and some others, clearly struck Mr. Alboim as extremely troublesome and threatening to the well-being of the body politic. And although he, and according to him, other media folk, recognized the extreme danger, he believed that most people during the early stages of the agreement, were hoodwinked by the common front of the federal and provincial government leaders.

When confronted with that sort of reality plus a clear understanding of the fragility of the deal and the rush to text and passage, we began a search for dissent ... you look for someone who will question the deal ... We went to Chrétien, we went to Romanow. We looked for constitutional experts. I looked around the country, searching for people who were going to say in that first week or two, boy, there's something wrong here. But what I got was, 'got to wait for the text, not quite sure.' ... The Trudeau watch started. Every day we sent a reporter down to Trudeau's office. Will he do it today? (p. 241)

Elly Alboim's account furnishes a number of germane insights into media, and, specifically, CBC behaviour during the Meech Lake era. It also cries out for critical reactions.

In the first place, they make it patently obvious that, whatever may have occurred in the summer of 1990, at first, when the Accord was being negotiated and refined, the CBC was bitterly hostile and was vigorously trying to drum up commentators who would attack it. The line between arranging for a balanced coverage and engaging in partisan journalism is not always easy to draw and one must therefore be careful before condemning the position taken by the corporation. Alboim's account, however, certainly explained my impression that the Accord was persistently presented in a negative light.

More important, I was aghast and shocked by what struck me as the appallingly arrogant and facile stance of one of the most senior CBC journalists. To have assumed that the government was driven solely by one motive and one man ("That was ... the *sole* motivation for the federal initiative"), to have been implacably convinced that the motives of Brian Mulroney were merely petty, peevish rivalry with Pierre Trudeau (flying in the face of substantial contrary evidence), to have convinced himself that the search for a new constitutional arrangement "wasn't a nation-building exercise," and then to have devised a strategy reporting the ongoing events accordingly ("the cynicism behind the politics of the deal ... had to be dealt with" (p. 240) revealed, to my mind, not only extremely questionable judgement but also constituted a quite inexcusable attempt by a key media player to engage in the political process. Convinced that the party opposition to what he saw as a cynical and dangerous government initiative was inadequate, Alboim proceeded to do what he could to provide an alternative ("we began a search for dissent").

Two features of Mr. Alboim's account are, no doubt, responsible for my reaction being so very negative: I find it frightening that anyone could feel so sure of himself in his reading of a government's and prime minister's motives—never mind that I find the reading to be ludicrous—that he would feel confident enough to plunge the medium for which he is responsible into the political process with the aim of offsetting the perceived cynicism and irresponsibility of the government. Second, I am deeply troubled by any journalist in possession, so to speak, of an immensely powerful instrument of opinion formation arrogating so critical a role to himself or herself, without being in any way accountable to anyone. My anxiety is all the more acute when the instrument is the public broadcaster.

Without diminishing the force of the foregoing comment, it is nevertheless only fair to add one or two qualifying observations. Mr. Alboim's remarks were made at a conference—his piece in the book cited reads very much like the transcript of an oral presentation based on notes rather than on a written text. Under such circumstances it is easy to be carried away by the excitement of the moment and to overstate one's case. It is possible that, had he edited his comments, the overall impression might have been slightly different. Second, Mr. Alboim never refers specifically to actual CBC policies or decisions. I am assuming that what he says about the media generally applies to his own news service. And while the views he expresses indubitably represent the positions he took during discussions within the corporation on how to deal with the evolving Meech saga, others must have been involved in the decisions, whose views were almost certainly not always identical with his. It is, therefore, risky to tar the whole of CBC news with the Alboim brush.

Evidence is in fact available, albeit for the coverage of the last stages of the Meech episode, not its beginning, indicating that the CBC went to quite extraordinary lengths in its efforts to provide competent and balanced accounts of the developments. The corporation's TV news and current affairs director reported (unwittingly putting some of Mr. Alboim's comments into a broader context) that because most government people, who usually have easy access to the media, supported the Accord, those who opposed it received extra time. "Between January and June," she reports, "Clyde Wells appeared on "The National" and "The Journal"

69 times; well-ahead of the second most interviewed leader, Robert Bourassa, who was on 45 times."[20] These attempts at correcting for certain "structural" biases in the situation are also documented by Lydia Miljan's studies.[21] The CBC created a formidable information depository on the Accord, to which reporters from across the country contributed regional and national views for months. "The CBC's Meech file is probably the most extensive intelligence dossier existing on the national public debate over Meech."[22] At the time of the first ministers conference, quite extraordinary measures were taken, as was noted above, to ensure full coverage.

In all, 25 journalists were assigned to the First Ministers Conference. Most of them did not appear on camera. But they fed back to the anchors a constant stream of information about the closed door sessions from dozens of sources in the delegations—senior people at both the bureaucratic and political levels. Any information that went on air was triple checked. In addition, our rule was that nothing could be said that had not been confirmed by at least one pro- and one anti-Meech delegation.[23]

What can we conclude from the above about the performance of the CBC during the Meech Lake episode, other than that the corporation played a dominant role in its coverage, setting the tone of much that was reported, and being perceived by the public as the most balanced medium informing it about the ongoing developments? Had the CBC really earned the confidence accorded it or was its fairness illusory? The question can best be answered by dividing the Meech era into two phases: the early period, starting in April 1987, and the concluding one, culminating on 23 June 1990, the day on which, according to the Constitution Act, all the legislatures had to ratify the Accord. It is difficult and unnecessary to pinpoint the end of one phase and the beginning of the other, except to link it to the time, in late 1988 or early 1989, when a turnaround in opinion led to more Canadians being opposed to the Accord than favouring it.[24] Taras has shown that the CBC, and Miljan that both English national television networks, failed to provide adequate coverage during the early period because they emphasized the process, the politics of the Accord too much, and the substance of it too little. Television's character as, above all, an entertainment medium and its practitioners' penchant for abetting this aspect have also encouraged broadcasters to present the controversies and their discussions in a dialectic format in which those who subscribe to extreme views, on either side, receive much more air time than middle of the road moderates.

Another element in part explaining the CBC's rather hostile manner of reporting the first phase relates to the tendency of all media, from which television is not immune, of giving greater scope to those opposing the government than to the government itself. It is assumed that livelier "copy" emerges from those who attack governments than from those who defend them, and so more time or space is usually devoted to critics than to proponents. It is this that is deemed to make news.

Elly Alboim's and Trina McQueen's articles cited earlier have also indicated that the CBC's attempts always to present both sides of the argument (since during the first phase, only very few political figures opposed the agreement), led the corporation to seek far and wide for opponents, thereby creating the impression that it was going out of its way to oppose the Accord. This policy may have been strengthened and made more vigorous by views like Mr. Alboim's, which, as we noted earlier, saw the whole Meech episode as a total sham launched by the prime minister for reasons related to his vanity. At any rate it is possible, although by no means established, that early in the game, in the spring of 1987, the CBC, perhaps like other media, contributed to the process that ultimately scuppered constitutional reform by seeking out and encouraging attacks against the Meech project by people who could be expected to attract a lot of public attention. Richard Simeon, in an essay exploring why Meech Lake failed, notes that in the few weeks after the breakthrough agreement of 30 April 1987, opposition to the Accord started to mount.

> Much of it was crystallized by former Prime Minister Trudeau, who attacked the Accord root and branch. It was a betrayal of all he had fought for: "Those Canadians who fought for a single Canada, bilingual and multicultural, can say goodbye to their dream."[25]

Although Trudeau's first salvo against the Accord was launched in the pages of *Le Devoir* and *The Toronto Star*, and not on the CBC as Elly Alboim no doubt hoped, the corporation gave the former prime minister every conceivable encouragement and opportunity to air his views subsequently, including in an extensive interview on "The Journal." It is impossible to estimate the effect of Trudeau's interventions but they likely had considerable impact on the ultimate position adopted toward the Accord by a great many English-speaking Canadians.

On the basis of the present review, it is reasonable to conclude that, overall, the CBC handled the Meech Lake events competently. Radio coverage succeeded better than television in finding an appropriate balance between focusing on the substance of the Accord and on the political processes involved in negotiating and ratifying it. In the early phase, both CBC radio and television appeared to me to have been rather more negative than positive, possibly because of the influence of Mr. Alboim or because his views were shared by colleagues in the corporation. But the one-sided approach was not displayed uniformly by all public affairs programmes, some of which went to considerable lengths in seeking balance.

Since I thought at the time, and still do, as I indicated above, that failure to reach a constitutional accord undoing the flaws of 1982 would threaten the survival of Canada as we know it, I did believe that not to ratify the Accord would plunge the country into a serious crisis. In the light of this reading of events, the "crisis atmosphere" with which the corporation endowed the events of June 1990 seemed to me appropriate and did not constitute the misuse of the services of the public broadcaster. The coverage itself struck me as eminently fair and even-handed, particularly on radio and such major television programmes as "The National" and "The Journal."

As for the charge that the CBC and *The Globe and Mail* were in cahoots in selling the federal government line, this struck me as laughable. In some areas the two media did collaborate, as we noted, but there is simply no evidence to suggest that they were in pursuit of a shared media agenda. The idea also lacks any plausibility in the context of the *modus operandi* of the corporation and the government, and the relations that prevail between them. It is nevertheless the case that Jeffrey Simpson's shared presence, Newsworld's use of *The Globe and Mail*'s business reports, and the CBC News/*Globe and Mail* poll do reinforce the reach and appeal of both media and hence enhance the quality of available news coverage in Canada. The combination also may strengthen the impression of some that the CBC is a medium catering to elites. This view is, however, flawed for two reasons. It overlooks the very wide range of CBC programming and it presupposes that a serious approach to covering public affairs, a determined effort to show Canadian programmes, including drama, and striving for high quality, are elitist. They are anything but, assuming as they do, that large audiences will go for excellence if they have an opportunity to find it.

RECOMMENDATIONS

The session of the "After Meech Lake" Conference at which this, and the other two media-oriented papers in this volume were presented, was entitled "The Media and Constitutional Reform in Canada." This theme invited consideration not only of how the Meech Lake episode was covered but also imposed the task of looking at how the media are likely to deal with future constitutional negotiations. In addressing this question, it is unavoidable that one should both draw some lessons from the past and consider recommendations for the future. The latter will, alas, for the most part here fall into the "motherhood" category and relate to the improvement of media performance of any sort, whether related to constitution making or any other subject. But they are relevant nevertheless. Because the manner in which the media serve the political community depends not only on themselves but also on government policies and some general societal factors, the observations that follow apply to a number of possible actors.

1) Despite the immense importance of information about public matters in a democratic society, and despite the notorious narcissism of the media, very little attention is paid to their performance in relation to political events. The situation is, however, improving; the notes underpinning some of the observations made in this paper indicate that several probes were undertaken during and after the Meech Lake debate, but there is still a woeful lack of hard information about how the media affected the politics of constitution making. The critical examination of how politics are covered requires two strategies applied by two sets of distinct actors.

In the first place, the media themselves ought to be much more self-critical, not only internally but also with respect to the performance of other newsgathering and opinion-dispensing organizations. The concentrated attack by the Southam papers on the CBC in June 1990 serves as an example of what is needed, although I think that this particular onslaught was ill-founded. An exemplary model of what can and should be done on a larger scale is CBC radio's "Media File," which regularly subjects some of the information industry to critical analysis. More such programmes, and on a variety of media, including television, would act not only as a corrective in the event that weaknesses develop but also would likely prevent flaws developing by keeping everyone on their toes in fear of having their knuckles wrapped in the future. It is interesting to recall, in this context, that the Reid study showing that the electronic media were generally found to have provided more balanced coverage than newspapers was largely ignored by the latter and so unnoticed by the public.

A seemingly effective and decidedly promising strategy ensuring balanced coverage was described to the "After Meech Lake" Conference by Graham Fraser of *The Globe and Mail*. He and Susan Delacourt were the principal people on the Meech beat and they held opposing views toward the Accord. They were in constant touch and frequently checked one another's perceptions and reactions, thereby acting as mutual correctives. This no doubt greatly enhanced the balance of their reports.

At any rate, a high degree of self-awareness, and self-criticism by media personnel would enhance the quality of reporting and commenting upon developments. Such introspection should take the form of regularly scheduled programmes reviewing press coverage and also, particularly on television, the equivalent of the printed media's "correction" notices which would alert viewers of past sins of commission and omission. News and public affairs programmes have loyal audiences, most of whom would "catch" the corrections.

Second, the work by Taras and by Miljan, cited above, and other such research, illustrates how useful academic or otherwise analytical media studies can be. But we need more of them, undertaken within diverse disciplines and by a variety of scholars and research institutions, and addressing, *inter alia*, some of the aspects identified in the opening paragraph of the section above, entitled "The Need to Distinguish Between Diverse Media." One useful framework for the study of media effects that has so far not been tried is an adaptation of "the Funnel of Causality" as applied to the voting decision many years ago by scholars at the University of Michigan. This metaphor directs researchers toward distinguishing between events affecting the voting decision on the basis of how close they are in time to the final act, and how directly relevant they are to it.[26]

2) One of the lessons the CBC learnt from the Meech experience is related to a suggestion noted above. It is that live political television would henceforth be closely scrutinized "by journalists outside the process." That scrutiny, according to Trina McQueen, is important to public broadcasting and calls for openness and candour on its part. "Just as we reveal the methodology behind public opinion polls we report, the CBC must now also report the methodology behind our journalism."[27] In doing so, it will be desirable to specify not only the "mechanics" of covering a major political event, as was done by Ms. McQueen, but also to indicate

what assumptions led the news and public affairs crews to deploy their resources in a particular manner. Viewers would have been much better able to evaluate CBC coverage of the early Meech Lake phase had they known something of the thinking Elly Alboim revealed in his contribution to *Meech Lake and Canada*[28] and had they known how others making key decisions reacted to it. In the future, the audiences of the public broadcaster in particular, but of others as well, should know by what particular mission the major media are animated, and how they intend to guide the public in interpreting the news, if, like Mr. Alboim, they believe that such guidance is necessary.

Some media organizations—the CBC is among them—have an internal procedure (in which outsiders may participate) designed to review, from time to time, the quality of their work. Reports of these periodic checks should be made public and the practice should be adopted by all major broadcasters and newspapers.

3) The superior quality of the CBC's radio service during the Meech days provides a reminder that public radio may have a special role to perform in informing the interested citizenry of current issues and developments. It is well to remember this in times of evermore menacing budget cuts. Many critically important local television news services have already been eliminated. To tamper with the capacity of CBC radio to cover public affairs at all times of the day—a prospect that cannot be ruled out, given the attitudes toward the corporation of successive Canadian governments, and internal CBC moves to "popularize" the radio service—would seriously diminish the responsible and concerned public's ability to keep abreast of constitutional and other developments. Governments and CBC management must always bear in mind that measures seemingly remote from the constitutional game may have implications for it and that services that may be considered elitist by some nevertheless may perform a critical function in the political process.

4) Few dispute that a competent and lively press is a *sine qua non* of democracy. And widespread trends toward increasing concentration of ownership notwithstanding, it is equally beyond doubt that the press is the most effective when it consists of a multiplicity of competing performers, compensating for one another's biases and collectively providing information to every stratum and cranny of society. Domination by one medium is possible, even when there is competition, as we saw. But while this is not an ideal situation it still offers a variety of perspectives on current developments, making it possible to choose from among available news sources.

Canadians have on several occasions become concerned about the monopolistic tendencies in the media and have sought to counter them. The last effort, headed by Tom Kent, recommended legislation that would have prohibited further concentration of ownership and control of daily newspapers.[29] Nothing came of the Kent report, partly because of the implacable opposition of the press and because of its political clout, and partly because of the lack of will on the part of governments to deal with the situation. But if future constitution making is to benefit from appropriate media coverage, the country would do well to return to the recommendations of previous inquiries probing the media, notably those headed by Kent, Davey, and Caplan and Sauvageau.[30] Independent newspapers and locally owned television stations continue to be gobbled up by the biggies, and serious thought should be given to what measures might be taken to protect media diversity. The inquiries cited offer numerous useful suggestions.

5) This is not the place in which to discuss the quality of Canadian journalists. But the foregoing discussion of Meech Lake coverage makes it abundantly clear that not only journalistic competence is essential, particularly when such complex matters as constitutional review are reported upon, but that the ethics, integrity, and sense of responsibility (and humility?) of journalists and their bosses are also essential. We saw above that these qualities were not always in evidence during the Meech era. They should have been. Schools of journalism should take particular care to impart them to their students.

6) Media effects depend on the manner in which information is received by the public as much as on what the media do. It is valid to ask to what extent the limited knowledge of the content of the Accord by the public reflects negatively on the media and how much the public itself is to blame. In this context it is well to consider whether the Canadian educational system is doing enough to teach our children how to "read" the media. It is my guess that, with some exceptions, the answer is negative and that this too is an area crying for remedies.

7) The earlier discussion of the media in the broader constitutional context concluded with an admonition to newspapers to prevent the constant repetition of factual error by zealots invading the letters-to-the-editor sections of their papers. This too is an area of possible action calling for consideration. It is obviously a matter of considerable delicacy but it is nevertheless incumbent on the media somehow to prevent being hijacked by malevolent forces wishing to foment social hatred and discord.

CONCLUSION

The title of this piece asks whether, in the period under discussion, the media reflected events, illuminated them, or invaded the arena and themselves became actors. The answer, as we saw, is that they did all three. There were differences among them, in this respect, and the same service or paper varied its approach over time. But overall one can conclude that though there were shortcomings, and criticism on the part of various observers—some of it clearly justified—any Canadian seeking to discover both the content of, and the politics surrounding, the Meech Lake Accord could succeed without too much trouble. That a high proportion of Canadians failed to be better informed must be ascribed in part to general social conditions and in part to media performance. Like most people everywhere, Canadians are not highly politicized; they are not voracious readers of elite newspapers or serious periodicals, and they tend to expect from their primary leisure time activity—watching television—mostly to be entertained, not informed. Even news and public affairs programming increasingly packages its content as much as possible as entertainment. It is widely assumed in the industry that if it did otherwise, it would lose audiences. The media could have done better in some respects, as we noted, but it is doubtful whether this would have led to substantially different results insofar as knowledge and comprehension of the Accord were concerned. In this view, media impact could only have been improved if other societal conditions had been different: had politicians and officials been held in higher regard; had nonpolitical opinion leaders played a more active part;[31] had the schools considered it important to involve the students in informed discussion of the issues; if the business community had acted earlier and more vigorously, and so on. There were shortcomings on both sides—the media and their audiences. During the next round of constitution making (or unmaking), greater efforts may be made to avoid some of the failings of the past. But, while the media themselves could fairly quickly adopt more effective ways of covering the constitutional debates, the equally important societal context can change only exceedingly slowly. It is doubtful whether there will be enough time to allow for the necessary changes and adaptations. We are therefore compelled to conclude that when Canada confronts the next phase of its national redefinition, the citizenry will likely not be much better informed than it was in the late 1980s. If this is to be minimized, interested opinion leaders, in a wide range of sectors of society, including those not normally active in politics, will have to become expositors of the proposed arrangements.

NOTES

* I am grateful for the assistance in the preparation of this paper of Margaret Day, Joan Harcourt, and Patrick McCartney.
1. Trina McQueen, "How the CBC covered Meech Lake," *The Toronto Star*, 25 July 1990, C3.
2. Peter Mansbridge, CBC's "Sunday Report," 11 February 1990. CBC Transcript, 4.
3. Lydia Miljan, "A Year in Review: CBC and CTV National News coverage," *On Balance*, III:1, (1990).
4. Miljan, "Network Coverage of the Meech Lake Accord," A paper presented to the annual meeting of the Canadian Political Science Association, Victoria, B.C., May 1990, 3–4.
5. David Taras, "Television and Public Policy: The CBC's Coverage of the Meech Lake Accord," *Canadian Public Policy—Analyse de Politiques*, XV:3, 322, 324. For the author's recent thoughts on this subject, see his chapter in the present volume.
6. Miljan, "Network Coverage," 5, 6. The reference she gives for the Mansbridge statement is *The Globe and Mail* of 26 January 1990.
7. For a brief overview, see idem, *The Newsmakers: The Media's Influence on Canadian Politics* (Scarborough: Nelson Canada), chap. 1.
8. Lise Bissonnette, "Coverage of Meech illustrates divisions," *The Globe and Mail*, 9 June 1990, 2.
9. Richard Mackie, "Peterson makes pitch to Québec journalists," *The Globe and Mail*, 8 June 1990, A5.
10. A whole string of writers in Southam-owned newspapers unleashed a barrage of attacks on the CBC. See, for example, Jamie Portman, "The CBC: How the network set the tone for coverage of constitutional crisis," *The Ottawa Citizen*, 12 June 1990, Op.Ed page; the same piece in the *Montréal Gazette* bore the subtitle: "Network helped set conference agenda"; idem, "CBC's

gloom over Meech compromises its impartiality," *Kitchener-Waterloo Record*, 7 June 1990, A7. Don McGillivray, a Southam stable mate of Portman's, wrote similar stories lambasting the national broadcaster. John Dafoe, the editor of the editorial page of the *Winnipeg Free Press*, Ramsay Cook, the strongly centralist historian, and Tom Kent, former editor of the *Winnipeg Free Press*, and of *Policy Options*, and former Liberal honcho and government official, were among those who also criticized the CBC for creating a crisis.

11. For a discussion of this phenomenon, albeit in quite a different context and sense, see Elisabeth Noelle-Neumann, *The Spiral of Silence: Public Opinion—Our Social Skin* (Chicago: University of Chicago Press, 1984).

12. Arnold Amber, interview, Toronto, 13 October 1990. See also Antonia Zorbisias, "Seems 64 per cent of you didn't see CBC bias either," *The Toronto Star*, 15 June 1990, D18; Tony Atherton, "Meech bias or Meech overkill?", *The Ottawa Citizen*, 16 June 1990, C6; Trina McQueen, "How the CBC covered Meech Lake."

13. Zorbisias, Ibid. More attention is given to the CBC in my paper than to CTV. The imbalance results from the preeminent and sometimes controversial role of the CBC. CTV aroused less comment but did provide an important alternative to the coverage provided by CBC.

14. Miljan, "Key Journalists Accuse Networks of Meech Lake Coverage Bias," *On Balance*, III:7 (July/August 1990), 1–7. The percentages given here are presented on p.4.

15. Julia Nunes, "TV news tightens its belt," *The Globe and Mail*, 13 June 1990, C1.

16. Rick Salutin, "Brian and the Boys," *Saturday Night*, CV:9 (November 1990), 15–17, 85–87. See also Morris Wolfe, "The Globe and CBC as Mulroney apologists? Not on your dice," *The Globe and Mail*, 11 November 1990, C1.

17. Douglas Fisher, "Massaging the Meech 'crisis,' " *Ottawa Sun*, 15 June 1990.

18. Elly Alboim, "Inside the News Story: Meech Lake As Viewed By An Ottawa Bureau Chief," Roger Gibbon, ed., *Meech Lake and Canada: Perspectives from the West* (Edmonton: Academic printing and Publishing, 1988), 236. Emphasis added.

19. Throughout this piece, Alboim does not speak for the CBC alone but for "political journalists," the parliamentary "press gallery," and "reporters" in general. Although he notes that "the gallery" was divided generationally and linguistically on how it perceived the Accord (p. 240) one must assume that the views he expounded in his conference contribution governed his own actions as the CBC news Ottawa bureau chief.

20. McQueen, "How the CBC covered Meech Lake."

21. Miljan, "Key Journalists Accuse Networks," 3–4.

22. McQueen, "How the CBC covered Meech Lake."

23. Ibid. This rare insider account was prompted by Ms. McQueen's awareness that since the CBC had played so important a role in the coverage of Meech, it was incumbent on it to describe its methods. She likened this responsibility to that the corporation assumes with respect to the publication of the details of its opinion polls. This is a notion to which we shall return.

24. For a graph tracing the shifts in opinion from 1987 to 1990 see Figure 5.6 in Michael Adams and Mary-Jane Lennon, "The Public's View of the Canadian Federation," in R.L. Watts and D.M. Brown, eds., *Canada: The State of the Federation 1990* (Kingston: Queen's University, Institute of Intergovernmental Relations, 1990), 107.

25. Richard Simeon, "Why Did the Meech Lake Accord Fail?" in R.L. Watts and D.M. Brown, eds., *Canada: The State of the Federation 1990* (Kingston: Queen's University, Institute of Intergovernmental Relations, 1990), 21.

26. A. Campbell, P.E. Converse, W.E. Miller, and D.E. Stokes, *The American Voter* (New York: John Wiley & Sons, 1960), 24–32 and passim.

27. McQueen, "How the CBC covered Meech Lake."

28. Alboim, "Inside the News Story."

29. Royal Commission on Newspapers, *Report* (Ottawa: Minister of Supply and Services, 1981), 237.

30. Ibid.; Gerald Caplan and Florian Sauvageau, chairmen, *Report* (Ottawa: Minister of Supply and Services, 1986). Special Senate Committee on Mass Media, (Hon. Keith Davey, chairman) *Report* (Ottawa: 1970).
31. The cultural community, for instance, which had been extremely active in the free trade debate, was rarely heard from.

How Television Transformed the Meech Lake Negotiations

DAVID TARAS

UNIVERSITY OF CALGARY

One can argue that there were two ways in which television coverage of the Meech Lake constitutional negotiations influenced the final outcome. First, television coverage was likely to have played an agenda-setting role; certifying which issues and events were seen as important by the public and which were not. Well aware of the singular power of television to convey moods and impressions to a vast audience, if not information and analysis, the first ministers missed few opportunities to appear on television with their messages and versions of events. Media managers and senior journalists acted as "gatekeepers" deciding which aspects of the unfolding Meech Lake drama would become leading news stories, the context in which the stories would be presented, and the stories' slant or spin.

Second, television seemed to become another platform for negotiations among the first ministers. The first platform, of course, was the actual face-to-face negotiations involving the prime minister and the premiers; a process that had acknowledged procedures and well-defined structures, symbols, and etiquette and included an elaborate "backchannel" of visits and emissaries, making side deals and forming coalitions. Less is known, however, about the rituals and routines that surrounded the "negotiations" that occurred on television. When first ministers were asked to respond instantly to the positions or comments of other first ministers, talked to each other directly while seeing each other only on television monitors, and presented and reacted to new proposals or information communicated to each other for the first time through journalists, a kind of negotiating process was, in fact, underway. Indeed, Mark Starowicz, the executive producer of CBC's "The Journal," once described his programme as "part of the system. It is the method by which with Parliament a national consensus is obtained. We are the perpetual emergency debate."[1] While great attention is now being paid to reforming the formal structures of power, there seems to be little concern about what A.W. Johnson has called the "parallel government," which includes the enormous power of the mass media. [2]

TELEVISION AND AGENDA-SETTING

A vigorous scholarly debate has been underway for some time concerning the effects television coverage has had on the formation of public attitudes. Most researchers would agree with the conclusions reached by Bernard Cohen in his influential study on press reporting conducted in the 1960s: "The press is significantly more than a purveyor of information and opinion. It may not be successful much of the time in telling people what to think, but it is stunningly successful in telling its readers what to think about." [3] It was Maxwell McCombs and Donald Shaw who first coined the term "agenda-setting" to describe the power of the mass media to influence voters' perceptions about which issues were important. [4] Their studies, carried out during the 1968 and 1972 U.S. presidential elections, found a correlation between the issues that were covered extensively on television news and in the press and the attitudes that voters had about which issues they considered important. A more recent study on the impact of television goes even further. Iyengar and Kinder concluded that "television is now an authority virtually without peer," with the capacity to "prime" viewers by setting "the terms by which political judgements are rendered and political choices made." [5] The key to television's power is its ability to convey an impression of almost impregnable authority. Viewers have the feeling that they are witnesses, that they are seeing things for themselves. Viewers trust what they see. Moreover, television news is encased in trappings of authority. Iyengar and Kinder quote P.H. Weaver's description of the role played by the TV reporter who "towers" over issues and events and speaks "authoritatively and self-confidently about everything that comes into his field of vision: men, events, motives, intentions, meanings, significances, trends, threats, problems, solutions—all are evidently within his perfect under-standing, and he pronounces on them without any ifs, and, or buts." [6] Todd Gitlin has described the influence of television journalists in the following way: "They name the world's parts, they certify reality as reality." [7]

Paradoxically, the scholarly literature also suggests that while television may have the power to reorder the perceptions and priorities of its viewers, audiences actually learn very little about the issues being reported. The accepted wisdom is that TV is far better at conveying drama and emotions than it is in presenting facts and information. Indeed, some scholars have gone as far as to argue that television news is so thin, so focused on visuals, personalities, and entertainment that it fails entirely as a vehicle for educating the public. For instance, Patterson and McClure were able to claim in their study of television coverage during the 1976 U.S. presidential election that "since the nightly news is too brief to treat fully the complexity of modern politics, too visual to present effectively most events, and too entertainment-minded to tell viewers much worth knowing, most network newscasts are neither very educational nor very powerful communicators."[8] A study published in 1990 by John Robinson and Dennis Davis suggests that while viewers may believe they are getting most of their information from television, in fact, newspapers and conversations are far more effective in transmitting information.[9] They conclude that television is primarily an entertainment medium that while conveying vast amounts of visual material that shocks and sensationalizes, stimulates and pacifies, does not normally produce anything beyond superficial learning.

A *Globe and Mail*-CBC News poll taken after the collapse of the Meech Lake agreement found that a majority of respondents knew "nothing at all" or "not very much" about the Accord.[10] An astonishing illiteracy about constitutional issues prevailed despite saturation television coverage; during a one-week period at the height of the final round of negotiations, the week of 4–10 June, CBC produced 882 minutes of live coverage excluding the time allotted for "The National" and "The Journal" preempting regularly scheduled programs 20 times. CTV produced 528 minutes of coverage during that same decisive week.[11] Each of the major networks made a decision to forgo substantial advertising revenue and dug deep into their budgets to pay overtime, use extra equipment, and follow the Meech Lake drama as it unfolded often in several locations at once across the country. At one point CBC television had as many as 14 or 15 reporters assigned to the story.[12]

The national news programmes reached a sizeable audience. CBC's "The National" registered an average audience of 1,189,000 during the week of 4–10 June, while "The CTV National News" was watched by an average of 759,000 viewers. Radio Canada's "Telejournal" reached an average audience of 841,000 during May and June.[13] It is also interesting to note that television is the exclusive source of news for 28% of adults aged 25–49.[14]

Knowing little about the contents of the Accord, however, did not prevent people from having views. In Québec, opinion seemed to harden as Meech Lake became a symbol the province's need for recognition and identity. The Accord became a touchstone for the deepest sentiments, for arousing the most naked passions. One is left to conclude that television, with its sizeable audience reach and authoritative power, helped set the public agenda although it failed to educate much of the public in any meaningful way.

This lack of knowledge cannot be dismissed as peculiar to Meech Lake: the complexity of the Meech Lake conundrum overwhelming the capacities of average citizens. Canadians know surprisingly little about most national institutions and issues.[15]

The educational failure stems from the very nature of television news. In a study of CBC television's coverage of the making of the Meech Lake deal as it unfolded from late April to early June 1987, I argued that reporting was limited and distorted by the television news "frame"; a system of reporting as much by the need to entertain as to inform.[16] According to Todd Gitlin "Frames are principles of selection, emphasis and presentation composed of little tacit theories about what exists, what happens and what matters."[17] Although Gitlin claims that the frame is based on ideological assumptions designed to promote established interests, the frame is also tailored to appeal to what media managers perceive to be audience tastes and to the routines and imperatives of news organizations. The frame is "clamped" over the event being covered, highlighting some aspects of the story and downplaying or ignoring others. While scholars differ over what constitutes the frame, some scholars using other terms to describe the same phenomenon and each proposing their own definitions, I used only the most obvious criteria.

1) News takes place in the "continuous present tense" and is concerned with what is happening in the here and now. It is ahistorical to the extent that little historical context can be provided.

2) News stories need conflict. In order to enhance the drama that is required to make stories exciting and appealing, television news celebrates stories that involve clashes between two distinct groups or positions, have clear winners and losers, and have an emotional human element. Stories that don't feature sharp conflict are unlikely to remain news stories for long.

3) Limited by time and budgetary constraints, the news "net" rarely reaches beyond reporting a restricted number of people and locations. Reporters tend to be placed at strategic "listening posts" such as on Parliament Hill so that party leaders, cabinet ministers, and MPs tend to dominate the news. The activities or reactions of business or labour, or regional or ethnic interest groups—those beyond the immediate news net—are almost never covered to the same extent.

4) Television news thrives on personalities. Individuals come to symbolize entire issues or events. News analysis is almost always a discussion about the motivations, desires, emotions, and strategies of individuals. The focus is usually on leaders in triumph, leaders in conflict, or leaders in trouble. Larger political, societal, or economic forces are hardly ever touched upon.

5) Stories must be easily labelled and condensed. The average news story is roughly 90 seconds long and amounts to no more than 150 to 250 words. The average length of a "clip" of someone being interviewed is 12 seconds. Issues that require complex explanations or extensive background information or are tedious and legalistic are either ignored or brutally condensed.

6) Television is a visual medium. The best stories for television journalists are ones that contain exciting visual material: shouting matches in the House of Commons, angry demonstrations, natural or human-made disasters and dramatic backdrops. Stories that don't have exciting visuals are unlikely to receive extensive coverage and may be ignored entirely.

My study concluded that, operating within the limits of an *infotainment* format, "The National's" coverage was highly condensed and truncated, focused on conflict, was obsessed with personalities, and conveyed little actual information about what was in the Accord. The Meech Lake Accord was presented as if it had sprung suddenly out of nowhere, as if there had been no prior history of constitution making. Reporting was so abbreviated that out of Québec's five demands only one was mentioned on the news. The most complete description of the agreement's provisions was offered by David Halton in the following manner:

172

Constitutional experts were also mulling over the first ministers' agreement yesterday which not only recognizes Québec as a distinct society, but also gives all provinces increased powers. Those powers give the premiers a veto over changes to some federal institutions, and a big say in Supreme Court and Senate appointments. [18]

Well over one-third of the news stories dealt with splits within the Liberal party and the party's turmoil over the Accord, and how it all would affect John Turner's leadership. The consequences that the Accord might have for Canadian identity, on how the country would be governed, and on the evolution of Québec nationalism were not discussed or referred to in any way. In short, "The National's" news format, its adherence to the frame, did not allow it to educate its viewers in any meaningful way.

Troubled by criticism that they had not explained the Accord adequately, senior CBC journalists attempted a series of innovations. In winter 1990 "The National" ran a series of special segments: five-minute reports on a different aspect of the Accord for four consecutive nights. Charts and graphics were used to explain the main points in the Accord and the issues that had caused so much controversy. Whenever there were new developments "The National" would prime its viewers by again explaining the significance of the Accord. In addition, "The National" and "The Journal" combined to produce a two-hour documentary that took a gloomy panoramic look at the strains caused by the Meech Lake drama.

"The Journal" also produced two shows entitled "In Search of Ourselves." Both programmes had a haunting foreboding quality. Rick Salutin has described the atmosphere created by the producers: "Guests were shot against darkness, with perhaps a single source of light. The many bridging shots were haunting landscapes of a stagnant river, a wave-beaten coast, a lonely lighthouse, a city in fog, all photographed through filters to give the impression of perpetual twilight, plus repeated images of Canadians walking slow motion, perplexed and ghostly, through their cities' streets." [19] Brian Stewart, the host, intoned mournfully about a country immobilized by doubt, bitterness, and despair. [20]

Yet these attempts to move beyond the frame proved frustrating and futile. As CBC correspondent and national anchor Peter Mansbridge has described the problem:

> It wasn't our stories, our reporters, or our presentations. I think they were all first rate. It was our medium television ... Here's where print has the edge over television. When you pick up a newspaper and read about Meech Lake, you can read a complicated constitutional story over and over until it makes sense. With television news, you've got just one shot. If the explanation isn't clear, we've lost you. That's what our research seems to indicate happened when we ran our series on Meech Lake. We tried, but it didn't seem to work. [21]

One also can argue that the problem was not with the limitations of the medium but with constraints imposed by the current format of television news. Education often requires frequent repetition, something that goes against the grain of the television news format. It also needs more words and ideas than are available in a 90-second news report. In addition, newscasts tend to be highly fragmented and disjointed as news shows in order to maintain a fast exciting pace move breathlessly from one story to another. Stories flitter by one after another, engendering, some scholars contend, a sense of distracted passivity in viewers. One also can argue that audiences are conditioned to see television as primarily an entertainment vehicle and are psychologically unprepared when watching TV to make the effort that real learning requires. What is presented to and received by the viewers in the end are the "coronas" of issues and events—their glow, rather than their substance.

News coverage of the Meech Lake negotiations produced another educational problem. Focus group testing conducted by the CBC in spring 1990 revealed that viewers were beginning to tire of the issue. They saw it as the concern of an elite group and were losing interest in what seemed to be an endless series of threats, manoeuvres, and squabbles. Audience interest had evaporated to some degree by the time the networks launched their last intensive rounds of coverage. The sentiment was captured in a cartoon that appeared in *The Globe and Mail* that showed a nurse presiding over the Meech Lake Accord Overexposure Trauma Centre. She was issuing a warning: "Attention all units, CBC's just run another in-depth analysis." [22]

Some scholars would argue that viewer boredom is the inevitable by-product of "jolts" television.[23] As audiences are constantly bombarded by sudden bursts of action on dramatic shows, powerful visuals, an endless kaleidoscope of new fresh faces, and a widening array of channels at their fingertips, tolerance for the "old" and mundane is at a low threshold. Studies conducted in the U.S. have found that more than half of those under 34 years of age routinely watch at least two programmes at the same time.[24] Even popular shows have relatively short lifespans. And Meech Lake was hardly a hit series.

But television is much more than fluff and puff. Television is, as described earlier, an immensely powerful medium that undoubtedly played a role in influencing the Meech Lake negotiations. Of course, television news did not create the agenda; the prime minister and the premiers, senior civil servants, political parties, and interest groups all had the capacity to "build" the agenda. Media gatekeepers, however, had and have the power to decide the issues and perspectives that are the most newsworthy, whether new developments will be portrayed in a positive or negative light and to declare "winners" and "losers." As Edwin Black has put it, "The new reality for federalist politics in Canada can be stated simply: so far as the voters are concerned, if it's not on TV, it doesn't exist."[25]

One can argue that there were at least three instances in which television news reporting influenced the shape of the negotiations. The first was when Prime Minister Brian Mulroney asserted that failure to ratify the Accord could lead to Québec's separation. A steady stream of statements from Mulroney and by cabinet ministers predicted dire consequences and even a return of FLQ-style terrorism. The strategy in raising the stakes, in heating up the political temperature, was to pressure the Accord's opponents into relenting by making their objections to the Meech Lake agreement seem narrow and self-indulgent. Some would contend, however, that in setting this tone for the negotiations Mulroney created a self-fulfilling prophecy. By putting the issue in such stark terms, and by making the "acceptance" of Québec the main issue, Mulroney contributed to the unleashing of nationalist sentiment in Québec.

By reporting these ominous forecasts as a way of hyping the Meech Lake story and without pointing out the larger strategy that lay behind these statements, journalists helped produce the harsh climate that surrounded and ultimately consumed the negotiations. What is significant in this case is that journalists seemed to abrogate accepted standards of media responsibility. During elections, for instance, journalists feel that analysing the election strategies of the parties, unmasking the pretensions of party leaders, and exposing the hollowness of political promises or policies are almost sacred obligations. The intentions and characters of party leaders are put under an intense burning spotlight. Yet these same standards of critical observation were largely absent with regard to many of the prime minister's pronouncements on Meech Lake. It was perhaps that Mulroney's hyperbole fit the frame; it had the sensational elements that TV news cherishes and requires.

A second example of the capacity of TV news to affect the political agenda was the swath of sensational coverage given to the defection of Mulroney's Québec lieutenant Lucien Bouchard in May 1990. Bouchard's resignation from the cabinet came in response to a unanimous report on how to resolve the Meech Lake impasse by a parliamentary committee headed by Jean Charest. The Charest Report proposed that there be a companion resolution that would affirm the supremacy of the Charter of Rights and Freedoms while acknowledging Québec's role as a distinct society. The report also recommended that the federal government be given the power to "promote" as well as preserve the English and French languages, and that Senate reform, if not agreed to within a specified period, could then be implemented with less than unanimous consent. One cannot dispute that Bouchard's dramatic exit was an important event that required extensive news coverage. His departure had enormous implications for Conservative prospects in Québec and indeed for Mulroney personally. It had all the elements that make for a first-rate television news story: personalities in conflict, charges of betrayal, raw human emotions, and exciting visuals.

Yet Bouchard's actions were given such extensive coverage that it allowed the Québec MP to "hijack" the negotiating process. Cameras followed Bouchard's "passion play" for days as he gave vent to his feelings of anguish and anger. The effect was to bury the Charest proposals amid an avalanche of publicity. The dry, detailed, and complex report, however crucial it might have been in moving the negotiations forward, was no match for the Bouchard story with its elemental human emotion. By not giving the Charest proposals significant coverage, and by leaping on the Bouchard story with such vehemence, the media probably influenced events. Certainly the lionization of Bouchard stirred the fires of Québec nationalism, and Bouchard's dire warning to Premier Bourassa that he not go to Ottawa to negotiate

175

because of the traps that were being laid for him left the premier with little room for compromise; his back was against the wall.

A third example of agenda-setting was the play given on French-language television to the desecration of the Québec flag by English rights extremists: the so-called Brockville incident. A 10-second clip showing the Québec flag being trampled on and burned by outraged anglophones caused a sensation in Québec. The scene became a metaphor, a symbol, for many Quebeckers of English Canada's "rejection" of Québec during the Meech Lake negotiations. This was a kind of "demon clip," the Canadian equivalent of the "Willie Horton" ad shown by Republicans during the 1988 U.S. presidential campaign; a scene that terrifies, strikes a raw nerve, evokes a heated emotional response. Some observers question why TV journalists in Québec found it necessary to use such explosive material and give such extraordinary coverage to the actions of a fringe group. The clip certainly fit the visual agenda of TV reporting, it also may have fit the personal biases and political agendas of some journalists. It also may have been a blind adherence to the Werner Von Braun theory of journalism. Braun, a rocket scientist who worked for Hitler and later for the Americans, supposedly said, "I just make the rockets, I don't care where they land." Interestingly enough when the national anthem was booed at a Montréal Expos baseball game, an incident that was at least as ugly as the flag desecration, it received little attention in the English language media. While it is difficult to know the effects of this kind of coverage, in a recent study Doris Graber found that "on television seeing is believing" because when it comes to TV "learning is shaped by the vistas gleaned by the human eye."[26]

TELEVISION AND CONSTITUTION MAKING

The Meech Lake negotiating process was, on one level, private and secretive. The actual face-to-face negotiations were not televised or open to the press. Much of the negotiations took place through a "backchannel" of phone calls and meetings, a process that was intimate and highly charged. At several stages in the negotiations a veritable constitutional shuttle service was at work carrying officials from capital to capital, and "rolling drafts of documents" were circulated across the country. First ministers were often on the phone to each other three or four times a day. The closed nature of the negotiations aroused suspicion and anger among groups that believed that only an open process would guarantee their positions received a fair hearing and to some degree amongst a public accustomed to watching constitutional conferences on television. The Meech Lake negotiating process was the very opposite of Woodrow Wilson's call for "open covenants openly arrived at."

Yet the Meech Lake negotiations became, despite the shrouds of secrecy that surrounded them, a major television spectacle. Television was an intrusive partner in the negotiations. It was at times a common ground for exchanges among the first ministers, the messenger that brought news of the latest developments to the negotiators, and the vehicle by which the first ministers communicated their positions to their publics. The television cameras could be likened to the wall in a squash court; negotiating positions would have to be hit against the media wall to keep them in play and to give them legitimacy.

There were three ways in which media coverage played a role in the negotiations. First, there were instances where information was received by the negotiators for the first time via the media. Whether through leaks or at press conferences and briefings, proposals or positions were presented to journalists before they were communicated to the other negotiating partners. The Ottawa bureau chief for CBC television news, Elly Alboim, has described the utility of leaking information to journalists as, "a way of getting things moving around, trying to screw things up or move things forward. It was a way of seeing what kind of bite there would be." [27] There were a number of instances where proposals were floated as "trial balloons" or "road tested" to see if they were acceptable. For example, the proposition that the federal government should be allowed to "promote" as well as preserve English and French was hit against the media squash court walls several times before it emerged as part of the Charest proposals. The dispute between Alberta, British Columbia, and Saskatchewan, on one hand, and Manitoba, on the other, over whether there would be "sunset" or "sunrise" provisions on the issue of how to override the unanimous consent needed to bring reform of the Senate, led to some of the players "getting stuff out to force people's hands." [28]

In late May 1990, an Ontario government strategy paper was leaked to Southam news. It described a plan to "discredit the holdout premiers" should the First Ministers Conference that was about to take place fail to break the constitutional logjam. The strategy advised Premier Peterson to ensure "that the blame for failure falls squarely on the dissident provinces and not on Québec." Peterson was to "insist that Clyde Well's concerns were 'out of proportion' and that he was fueling the crisis." The media were to be discouraged from delving too deeply into legal issues or "those involving popular parts of the dissident's positions, e.g., individual rights, regional development, aboriginals, perceived lack of compromise by Québec." [29] The purpose in leaking the document was obviously to embarrass Peterson and foil the strategy.

The secrecy encrusting the formal negotiations that took place during the crucial week of 4–10 June seemed to produce feverish attempts by various governments to get messages out to the media. Rick Salutin claims that the Mulroney government successfully managed the news through leaks. As Salutin has put it, "The government leaked in torrents—to the Globe and the CBC. The phrase 'CBC news has managed to learn' became equivalent to 'The government would like us to say ...' " [30]

Of course once information is in the hands of journalists, negotiators have little control over the play or "spin" that a story will receive. Stories that have been put through the media mix-master often lose their original thrust. Constitutional players rely on journalists to present their stories in a favourable light and not downplay, dismiss, or distort their messages or plans.

Second, there were many instances when first ministers found themselves in the midst of a media scrum and pressed to comment on the latest developments without time to think, compose themselves, or consult with colleagues and advisers. Surrounded by journalists who were seeking to heighten conflict, first ministers could, if not careful, give answers that were only partly thought through or make off-the-cuff impromptu remarks. On more than a few occasions Clyde Well's temper seemed on the verge of boiling over as he reacted sharply to statements made by Brian Mulroney or Robert Bourassa, statements conveyed to him by hovering journalists. Of course the politicians are often the ones who seek out journalists, who crave the intoxicating glow of publicity. In a moment of reckless candour Mulroney told journalists from *The Globe and Mail* that he had "rolled the dice" in plotting his strategy during the last weeks of the constitutional negotiations; words that undermined his credibility with some of the key players.[31] What is particularly noteworthy about television is that it requires politicians to respond. Once in front of the cameras, politicians must address reporters' questions or risk appearing indecisive or as if they have something to hide. Television in particular but journalists in general sometimes forced events, intruded, literally pushing their way into the process.

Third, having staked out a constitutional position and having that position described to millions of viewers on television, first ministers could not change or modify those stands without appearing to have betrayed their principles. Amid the glare of publicity negotiators were locked into positions from which they could not easily retreat. Making matters worse was the tendency of some journalists to declare "winners" and "losers," treating the negotiations as if they were a hockey game or a boxing match. The first ministers may have come to believe that any substantial compromises that they might make were likely to be portrayed as a personal defeat. They could read and hear the next day about how they had been outmanoeuvred or had fallen into traps that had been laid for them. Face saving, an essential element in any successful negotiation, is made exceedingly difficult. Small wonder that Mulroney, Bourassa, and Wells among others came into the final round of negotiations with backbones steeled by public expectations; backbones that couldn't be bent.

CONCLUSION

Much more research on how media reporting affects federal-provincial and constitutional relations in Canada needs to be conducted. Little is known about how television in particular, by influencing political agendas and intruding onto the negotiating landscape, alters the bargaining process. We may find that television does not fundamentally transform or reshape events; events galvanized for the most part by hard traditions and history, large vested interests, and deeply held convictions. We may conclude that television coverage affects outcomes only at the margins, style not substance. Yet the evidence may suggest, as I have argued, that television not only reports on the negotiating process but has become part of it.

If this is the case then the power of television to transform outcomes must be addressed in some way. Informal groundrules might be devised so that journalists do not exacerbate conflict by hyping and sensationalizing disagreements. The TV news frame might be altered under some circumstances to accommodate a slower pace, some degree of repetition and longer explanations of complex issues. The first ministers might agree on mechanisms for dealing with the media; perhaps a single spokesperson could be appointed to deal with reporters' questions so that the usual orgy of threats and bravado, self-congratulations and grandstanding could be avoided. Ultimately there is an educational mandate and a responsibility for caution and self-restraint that must be exercised by both journalists and politicians. The alternative is to have the mass media transform the debate according to its own rules and requirements. Given the destructive nature of Canadian constitutional politics one is tempted to repeat Todd Gitlin's observation about American politics during the Vietnam War: "above the battle only the spotlight will remain." [32]

NOTES

1. Interview with Mark Starowicz, Toronto, 21 May 1986.
2. Interview with A. W. Johnson, Ottawa, 21 August 1990.
3. Bernard Cohen, *The Press and Foreign Policy* (Princeton, N.J.: Princeton University Press, 1963).
4. Maxwell McCombs and Donald Shaw, "The agenda-setting function of the mass media," *Public Opinion Quarterly* 36 (1972): 176–187.
5. Shanto Iyengar and Donald Kinder, *News that Matters* (Chicago: The University of Chicago Press, 1987).
6. Ibid., 126.
7. Todd Gitlin, *The Whole World Is Watching* (Berkeley: The University of California Press, 1980), 2.
8. Thomas Patterson and Robert McClure, *The Unseeing Eye: The Myth of Television Power in National Elections* (New York: Putnam, 1976).
9. John Robertson and Dennis Davis, "Television News and the Informed Public: An Information-Processing Approach," *Journal of Communication* 40 (1990): 106–119.
10. "The Globe and Mail-CBC News/Poll," *The Globe and Mail*, 9 July 1990, A4.
11. Interview with Kara Switzer, CTV research, 18 October 1990, (phone).
12. Interview with Elly Alboim, 26 October 1990, (phone).
13. Interview with Ken Leclair, CBC research, 16 October 1990, (phone). See also Julia Nunes, "TV news tightens its belt," *The Globe and Mail*, 13 June 1990, A13.
14. *Canadian Facts*, 1990.
15. Particularly damning evidence about general educational awareness can be found in Edna Einsiedel, *Scientific Literacy: A Survey of Adult Canadians*, report prepared for the Social Sciences and Humanities Research Council and Industry, Science and Technology Canada, 1990.
16. David Taras, "Television and Public Policy: The CBC's Coverage of the Meech Lake Accord," *Canadian Public Policy* 15 (1989): 322–334.
17. Gitlin, "The Whole World is Watching," 7.
18. Taras, "Television and Public Policy," 328.
19. Rick Salutin, "Brian and the Boys," *Saturday Night* (November 1990), 17.
20. Ibid., 17, 85.
21. Peter Mansbridge, "Even if it's boring, it's time to pay attention," *The Globe and Mail*, 26 January 1990, A7.
22. Ibid.

179

23. See Morris Wolfe, *Jolts: The TV Wasteland and the Canadian Oasis* (Toronto: James Lorimer, 1985).
24. John Stackhouse, "Izzyvision," *Report on Business Magazine*, (May 1990), 81.
25. Edwin Black, " 'Going Public': Mass Communications and Executive Federalism," in David Shugarman and Reg Whitaker, eds., *Federalism and Political Community: Essays in Honour of Donald Smiley* (Peterborough: Broadview, 1989), 358.
26. Doris Graber, "Seeing Is Remembering: How Visuals Contribute to Learning from Television News," *Journal of Communications* 40 (1990), 154.
27. Interview with Elly Alboim.
28. Ibid.
29. Joan Bryden, "Plot to discredit holdouts," *Calgary Herald*, 30 May 1990, A1.
30. Salutin, "Brian and the Boys," 85.
31. "It is a tough country to govern," *The Globe and Mail*, 20 June 1990, A21.
32. Gitlin, "The Whole World is Watching," 192.

Canadian Broadcasting, Canadian Nationhood: Two Concepts, Two Solitudes, and Great Expectations

MARC RABOY

UNIVERSITÉ LAVAL

As social institutions subject to the tensions and pressures that characterize a given society at any point in time, mass communication systems provide a good indication of how a society sees itself and where it perceives that it is headed. This has been particularly true in the case of Canadian broadcasting, whose evolution over the past 60 years has closely paralleled the continuing debate over Canadian nationhood.[1]

Various combinations of political and economic factors have come into play in the federal government's attempts to develop a policy on broadcasting since the late 1920s, but the national question has never been far from the heart of the matter. In this respect, the following characteristics are important to bear in mind:

1) despite often vigorous claims from the provinces, especially Québec, broadcasting has been staked out and maintained as an area of exclusive federal jurisdiction

2) despite the centralist, unitary nature of the system's governing policy framework, broadcasting services have developed along parallel lines in English and in French

3) despite the system's formal autonomy, Ottawa has tended to view broadcasting as an extension of the state—particularly in ascribing to the Canadian Broadcasting Corporation a role in the promotion of national unity.

As this combination of contradictions might lead one to believe, broadcasting in Canada has been seen not only as a means of communication, but as an object of struggle, a contested terrain.

Looking at the evolution of Canadian broadcasting from its inception in the 1920s up to the recent Meech Lake debates thus can tell us a good deal about the nature of our constitutional and national dilemma.

1928–1945: CREATING A SYSTEM ... AND ITS PROBLEMS

Although broadcasting in Canada actually began in 1919, the basic framework of the Canadian broadcasting system was laid out by the Royal Commission on Radio Broadcasting (chaired by Sir John Aird) that reported in 1929.[2] Remarkably, the central issues in Canadian broadcasting today are essentially the same as they were at that time.

The Aird Commission recommended wholesale nationalization of the then largely commercial radio system, and creation of a national publicly owned monopoly to operate all broadcasting in Canada on a basis of public service for the information, enlightenment, and entertainment of the Canadian people. Even before its report was tabled, however, the Québec government of Louis-Alexandre Taschereau passed legislation authorizing Québec to erect and operate its own radio station, as well as produce programmes for broadcast by existing commercial stations.

Before acting on the recommendations, Ottawa asked the Supreme Court to determine whether jurisdiction over broadcasting lay with the Dominion or the provinces, and in 1931 the court ruled in Ottawa's favour. An appeal to the Judicial Committee of the Privy Council in London took another year to resolve, and so it was only in 1932 that Ottawa had a clear signal to legislate.

The Canadian Radio Broadcasting Act of 1932 created a national public broadcaster, the Canadian Radio Broadcasting Commission, which had the additional responsibilities of regulating the activities of the private broadcasters. (This double mandate would be transferred to the CRBC's successor, the Canadian Broadcasting Corporation, by the legislative reform of 1936.)

Aird had proposed broadcasting content be overseen by assistant commissioners in each of the provinces, but this interesting recommendation was not retained by the legislator. The CRBC, meanwhile, set out to create a national radio service in English and in French: a single service, using both languages alternately in such a way that both English and French audiences heard the same programme. Or, to put it another way, the CRBC took the approach that there was only one radio audience in Canada, made up of members of two different language groups.

In its submission to the Royal Commission on Bilingualism and Biculturalism some 30 years later, the CBC reflected on this aspect of its prehistory:

[This] alternative was tried in the mid-thirties as being the simpler in practice and more feasible in view of the limited human, technical and financial resources then available. Obviously, such an alternative was only workable as long as the program needs of both groups could be met by a single network. With the passage of time and the development of broadcasting techniques and resources, the demands of each group for a more complete service continued to grow, presenting the Corporation with a situation which could only be met adequately by duplicate networks, English and French. These the Corporation proceeded to establish and the pattern then adopted has prevailed to the present.

Needless to say, the transition was not as simple and orderly as the foregoing would suggest.[3]

Indeed, it was not. The most important factor in compelling the CRBC to move away from a single service using two languages to "parallel services" in each language as early as 1934 was the absolute, militant refusal of anglophone communities in the Maritimes, Ontario, and western Canada to accept the presence of French on the air. This has been documented in the memoirs of Canadian radio pioneers such as E.A. Corbett, Hector Charlesworth, and Austin Weir, according to whom French programming on national radio sparked "a queer mixture of prejudice, bigotry and fear."[4]

By 1941, separation of the two services was complete—although the original CBC news service, created to meet the demands of covering the Second World War, operated bilingually. Paradoxically, yet to be expected, the institution of separate services was welcomed by French-Canadian nationalists, who had feared becoming the marginalized minority within a single, nominally bilingual service. The French network achieved a degree of administrative autonomy because of "the need for national unity raised by the war," but no sooner was it in place than it became the focus of a national crisis.[5]

In January 1942 the government announced it would hold a plebiscite on conscription. In the ensuing campaign, the Québec-based Ligue pour la défense du Canada, a broad front of political and social leaders opposed to conscription, sought to use the public airwaves in order to urge their fellow citizens to vote "No." The CBC, by order of the government, denied the "No" voice access to its stations. The opponents of conscription were able to promote their cause by purchasing paid advertising on commercial stations, however, resulting in another paradox: the identification of "public" broadcasting as an oppressive agent of centralized federalism, and of French-Canadian entrepreneurial capital as a progressive force.[6]

1945–1963: CONSOLIDATING THE SYSTEM ... AND THE SYNDROME

Citing the educational nature of broadcasting, as "a powerful medium of publicity and intellectual and moral training," the government of Québec under Maurice Duplessis claimed that Québec had the constitutional authority to create a provincial broadcasting service, and passed legislation setting up Radio-Québec in 1945.[7] Duplessis's legislation was never put into effect, after C.D. Howe announced in the House of Commons that, "since broadcasting is the sole responsibility of the Dominion government, broadcasting licences shall not be issued to other governments or corporations owned by other governments."[8]

Meanwhile, outside Québec the "parallel services" of public broadcasting were developing unequally. While the CBC's English-language radio service extended from coast to coast by 1938, the same could not be said for French-language service in the 1950s. The Royal Commission on National Development in the Arts, Letters, and Sciences (the Massey Commission) reported in 1951 that French-speaking communities outside Québec were still poorly served by the CBC: "It has been pointed out to us repeatedly in different parts of Canada that the French-speaking

Canadian listener does not receive a broadcasting service equal to that intended for his English-speaking neighbor."[9] Six years later, the Royal Commission on Broadcasting (the Fowler Commission) found that many parts of Canada were still lacking French service, and suggested that this was more than a question of available resources: "It remains a moot question, however, whether Canada has yet reached the stage of complete national maturity where the introduction of French on the airwaves of Ontario ... would not be regarded by a substantial majority as an intolerable intrusion rather than the cultural complement that in truth it would be."[10]

The Conservative government elected in 1957 sought to build up the commercial side of Canadian broadcasting, and paid little attention to its role in the complexities of the evolving national dilemma. This was most apparent in its response to the historic Radio-Canada producers' strike of 1958–59, which saw, among other things, the rise to political prominence of René Lévesque. Gérard Pelletier has pointed out that much of the problem was attributable to the fact that the French network executives in Montréal lacked the authority to negotiate on behalf of the corporation, while the head office in Ottawa did not bother to take it seriously. The strike paralysed French-language television for 68 days (there was only one available Canadian channel in each language at the time), and became a symbol of the historic inequality of French and English Canada.[11]

1963–1980: NATIONAL UNITY AND STRUGGLES FOR POWER

By the time the Liberals returned to power in 1963, the situation had changed. In fact, early in its mandate the Pearson government publicly identified cultural policy in general and broadcasting in particular as strategic weapons in its struggle against the rising and increasingly radical nationalist movement in Québec. In the House of Commons on 13 November 1964, Secretary of State Maurice Lamontagne announced the government's intention to rationalize and centralize the activities of all federal cultural agencies under the jurisdiction of his office, and to create a cabinet committee on cultural affairs. Under the new policy, the national broadcasting service, the CBC, would play a central role:

> The CBC is one of Canada's most vital and essential institutions at this crucial moment of our history. The CBC must become a living and daily testimony of the Canadian identity, a faithful reflection of our two main cultures and a powerful element of understanding, moderation and unity in our country. If it performs these national tasks with efficiency, its occasional mistakes will be easily forgotten; if it fails in that mission, its other achievements will not compensate for that failure.[12]

This was the clearest enunciation of the CBC's mission, in the government's view, since the war. It became clearer still during the next few years. At parliamentary committee hearings in 1966, Liberal backbenchers from Québec and Radio-Canada middle-management executives sparred over their respective views of the CBC's role vis-à-vis the emerging question of "separatism." When a new broadcasting act was introduced in October 1967, it contained a clause that read as follows: "The national broadcasting service [CBC] should ... contribute to the development of national unity and provide for a continuing expression of Canadian identity."[13]

In the House, Secretary of State Judy LaMarsh said the national unity clause was "perhaps the most important feature of the CBC's mandate in the new bill."[14] This was the first time that Parliament had tried to spell out the goals and purposes of the CBC, she told the parliamentary committee: "[The CBC] is the instrument which Parliament has chosen with respect to broadcasting. Parliament is now, in this bill, saying to the instrument that this is one of its purposes, and as long as that purpose is there, to help weld the country together, Parliament is prepared to raise taxes from the people to keep it going ... I do not think there is very much more time for public broadcasting to prove itself, to prove to Canadians it is worth while spending the money on."[15]

After some vigorous debate, the broadcasting act passed, with the controversial clause intact. The NDP's R.W. Prittie expressed the fear of a witch-hunt. Gérard Pelletier admitted he had doubts about it "lead[ing] some people to believe that it is not a matter of promotion but of propaganda."[16] And an important observation on the implications of the clause came from Conservative MP David MacDonald:

> When we begin to move into areas such as ... national unity, we are in effect moving away from the concept of public broadcasting toward the idea of state broadcasting whereby the broadcasting system of the country becomes an extension of the state.[17]

Radio-Canada's interpretation of its mandate to promote national unity led to bizarre incidents such as keeping its cameras trained on the parade at the 1968 Saint-Jean-Baptiste Day celebrations in Montréal, while police and demonstrators fought a bloody battle on the sidelines. During the October Crisis of 1970, the federal cabinet closely oversaw what was and was not broadcast by Radio-Canada, and a few months later a string of management "supervisors" appeared in the corporation's newsrooms, with no apparent function other than political surveillance.[18] The former head of Radio-Canada news and public affairs, Marc Thibault, remembers one official whose job was to monitor all news programmes and count the number of times the word québécois was used.[19]

The situation culminated with Prime Minister Trudeau's instruction to the federal regulatory agency, the Canadian Radio-Television and Telecommunications Commission, to inquire into CBC news coverage in the wake of the election of the Parti Québécois in Québec in November 1976:

> Doubts have been expressed as to whether the English and French television networks of [the CBC] generally, and in particular their public affairs, information and news programming, are fulfilling the mandate of the Corporation.[20]

The CRTC dutifully investigated and reported, in July 1977, that the CBC had indeed failed "to contribute to the development of national unity"—but not in the sense anticipated by the prime minister. The problem was not a bias in favour of separatist politics, it said, but deficient representation of Canada's "two solitudes" to one another. In English and in French, the CBC did not pay adequate attention to the regions of Canada; it was too centralized and aloof, too influenced by commercial pressures, too bureaucratic. "In the modern world," reported the CRTC, "political and economic developments tend to centralize; cultural developments, on the other hand, tend to be regional, arising in much more sharply delimited areas."[21]

The 1977 CRTC inquiry appears to have been a turning point in the Liberal government's view of the role of media in Canada's constitutional struggle. By year's end it had created a new agency, the Canadian Unity Information Office, and a strategy for containment of the pressures of national fragmentation thereafter flowed through there. Political expectations of the CBC diminished, and in the important run-up to the Québec referendum of 1980, the corporation was left to establish and carry out an internal policy of news coverage according to rigorous journalistic standards and the principle of "the public's right to be informed."[22] Ultimately, the referendum campaign was covered by CBC as a straight news event, while the government sought to mobilize its constituency directly, particularly through advertising.[23]

The role of the CBC aside, political struggles surrounding the national question continued to mark the evolution of Canadian broadcasting in the 1960s and 1970s.

From 1968 on, renewed demands from Québec for constitutional powers in broadcasting highlighted the constitutional debates of the day and marked the evolution of communications in Canada. In its brief to the constitutional conference convened by Lester Pearson in February 1968, Québec claimed the right to play the role of a national state in matters pertaining to language and culture, including broadcasting. As instruments of education and culture, radio and television rightfully belong under provincial jurisdiction, the Québec brief argued. The court ruling of 1932 was "unacceptable"; federal agencies like the CBC should be made to reflect the "bicultural reality" of Canada; jurisdiction over broadcasting should not be the exclusive domain of the federal government.[24]

In the coming months, debate focused on the question of "educational broadcasting." The new broadcasting act stated that "facilities should be provided within the Canadian broadcasting system for educational broadcasting."[25] As we saw earlier, federal policy explicitly excluded provincial governments or their agencies from holding broadcasting licences. Yet, education was clearly under provincial jurisdiction. Who then would have control over educational broadcasting? Returning to Québec from the constitutional conference, Johnson declared that his government had decided to apply Duplessis's 1945 law establishing Radio-Québec.[26] The move was enough to upset Ottawa's design. By the end of 1969, Ottawa and the provinces had settled on a definition of educational broadcasting under which, in the 1970s, provincial public broadcasting agencies would begin operating in four provinces.

The growing complexity of communications in the late 1960s prompted Ottawa to create a Department of Communications (DOC) in April 1969. Determined to match Ottawa move for move, Québec created its own Ministère des communications six months later. In the early 1970s, negotiating a strong role for Québec in communications policy became one of the hallmarks of Robert Bourassa's programme for achieving "cultural sovereignty." In a series of policy statements authored by Communications Minister Jean-Paul L'Allier, Québec proposed "to promote and maintain a québécois system of communications,"[27] and to become "master craftsman of communications policy on its territory."[28]

The cornerstone of Québec's policy was to be the Régie des services publics, the regulatory authority for utilities falling under the province's jurisdiction. L'Allier saw the Régie becoming a Québec equivalent to the CRTC, extending its activities to areas such as cable television—which, Québec argued, were not covered by the Privy Council decision of 1932. In 1973, the Régie began to subject the 160 cable companies then operating in Québec to its own regulation as well as that of the CRTC, and within a year the inevitable occurred: in applications to serve a community near Rimouski, the Régie and the CRTC awarded licences to two different applicants. It took until November 1977 for the Supreme Court to decide the Dionne-d'Auteuil case in favour of the CRTC, ruling that Ottawa had exclusive jurisdiction over cable.[29] Oddly enough, the court split neatly along national lines, the three judges from Québec dissenting from the majority opinion. As constitutional scholar Gil Rémillard put it: "On the strictly legal level, both options were defensible. The decision was based on the judges' different conceptions of Canadian federalism."[30]

Under the Parti Québécois government, Québec did not directly engage with Ottawa over communications policy. The PQ carried over the policy thrust of the Bourassa government but basically abdicated due to its lack of power over communications under the existing system. In the view of Communications Minister Louis O'Neill, political sovereignty was the only solution to Québec's communications problems.[31] Paradoxically, the PQ was thus a lot less aggressive than its predecessors in seeking concrete gains from Ottawa in this area. It concentrated instead on developing the programmes and policies begun by Union Nationale and Liberal governments: Radio-Québec, now a full-fledged broadcaster, and the particular Québec form of participatory communication known as "community" media.

1980–1990: POSTNATIONALISM AND THE TRIUMPH OF THE MARKET

Both in Ottawa and Québec, communication policy took on a new—yet strangely similar—shape after the referendum of 1980.

In Ottawa, as we saw earlier, the view of the CBC as the centrepiece of Canadian cultural policy had begun to shift as of the late 1970s. With the referendum out of the way, the entire cultural sphere took on a distinctly economic vocation. In July 1980, the arts and culture branch of the Department of the Secretary of

State and ministerial responsibility for culture were transferred to the industry-oriented DOC. Communications Minister Francis Fox told the parliamentary committee that the diffusion of culture would henceforth depend increasingly on its industrial base and the DOC would be concentrating on the growth of "cultural industries." [32]

The new orientation was underwritten by the Federal Cultural Policy Review Committee (Applebaum-Hébert) that reported in 1982, and spelled out in detail in a series of policy statements signed by Fox in 1983–84. [33] Since then, federal policy has been marked notably by a gradual withdrawal of fiscal responsibility for public service broadcasting (CBC budget cuts), privatization of television production (through the Telefilm fund), and the introduction of a wide range of new commercial cable-delivered television signals (pay-TV and nondiscretionary subscriber-funded specialty services). In generic terms, the 1980s marked a shift from the political to the economic, and the eclipse of the traditional sociocultural objectives of broadcasting in Canada.

The new approach in Québec was strangely similar, as in the postreferendum context, Québec appeared to lose interest in the sociocultural possibilities of communications altogether, and placed its emphasis on industrial development during its second mandate. Québec Communications Minister Jean-François Bertrand signalled the new situation in June 1981: PQ communications policy would be based on economic development, and not on making jurisdictional demands from Ottawa. [34] Indeed, Québec under the PQ seemed determined to outpace Ottawa in shifting the accent in communications from the cultural and political to the industrial and economic spheres. [35]

So the Québec referendum not only changed the underlying basis for both Ottawa's and Québec's strategy in communications, and shifted the emphasis from the political and sociocultural to the economic and the industrial; it also changed the nature of jurisdictional conflict between Québec and Ottawa—competition over control of cultural development could change to collaboration in the name of economic development. [36] But such collaboration was not possible while the Liberals were in office in Ottawa, given the rigidity of their historic claim to exclusive jurisdiction over communications. It had to await the election of the Conservatives in 1984.

The most generous thing one can say about the new Conservative government's broadcasting policy is that it had none. In general, the government's early initiatives with respect to broadcasting coincided with its general thrust toward reduced public spending and expanding the role of the private sector in the Canadian economy. [37] But broadcasting and communications generally quickly emerged as one of the sectors on the cutting edge of the government's plan for "national reconciliation" after the institutionalized antagonism of the Trudeau years.

Brian Mulroney's choice of Marcel Masse to be his minister of communications was an astute one in this regard. Masse was not only a loyal Tory, but a reputed Québec nationalist who had been involved with the Union Nationale government of the late 1960s in its battle for more provincial power through agencies such

188

as Radio-Québec. He was the ideal minister for thawing relations with Québec while applying broad government policy to communications.

Tendering the olive branch to Québec, was not only an effective manoeuvre in terms of the government's thrust toward national reconciliation, it was also an early move to deflect criticism from its attitude toward national public broadcasting. In an interview with *Le Devoir* in December 1984, Masse said:

> The Conservative Party applies its theories in every sector, in communications as elsewhere ... the state is an important tool in economic affairs as in cultural affairs, but we are not about to have a culture of the state ... we are going to have a culture of Canadians. We have insisted, to the exclusion of everything else, that the defence of Canadian culture was the CBC's responsibility. We have insisted on this until everyone else wound up believing they had no responsibility. Perhaps it is time to redress the balance. Canadian culture belongs to the Canadian people, and it is up to them, through all their institutions, to see that it flourishes. [38]

In the same interview, Masse added that he saw provincial broadcasters as positive instruments for regional cultural development, not as usurpers of federal authority (the standard Liberal view).

Elsewhere, while his government administered crippling surgery to the CBC budget, Masse was fond of reminding audiences of the previous government's attitude toward public broadcasting: "We're not the ones who threatened to put the key in the door of the CBC because we didn't like its news coverage," he told a meeting of Québec journalists in Montréal. [39]

On 1 February 1985, Masse and Québec Communications Minister Jean-François Bertrand signed an agreement on communications enterprises development under which they jointly provided $40 million in seed-money to stimulate research and job creation by Québec-based communications firms. The industrial thrust of the accord was self-evident, aiming at technical innovation and support for the production, development, and marketing of communications goods and services, especially in export markets. [40]

It was the first-ever communications agreement between Ottawa and Québec since they created their respective communications ministries a few months apart in 1969. Masse and Bertrand also announced the setting up of a permanent joint committee, chaired by their two deputy ministers, to pursue further areas of collaboration. This committee has functioned successfully ever since, making communications one field where Ottawa and Québec actually function d'égal à égal. [41]

The committee's first effort produced an important report, "The Future of French-Language Television," made public in May 1985. [42] The report's central recommendation was crucial to the developing federal policy with respect to broadcasting, as well as strangely premonitory. It proposed "that the special nature of the French-language television system be recognized within the Canadian broadcasting system, and that government policies and regulations be adapted accordingly."[43] Such a proposal would recognize, for the first time, the historic reality of parallel development of Canadian broadcasting since the 1930s. It also would mark a major shift in Ottawa's official attitude that there is but one policy for Canadian broadcasting, not two.

Specifically, the report proposed the following areas as requiring distinct policy approaches:

—Radio-Canada should be allowed to evolve separately (*pouvoir connaître une évolution distincte*) from the CBC;
—the roles to be played by public and private networks in the evolution of the French-language system should not be assumed to be the same as in the English;
—a policy on French-language cable TV should be developed to protect emerging French-language specialty services against the massive influx of services in English and to foster their introduction by ensuring more favourable financing arrangements;
—private television stations should increase their investment in French programming;
—public television networks should make greater use of independent production houses and government funding agencies should increase their support for programme creation outside the system;
—public and private television networks should work together to maximize audience penetration and combat audience erosion by English-language stations;
—the status of Québec community television organizations should be clarified, funding sources increased, and experience used to promote development outside Québec;
—delivery of French signals to underserved areas should be promoted.

In addition, the report proposed general ongoing consultation between Ottawa and Québec. A "harmonization" agreement for the development of French-language television was signed soon thereafter.[44] Since then, areas of federal-provincial collaboration have included working groups on cable television, children's advertising, and computer software[45], and the idea of tailoring policy to meet the distinct needs of different markets has been reflected notably in CRTC decisions[46] and the policies of the Telefilm fund.[47]

Québec public opinion welcomed the new distribution of resources in communications, which was seen as a move away from the traditional approach of massive, and exclusive, federal involvement in cultural affairs.[48] This, it was recalled, had begun as a kind of benevolent state intervention in the 1950s in the wake of the Massey Report, only to be transformed into a strategic weapon for the promotion of national unity under the Pearson, and particularly the Trudeau governments.

The Mulroney government's first term in office was marked by a series of formal initiatives with respect to broadcasting policy: a comprehensive review by a Task Force on Broadcasting Policy[49], lengthy hearings, and a report by the parliamentary Standing Committee on Communications and Culture[50], a ministerial policy statement[51], and, finally, a new broadcasting act.[52]

The first stage of this process took the form of a ministerial task force headed by Gerald Caplan and Florian Sauvageau. Its terms of reference, announced in April 1985, were to propose "an industrial and cultural strategy to govern the future evolution of the Canadian broadcasting system through the remainder of this century," taking into account "the need for fiscal restraint, increased reliance on private sector initiatives and federal-provincial co-operation."

The Caplan-Sauvageau task force welcomed the proposals of the federal-provincial committee on French-language television[53], and reiterated many of its key proposals. It proposed "that the distinctive character of Québec broadcasting be recognized both in itself and as the nucleus of French-language broadcasting throughout Canada."[54] French- and English-language services within the CBC should be recognized as serving "distinct societies," and be allowed to take "different approaches to meeting the objectives assigned to public broadcasting."[55] The CBC's French network budgets should be reviewed "to establish hourly production costs that reflect the role assigned to the French network in the new television environment."[56] As for the CBC's national unity mandate, the task force found it "inappropriate for any broadcaster, public or private ... It suggests constrained attachment to a political order rather than free expression in the pursuit of a national culture broadly defined."[57] The task force proposed to replace it with "a more socially oriented provision, for example, that the service contribute to the development of national consciousness."[58]

The parliamentary committee that studied the Caplan-Sauvageau recommendations in 1986–88 made two pertinent proposals of its own. One concerned making the law reflect the CRTC practice of "tak[ing] into consideration the distinctive characters of French and English broadcasting when implementing broadcasting policy."[59] The other extended an important task force proposal, specifying that the budget for CBC production costs be established "so that the quality of the Canadian programs of the English and French networks would be comparable."[60]

The government's position was formalized in the policy statement *Canadian Voices Canadian Choices*, signed by Flora MacDonald and made public a few days after the report of the parliamentary committee in June 1988. Here it was recognized that

> the problems and challenges for English-language broadcasting and French-language broadcasting are not the same ... [and that] these differences between the English and French broadcasting environments necessarily require different policy approaches for each.[61]

The legislation tabled at the same time (Bill C–136) featured a half-dozen clauses referring to the linguistic duality of the system. The key clause, article 3.1.b., specified that "English and French language broadcasting, while sharing common aspects, operate under different conditions and may have different requirements."[62] The CBC's mandate was changed to read that "the programming provided by the Canadian Broadcasting Corporation should ... contribute to shared national consciousness and identity."[63] (An amendment introduced at third reading added that it should "strive to be of equivalent quality in English and in French" as well.)[64]

Bill C-136 died in the Senate on 30 September 1988, as Parliament was dissolved for the national elections.[65] It was reintroduced virtually intact, however, as Bill C-40 in October 1989.[66] This bill had an even more bizarre itinerary, especially insofar as the aspects that interest us here are concerned.

In retrospect, one of the interesting aspects of the policy evolution between 1985-88 was just how little controversy was provoked by issues with constitutional implications.[67] In spite of an unprecedented outpouring of public discussion and production of official policy documents[68], there was almost no contradictory debate surrounding constitutional matters. The opposition political parties were especially silent[69]—particularly in view of how vocal they had been on these questions in the past, and would soon be again.

The situation changed suddenly when Bill C-40 went to legislative committee in January 1990. The minister, once again, was Marcel Masse. He reiterated the general thrust of the legislation as it had been expressed in Flora MacDonald's policy statement of June 1988:

The new proposed legislation recognizes the distinct character of francophone audiences. It is clear that English and French-language broadcasting differ in their operations and in their needs.[70]

Masse then explained the rewording of the CBC's national unity mandate, in terms borrowed from Caplan-Sauvageau:

I have removed from the CBC its obligation to promote Canadian unity because it is, first, maintaining this political value artificially, and second, it was a constraint on freedom of expression. This obligation also opens the door to an intolerable interference. In removing it, we will rather place greater emphasis on the capacity of Canadians to recognize each other through their values.[71]

The issue was picked up by the NDP's Ian Waddell:

Waddell. ... you are now 'Meeching' [the CBC]; you are now applying the doctrine of the Meech Lake agreement to this.

Waddell asked Masse to explain what he meant by the CBC's old mandate "maintaining this political value artificially."

Masse. A public broadcaster must reflect society, its sociological aspects as well as its cultural aspects. It is not a propaganda instrument. To become the promoter of one aspect of our reality might easily produce consequences that would limit freedom of expression. You may be too young to remember the time when Liberal governments, before our time, asked the CBC to report on the number of separatists who worked at or did not work at promoting Canadian unity. We lived through those times. They certainly were not the most conducive to freedom of expression in our country.

Waddell. The intolerable interference with the CBC was when the [Liberal] government of the day issued directions that it did not want separatists in the CBC. That is what you mean by intolerable. Is that why you are changing?

Masse. Do you support the government in issuing a directive to Radio-Canada in a sense like that?

Waddell. Yes, yes, yes.

Masse. Do you support that?

Waddell. I believe in Canada. I believe in national unity.

Masse. Do you believe in it to the degree that you want to muzzle la liberté d'expression in this country?

Waddell. Je ne suis pas séparatiste, monsieur le ministre. Etes-vous séparatiste?[72]

The reader will understand if I abandon the narrative at this point, although the discussion continued through several more exchanges of a similar nature.

At subsequent hearing meetings, Liberal and NDP committee members sought to draw out the views of prominent parties with respect to the national unity mandate—although not a single intervenor raised the question on his or her own steam.

Under questioning from Liberal member John Harvard on 15 February, broadcasting historian and former CBC producer Frank W. Peers, appearing for the Friends of Canadian Broadcasting, stated:

> I tend to think the wording in the existing act, whereby the CBC is asked in effect to promote national unity, can be a source of difficulty for a public broadcaster which is expected to reflect opinions from all elements of the population.[73]

The head of the CRTC, Keith Spicer, responding to a question from Waddell, stated on 22 February:

> I would agree with the government on this one. I think the words 'national unity' had a historic value at the time ... I think this new wording is probably more appropriate to the times we live in.[74]

The CBC's designated chairman Patrick Watson, responding to Liberal member Sheila Finestone, stated on 12 March:

> I felt at the time of the passage of the previous law in 1968 that the introduction of the requirement to promote national unity was inappropriate and verged on requiring of the CBC that it become an instrument of propaganada ... there is a widely held feeling [within the CBC] that the real obligation of this corporation, of this institution, is to reflect realities.[75]

So, as in 1968, there was no apparent sign of a public interest (or indeed, of public interest) in the CBC's national unity mandate. It was strictly an affair of politicians.[76] When Bill C-40 returned to the House for third reading, the government voted down two opposition amendments on the question, one by Sheila Finestone proposing a return to the *status quo ante* ("... contribute to the development of national unity and provide for a continuing expression of Canadian identity"), and a hybrid proposal by Ian Waddell ("... contribute to national unity, shared national consciousness and identity").[77]

The new Broadcasting Act was finally adopted on 5 December 1990—just as the CBC president was announcing draconian cuts in staff and services that would eliminate public broadcasting at the local level.[78] The combination of cynicism and irony evident in this coincidence stood as a reminder that its ministers' lofty pronouncements on the sociocultural importance of broadcasting notwithstanding, the Conservative government's lack of support for public broadcasting demonstrated its view of broadcasting as just another business.

CONCLUSION

The distant and recent history I have just outlined is of interest to communications and constitutional scholars alike. For communications scholars, it shows how media systems, institutions, services, and policies evolve according to the political and economic agendas of the surrounding society and its elites. For constitutional scholars it shows the strategic importance of the media system and pertaining policy issues to the evolving constitutional context.

Aside from what it tells us about media, this history is rich in illustration about governments' conception of media—and of the link between their constitutional agendas and their overall agendas.

Most of the time, Canadian politicians have tended to see broadcasting as an instrument of nation-building, and have thus been quick to blame broadcasting for failing to contribute to national unity. The blame is misplaced and the expectation unreasonable.

As a forum of public discussion, a mirror of social life, a system in which problems of jurisdiction, allocation of resources, and other areas of conflict are played out, Canadian broadcasting has reflected the lack of consensus about fundamental nature of Canadian nationhood.

In this sense, it is a microcosm of Canadian society, and of the quintessential Canadian dilemma of how to accommodate divergent sociocultural demands within a "national" framework when the question of "nationhood" remains unresolved.

NOTES

1. The reader desiring more historical detail is referred to Marc Raboy, *Missed Opportunities: The Story of Canada's Broadcasting Policy* (Montréal and Kingston: McGill-Queen's University Press, 1990) from which most of the material in this paper is drawn.

2. Canada, Royal Commission on Radio Broadcasting, *Report* (Ottawa: King's Printer, 1929).
3. Canadian Broadcasting Corporation, *Submission to the Royal Commission on Bilingualism and Biculturalism*, Ottawa: CBC, 1964, 5.
4. E. Austin Weir, *The Struggle for National Broadcasting in Canada* (Toronto: McClelland and Stewart, 1965), 151.
5. See, e.g., Gérard Lamarche, "Radio-Canada et sa mission française," *Canadian Communications* 1, 1 (summer 1960): 6–15.
6. See André Laurendeau, *La Crise de la conscription* (Montréal: Editions du Jour, 1962), (summarized in Raboy, *Missed Opportunities*).
7. Québec, Statutes, Loi autorisant la création d'un service de radio-diffusion provinciale, SQ 1945, c. 56.
8. Canada, Parliament, House of Commons, *Debates* (1946), 1167.
9. Canada, Royal Commission on National Development in the Arts, Letters and Sciences, *Report* (Ottawa: King's Printer, 1951), 297.
10. Canada, Royal Commission on Broadcasting, *Report* (Ottawa: Queen's Printer, 1957), 242.
11. See Gérard Pelletier, *Les années d'impatience (1950–1960)* (Montréal: Stanké, 1983), (summarized in Raboy, *Missed Opportunities*).
12. Canada, Parliament, House of Commons, *Debates* (1964–65), 10084.
13. Canada, Statutes, Broadcasting Act, SC 1967–68, c. 25, article 3.g.iv.
14. Canada, Parliament, House of Commons, *Debates* (1967–68), 3754.
15. Canada, Parliament, House of Commons, Standing Committee on Broadcasting, Films and Assistance to the Arts, *Minutes* (1967–68), 13, 54.
16. Canada, Parliament, House of Commons, *Debates* (1967–68), 6017.
17. Canada, House of Commons, *Debates* (1967–68), 6025.
18. See Raboy, *Missed Opportunities*, 204–208.
19. This was related by Marc Thibault in comments at the National Archives of Canada Conference, "Beyond the Printed Word," Ottawa, October 1988.
20. Canadian Radio-Television and Telecommunications Commission, Committee of Inquiry into the National Broadcasting Service, *Report*, Ottawa: CRTC, 1977, p. v.
21. Ibid., 9.
22. See, e.g., Canadian Broadcasting Corporation, *The CBC—A Perspective*, Ottawa: CBC, 1979, 377–424.
23. See A.W. Johnson, "The Re-Canadianization of Broadcasting," *Policy Options* 4, 2 (March 1983): 6–12; and Frank Stark, "Persuasion, Propaganda, and Public Policy," paper to the fourth annual conference of the Canadian Communication Association, Vancouver, June 1983, typescript.
24. Québec, "Ce que veut le Québec," brief submitted by Daniel Johnson to the Constitutional Conference, first meeting, Ottawa, 5–7 February 1968.
25. Canada, Statutes, Broadcasting Act, SC 1967–68, c. 25, article s.2.i.
26. Québec, National Assembly, *Journal des débats* (1968), 3.
27. Québec, Ministère des communications du Québec, *Pour une politique québécoise des communications*, Québec: MCQ, 1971.
28. Québec, Ministère des communications du Québec, *Le Québec, maître d'oeuvre de la politique des communications sur son territoire*, Québec: MCQ, 1973.
29. Canada, Supreme Court, *Supreme Court Reports* (1978), vol. 2, 191–210.
30. Gil Rémillard, *Le fédéralisme canadien: Eléments constitutionnels de formation et d'évolution* (Montréal: Québec-Amérique, 1980), 349.
31. Québec, National Assembly, Journal des débats (1977), B–2095.
32. Canada, Parliament, House of Commons, Standing Committee on Communications and Culture, *Minutes* (1980–83), 2,9.
33. Canada, Federal Cultural Policy Review Committee, *Report* (Ottawa: Minister of Supply and Services Canada, 1982); Canada, Department of Communications, *Towards a New National Broadcasting Policy* (Ottawa: Minister of Supply and Services Canada, 1983); *Building for the*

Future: Towards a Distinctive CBC (Ottawa: Minister of Supply and Services Canada, 1983); *The National Film and Video Policy* (Ottawa: Minister of Supply and Services Canada, 1984).

34. See Québec, National Assembly, *Journal des débats (1981)*, B–326–329.

35. *See, e.g.*, Québec, *Ministère des communications du Québec, Bâtir l'avenir* (Québec: Gouvernement du Québec, 1982); and *Le Québec et les communications: Un futur simple?* (Québec: Gouvernement du Québec, 1983).

36. See Gaétan Tremblay, "La politique québécoise en matière de communication (1966–1986): 'De l'affirmation autonomiste à la coopération fédérale-provinciale,' " *Communication information* 9, 3 (summer 1988): 57–87.

37. See Canada, Task Force on Program Review, *An Introduction to the Process of Program Review* (Ottawa: Minister of Supply and Services Canada, 1986).

38. Bernard Descoteaux, "Marcel Masse: Radio-Canada prend trop de place dans le budget culturel," *Le Devoir*, 20 December 1984.

39. Comments to a meeting of the Fédération professionnelle des journalistes du Québec, Montréal, 10 December 1984.

40. Canada/Québec, *Canada-Québec Subsidiary Agreement on Communications Enterprises Development 1984–1990* (Ottawa and Québec: Government of Canada/Gouvernement du Québec, 1985). See also Tremblay, "La politique québécoise."

41. This view was expressed to the author in these words by a senior official of the MCQ in June 1990, a few days before the collapse of the Meech Lake Accord.

42. Canada/Québec, Federal-provincial committee, *The Future of French-Language Television* (Ottawa and Quebec: Government of Canada/Gouvernement du Québec, 1985).

43. Ibid., 2. The French version read: "... *que le système télévisuel francophone soit reconnu comme une entité spécifique du système canadien et qu'en conséquence des politiques distinctes lui soient appliquées,*" 10. According to the MCQ official referred to in note 41, "C'était Meech avant la lettre"—it was a precursor to Meech.

44. Canada/Québec, "Canada-Québec Memorandum of Understanding on the Development of the French-language Television System," Ottawa and Québec: Government of Canada/Gouvernement du Québec, 13 February 1986.

45. Tremblay, "La politique québécoise," 83.

46. E.g., Canadian Radio-Television and Telecommunications Commission, *More Canadian Programming Choices*, Ottawa: CRTC, 30 November 1987.

47. However, the functioning of the Telefilm fund is now being contested by Québec. See, e.g., Paule des Riviéres, "Les coproductions avec la France vont bien ... mais en anglais," *Le Devoir*, 22 October 1990.

48. See, e.g., Lise Bissonnette, "L'envers du décor," *Le Devoir* editorial, 23 March 1985.

49. Canada, Task Force on Broadcasting Policy, *Report* (Ottawa: Minister of Supply and Services Canada, 1986).

50. Canada, Parliament, House of Commons, Standing Committee on Communications and Culture, *A Broadcasting Policy for Canada (Report)*, (Ottawa: Minister of Supply and Services Canada, 1988).

51. Canada, Communications Canada, *Canadian Voices Canadian Choices: A New Broadcasting Policy for Canada* (Ottawa: Minister of Supply and Services Canada, 1988).

52. Canada, Unpassed Bills, Broadcasting Act, Bill C–136, first reading, 23 June 1988.

53. Task Force on Broadcasting Policy, 157.

54. Ibid., 223.

55. Ibid., 217.

56. Ibid., 253.

57. Ibid., 283–284.

58. Ibid., 285.

59. Canada, Parliament, House of Commons, Standing Committee on Communications and Culture (1986–88), *Sixth Report*, recommendation 65 (*A Broadcasting Policy for Canada*), 418.

60. *A Broadcasting Policy for Canada,* recommendation 34, 363.
61. *Canadian Voices Canadian Choices,* 6–7.
62. Bill C–136, article 3.1.b.
63. Ibid., article 3.1.n.iv.
64. Canada, Unpassed Bills, Broadcasting Act, Bill C–136, third reading, 28 September 1988, article 3.1.k.iv.
65. See Raboy, *Missed Opportunities,* 329–334.
66. Canada, 34th Parliament, second session (1989–), Broadcasting Act, Bill C–40, first reading, 12 October 1989.
67. A rare exception came from newspaper columnist William Johnson, for whom Bill C–136 stood for the "meeching" of Canada. By reflecting "the view that Québec is a distinct society," he wrote, the bill would "break the national coherence of the CBC." William Johnson, " 'Meeching' of Canada takes another step forward," *The Gazette* (Montréal), column, 21 September 1988.
68. See Marc Raboy, "Two Steps Forward, Three Steps Back: Canadian Broadcasting Policy from Caplan-Sauvageau to Bill C–136," *Canadian Journal of Communication* 14, 1 (1989): 70–75.
69. According to a research project in progress at Laval University, no Liberal or NDP intervention before the task force, the parliamentary committee, or the legislative committee hearings on Bill C–136 addressed the question of the distinct society or the CBC's national unity mandate (personal files).
70. Canada, Parliament, House of Commons, Legislative Committee on Bill C–40, *Minutes* (31 January 1990), 11.
71. Ibid.
72. Ibid., 17–18.
73. Ibid., 15 February 1990, 29.
74. Ibid., 22 February 1990, 17–18.
75. Ibid., 12 March 1990, 6.
76. See, e.g., the debate among members at the legislative committee's final public session in Canada, Parliament, House of Commons, Legislative Committee on Bill C–40, *Minutes* (15 March 1990), 69–84.
77. Canada, 34th Parliament, second session, House of Commons, Order Paper and Notice Paper no. 170 (23 April 1990).
78. See, e.g., Hugh Winsor, "Drop in funds cited in CBC cuts," *The Globe and Mail,* 6 December 1990; Gerald Caplan, "CBC cutbacks tear another hole in fabric of national unity," *The Gazette* (Montréal), 8 December 1990.

COMMENTARY

VAUGHN PALMER

VANCOUVER SUN

First, a confession: I did not attend the final conference on Meech Lake. I watched on television. I am comforted that most journalists had to do the same thing. You watched, you know what happened those seven ghastly days in June. The first ministers would arrive at the conference centre, talk to CBC reporters Don Newman and Wendy Mesley, go inside, get nowhere, and come out and talk to Don Newman and Wendy Mesley. Indeed this discussion could be retitled "Meech Lake and Don Newman and Wendy Mesley."

So, did Don and Wendy do a good job? Two of the three papers on the media say: "No." John Meisel and David Taras both say the news media did more than cover the final stages of Meech Lake: they became players in the proceedings, set the framework of debate, and influenced—even distorted—the outcome. Both men suggest remedies to make sure this does not happen in the future.

I say the remedies are unnecessary because the arguments do not stand up. Let me deal with a few of their examples.

John Meisel says the Québec media put pressure on Premier Robert Bourassa to prevent a compromise. He could not discuss changing even one comma of the Meech Lake Accord without his press corps accusing him of a "sellout." I am not familiar with the French-language coverage, but in English I heard Bourassa say repeatedly that Meech must not be amended. Premier Bourassa, not the Québec press, created the impression that to change one comma of the Accord would be a sellout.

David Taras says the media did not expose the prime minister's deliberate strategy of trying to force a settlement by raising the temperature of the debate. I suggest the reason we know about the strategy is because it was reported—and reported at the time it unfolded. Yes, the news media covered Meech in a crisis atmosphere. Most of the political leadership in the country said there was a crisis. Who were the news media to say there was no crisis?

Mr. Taras complains about the coverage of Lucien Bouchard's coup de process. He says the media allowed the ex-cabinet minister to "hijack" the negotiations and override coverage of the Charest Report. I think Bouchard's defection from the prime minister's side was one of the significant events of the year and deserved coverage as such. Whereas the Charest Report was buried because nobody liked it. Not Bourassa. Not Wells. Not Filmon. Not the public.

Mr. Taras's third complaint, and the most painful to address, is the demo "clip" of demonstrators trampling the Québec flag. I think the trampling was broadcast again and again because, regrettably, it fit. It accurately symbolized the anti-Québec sentiments in English Canada, as anyone who tuned in to a radio

199

phone-in show would realize. The clip fit the debate in Québec too because it played to the French-Canadian feelings of persecution. Just because the Québécois are paranoid does not mean they do not have enemies.

Although Marc Raboy's paper is not specifically about Meech, it still exposes the flaw in the argument that the news media must strive to keep the country together. Mr. Raboy details the attempt to make the CBC fulfil a mandate to promote national unity. The effort failed, though the government that pursued it controlled both the airwaves and the purse strings. I find that failure reassuring, an example of a free press struggling to portray the reality of its society against a well-intentioned effort to make it report something else.

Let me illustrate my point about the limitations of good intentions by referring to my own newspaper's coverage of Meech Lake. Over the life of the Accord, *The Vancouver Sun* blanketed the issue, running about 1500 pieces, more than any other national story except free trade, to which it devoted 2,200 pieces. Moreover, the coverage was constructive. The paper devoted about one-third of the space to analysis or opinion pieces, it supported the Accord editorially, and the negative stuff was not of the red-neck variety.

I hope that the *Sun's* coverage left readers better able to make up their minds about Meech Lake. I hasten to point out that it did not turn them into supporters. It is revealing that while the paper was devoting so much space to the Accord, it ran just 196 stories on the Reform Party, whose leader, Preston Manning, was one of the strongest anti-Meech voices. I am suggesting that Meech failed not through lack of reporting, but because people did not like it. Mr. Manning gained support not because of the publicity—he did not get very much—but because people agreed with what he had to say. In both cases the message, not the medium, is what counted.

I want to finish my remarks with a ship-of-state metaphor. I know they are tedious, but we commentators find them convenient. Here is mine. The news media are qualified to keep the log. We make a tolerable lookout as long as not too much of the iceberg is hidden from us. But we are temperamentally unsuited to issuing commands. Our powers of concentration are not good enough to steady the rudder for any length of time. And only the terminally irresponsible would expect us to swab the deck, mend the hull, or—God forbid—divert the river.

COMMENTARY

GRAHAM FRASER

THE GLOBE AND MAIL

I enjoyed all three of the papers: John Meisel for his insight, David Taras for his stimulating description of how the media work, and Marc Raboy for his fascinating glimpse of the differing cultural assumptions about the Canadian Broadcasting Corporation and Radio-Canada in English- and French-speaking Canada.

John Meisel called for our educational institutions to teach media literacy. While I think the idea is a valuable one, I do not think we should underestimate the degree to which our children are already extremely media-literate, and, as a result, highly sceptical of what they see on television. I recall the famous "Journal" documentary broadcast on 4 December 1989, on the Monday following the New Democratic Party convention that elected Audrey McLaughlin leader. I had just returned home from Winnipeg and was watching "The Journal" with my son, then 13. I was fascinated by the famous hidden microphone sequence, which showed Simon de Jong behind closed doors striking a deal with Dave Barrett, and was hanging on every word when my son asked, "How do we know they didn't overdub the voices?"

How indeed? As I reflected on the cynicism of the young, I realized that I am part of a generation that, despite years of experience to the contrary, believes that Wendy Mesley and Don Newman live in a magic box in the corner of our guest bedroom.

The Meech Lake Accord coincided with the age of Newsworld; it was the first Newsworld-era constitutional conference, just as the next election will be the first Newsworld election. Much of what John Meisel and David Taras referred to was a result of this fact.

John Meisel also referred to Trina McQueen's comment that the electronic media should explain better how they do what they do. In that spirit, it might be useful if I explained how I approached the coverage of the Meech Lake Accord.

I am somewhat bemused by the suggestion that has often been made, most recently by Rick Salutin in *Saturday Night*, that there was some kind of monolithic media conspiracy in support of the Meech Lake Accord. When the Meech Lake Accord was negotiated in 1987, I had been in Ottawa less than a year. I had come to Ottawa from Québec City, where I had spent seven years, after three years in Montréal. During that decade, I covered the 1976 Québec election, the 1980 referendum, the 1981 Québec election, the constitutional debates of 1981–82, the federal election of 1984, and the return to power of Robert Bourassa in 1985.

Coming from those experiences, my immediate instinctive thought was that Meech Lake was the best deal English Canada could ever hope to get with Québec. I still think so—and am prepared at some length, and with some heat, to defend

201

even the unanimity provision for the admission of new provinces, and the effect of Meech Lake in strengthening the hand of the federal government in the area of social policy.

But at that point, in the Ottawa Press Gallery, I was in a distinct minority. Most people seemed to feel that Meech Lake weakened the federal government. I concluded, in fact, that most critics of Meech Lake did not think the provinces should have exclusive jurisdiction at all. In fact, when the public opposition to Meech Lake began to grow, one senior federal official remarked to me that if a pollster asked English Canadians if they were prepared to grant Québec those powers now in the British North America Act—control over education, their own legal system, language guarantees—the answer would be an overwhelming no.

Although it may surprise theorists to hear this, I—like many reporters, I suspect—am actually uncomfortable when I find that there is too much congruence between my views and those of the editorial writers. As a result, I was relieved when I was joined in the coverage of the Meech Lake process by Susan Delacourt, whose instinctive reactions to the Meech Lake Accord were very different from mine. She is a superb reporter: careful, conscientious, and hardworking. I found the fact that we disagreed fundamentally about certain elements of the Meech Lake Accord, rather than creating difficulties in our working relationship, meant that we balanced each other, each of us seeing stories or angles or sources that the other was less likely to identify.

I enjoyed David Taras's description of the role that television played at the final meeting. However, I have a problem with his assertion that the cameras elbowed their way into the process. The meetings were held in a building owned by the federal government, and the cameras were given no more and no less access than the participants wanted. Had they wanted to, the prime minister and the premiers could have kept the cameras far away—just as the cameras were kept far away from the Reagan-Gorbachev meeting at Reykjavik, for example.

In fact, the politicians used the cameras to communicate, not only with the public, but in some cases with each other. When Brian Mulroney paused to speak to reporters and to try to explain the confusion of the night before over a clause that had been dropped from the draft, he was talking to Clyde Wells, who was still in his hotel room.

There are three important questions that must be asked about the media in the coverage of the Meech Lake process: Did we withhold information? Did we manipulate events? And would events have turned out differently if the coverage had been different?

I would argue that the correct answer to the three questions is no. However, there is perhaps an exception. The prime minister's interview with Jeffrey Simpson, Susan Delacourt, and me, the so-called "Roll all the Dice" interview, may have had an effect on events. But far from conspiring to manipulate events in a conspiratorial fashion, we did the reverse: we printed the interview and let the chips—or the dice—fall where they may.

The problem we faced, and that the public faced, was ordering the avalanche of information that poured out about the Meech Lake Accord. I must say, I distrust the polling data which suggest that people know little or nothing about the Meech Lake Accord. I suspect that there is a phenomenon that one might call "sophisticated ignorance." People know quite a lot—but they are unsure of whether the Meech Lake Accord is a good thing. This is an understandable concern, since I doubt if we could achieve an agreement at this conference on that.

However, there is a problem with the flow of information. Often, in the evolution of a complicated issue like Meech Lake or free trade, a great deal of information is published or broadcast before people are sufficiently interested to focus on it. Then, when they are interested, journalists find it difficult to go back and review issues that are no longer "news" in the classic sense.

That is a problem, but I do not see a solution that can be dealt with at this conference.

CONSTITUTIONAL CHALLENGES FROM ABORIGINAL PEOPLES AND WOMEN

After Meech Lake: The Ms/Representation of Gender in Scholarly Spaces

BEVERLEY BAINES
QUEEN'S UNIVERSITY

When I was invited "to present a paper ... exploring, if you wish, the constitutional development of women's issues in the aftermath of the demise of the Accord," it was further suggested that I "might like to speculate on how we could profit from the lessons of Meech Lake in devising better norms for the protection of gender rights in new constitutional arrangements."[1] In the best of all worlds, in my opinion, only one such norm would be necessary. I refer, of course, to the norm of equality.

In so saying, obviously I disagree with what I perceive as the sterile approach of commentators who have argued that equality is an empty concept.[2] For me, their nihilism (or is it denialism?) is utterly devoid of challenge. Almost as if to the contrary, what I find most demanding is to reflect on the possibilities for breathing life into the concept of equality, and then for nurturing it, while always remaining hopeful, albeit never blindly so, that equality will both survive and flourish, taking on as it were a fecundity of its own. I believe, in other words, that equality has the potential to be seen as the root, trunk, branch, leaf, and bark of the proverbial "living tree" of the Canadian constitution.[3] As this metaphor evidently suggests, and its other features notwithstanding, stasis could never be a characteristic that I would willingly attribute to a viable constitutional conceptualization of equality.

We have a long way to go however. Elsewhere I have argued that stasis, and more disquietingly the stasis of a particularly virulent conception of equality that seriously denigrated—indeed, denied—the legal personhood of women, prevailed in the minds of most Canadian judges throughout this century up to the advent of the Canadian Charter of Rights and Freedoms.[4] Moreover, given how easy it is to trace the lineage of this conception of equality backwards through the ages to the time of Aristotle, it should not come as any surprise that some feminist commentators who are doubtlessly more prescient than I have begun to seek out, and even to prefer, alternative routes to legal personhood for women.[5] I neither need nor want to disparage such choices.

Indeed, there are two pragmatic reasons that make it quite foolhardy even to contemplate doing so. In the first place, we are at such an early stage in the post-Charter interpretation of sex equality that its constitutional (and other) ramifications are as yet virtually unknown, and perhaps even unknowable.[6] At best, therefore, it might be said of our existing equality norms that we should still be prepared to give them a chance, particularly in view of the fact that so many Canadian women made such a concerted effort to ensure their existence.[7] That said, nevertheless, in the second place there is something that we now know and must address, which is that some judicial backsliding has already occurred. That much is evident from several sources; but it is particularly well-documented by the research in a recently released study of women's equality rights under the new Charter.[8]

Now it should be acknowledged immediately that while the forces that promote backsliding may simply be the alter ego of those that impel backlash, nevertheless these states are not completely identical. Probably the most efficacious way to distinguish them is to invoke the distinction that the courts themselves proffer when they differentiate between intent on the one hand and effect on the other. That said, then the import of this distinction is also available to illuminate what I want to suggest is the primary lesson of Meech Lake, at least for those of us who are preoccupied with the issues that relate to the constitutionalization of sex equality. This lesson is not new; it was available to be learned even during the lifetime of the Accord when many of the women who participated in the various academic and political forums argued that, without more, Meech Lake could have put women's Charter-based equality rights in jeopardy. These arguments were heard, quite rightly, as allegations of political and legal backsliding. That was, and still is to date, the most that could reasonably be contended given the almost pathological secrecy of the patriarchal process that ultimately gave us the final version of the Accord.

Under these circumstances, it became then all the more surprising, and certainly revealing, when various politicians and others who supported the Accord opted to choreograph their rectitude by contending that, amongst other things, they had never intended to jeopardize our equality rights.[9] Be that as it may, however, to the extent that the more salient lesson of Meech Lake was (and is) backsliding and not backlash, the remedy lay (and lies yet) in preserving the existing (if untested) constitutional norms, rather than indulging in further speculative (and possibly empty) exercises.[10] If it was never intended that the Accord jeopardize equality rights, then there were various simple and relatively expeditious ways of reflecting this. For example, clause 16 could have been amended to include the Charter in the list of provisions that were exempt from the reach of the Accord. But this proposition was always rejected as unnecessary, thereby putting the bona fides of the Accord's supporters into question. In most constitutional and all Charter adjudication, necessity takes much if not all of its force, not from the eyes of the beholders, but rather from its presence in, or indeed absence from, the written texts on which judges are required to ground their decisions.

It is quite likely that exempting the Charter as a whole from the reach of the Accord was of the greatest concern mainly to Québec. It is important, though, to be precise about the nature of that concern; it has not always been portrayed with accuracy or sympathy.[11] Québec neither rejected nor denigrated the Charter as a whole. At the Mont Gabriel Conference on the Canadian Confederation in May 1986, for example, when the Québec minister responsible for constitutional matters first outlined the five conditions that ultimately became the basis for, albeit not definitive of, the Meech Lake Accord, he also referred to the Charter as "on the whole a document of which we as Quebeckers and Canadians can be proud."[12] More significantly, however, the minister made one, and only one, reference to the circumstances in which the Accord should—his word was "must"—take precedence over the Charter. He was referring to the minority language rights provisions of the Charter—and more particularly, only to the language rights of Québec's anglophone minority—when he stated that "these rights must naturally be seen within the context of the francophone character of Québec society and the Government's firm desire to ensure its full development."[13]

Without more, in other words, the contention that Québec was either hostile to or threatened by the sex equality norms in the Charter cannot be sustained. In effect, women from Québec were forced to make this point repeatedly during the three-year lifetime of the Accord.[14] Moreover as the minister himself pointed out in his Mont Gabriel speech, when his government succeeded that of the Parti Québécois they immediately stopped the practice of systematically applying the override clause to Québec statutes to exempt Québec laws from sections 2 and 7 to 15 of the Charter. In his words, "we want Quebeckers to have the same rights as other Canadians"; furthermore, as he elaborated, "there is absolutely no question of depriving our people of such fundamental constitutional rights as the right to life, to security of the person, to a just and fair trial, and to equal treatment under the law."[15]

Under these circumstances, it may be convincingly argued there were other, similarly pragmatic, remedial options short of exempting the whole Charter that were also available to obviate the backsliding that the Accord might otherwise have caused in the context of sex equality rights. We need only to look, for a good example, to the precedent that had already been set by the aboriginal peoples when they agreed that their constitutionally protected aboriginal and treaty rights should be guaranteed equally to both sexes.[16] Similar provisions could have been drafted for insertion into clauses 1 and 16 of the Accord, hence ensuring continuing constitutional respect for the norm of sex equality as it had been entrenched in 1982. Moreover, not only is it clear that Québec had no particular reason to fear this norm; as well, it must be assumed that the same should have obtained for any multicultural groups who might have chosen to avail themselves of clause 16 of the Accord, and hence of section 27 of the Charter.

As I am sure most of you have already concluded by now, the problem with the foregoing analysis is that, at best, it leaves us with many unanswered and possibly irrelevant what-ifs. What if we had the best of all worlds, would it be sufficient to constitutionalize the norm of sex equality and then get on with other pressing matters? What if the Supreme Court of Canada had begun to render interpretations of our Charter-based sex equality rights, which I have already advocated awaiting, would we continue to be hobbled by the worst of stasis or might the best of the jurisprudence of the "living tree" precedent begin to take root and grow? What if the Meech Lake Accord had not died, would the risks perceived and foretold by national women's groups have become troubling realities? And finally, what if they had? Would we be any closer to knowing whether the real lesson of the Accord was only the reckless one of backsliding or the more heinous, intentional one of backlash? What is, in sum, the point of focusing on such normative arrangements, be they constitutional or otherwise, when they are and continue to be designed, delivered, and determined by political and legal regimes that are predominantly male dominated or, as they are more conventionally characterized, "patriarchal"?

Inherent in this last question is the most invidious lesson of Meech Lake and indeed of all the constitutional exercises that preceded it. We have a constitutional past, present and, it would appear, future in which it is taken for granted that men can and should represent the interests of women, not just politically but also constitutionally. Certainly that has always obtained with our first ministers and, as well, it prevailed throughout the Meech Lake process; every legislative entity, be it committee or assembly, that was charged with the arduous responsibility of reviewing the Accord was undeniably male dominated. For example, during the final contentious days of Meech Lake in June 1990, even though only 12 of the Senate's 93 occupied seats were held by women, that unelected body had the highest proportion of women in any federal or provincial legislature in Canada at that time; and even there, more than 85% of the senators were men.[17] It seems, in short, that our gender is not supposed to matter in political spaces and constitutional moments.

Of course not everyone agrees with that view. In 1970, for example, the members of the Royal Commission on the Status of Women in Canada not only thought it relevant to report that the "formulation of policies affecting the lives of all Canadians is still the prerogative of men"; as well, they decried this situation in the strongest of words by characterizing it as an "absurdity."[18] Since they also understood all too well how unlikely it was that the situation would spontaneously right itself, they concluded their chapter on women in public life by arguing for a "special effort" to change it.[19] Their animadversions notwithstanding, in the intervening decades no government has ever sponsored a proposal or policy, let alone a constitutional provision, that would even begin to address this issue. If it is by their deeds that politicians come to be known, then we must conclude that our politicians really do believe men represent the interests of women.

But what of the scholars? Since the politicians (the vast majority of whom are still male[20]) continue to act as if our gender does not matter, we must begin to pose the same question of their self-appointed critics, the academics who currently man the male-dominated fields of political science and constitutional law. Fortunately academics are almost as accustomed as politicians to having their views questioned. It is, however, important to make one difference very clear: the perspectives I intend to examine are those of academics functioning not in their personal, but rather in their scholarly, capacities. Accordingly, I must resist the temptation to ask those of you who are in this room for a show of hands on the question of gender representation. What I must examine instead are your scholarly publications and presentations, your faits accomplis as it were.

Presumably it will not disturb you to learn that I decided to analyse the presentations and comments that have been made until now by the academics at this conference. Lest it become debatable, let me make my underlying assumption explicit—to wit, that you would not be here were you not outstanding representatives of your respective scholarly fields. However, despite my earlier caveat about your scholarly standpoints, some of you may nevertheless feel that you should have been warned about your status as research objects when it was still pending. While I cannot offer to allay such concerns otherwise than by reporting my findings, I also want to assure you that, scholarly conventions notwithstanding, I would welcome being wrong about them. From my perspective, the results are uniformly bad as I shall now demonstrate.

In setting out to explore the relationship between representation and gender in your work, initially I took it for granted that you would make copious and detailed references to one of these concepts. Obviously I refer to the concept of representation. Thus I was quite surprised, and not pleasurably, to discover that I was wrong. Hardly anyone has chosen the conceptual route, even though I would have thought that discussing constitutional reform after Meech Lake had to involve, in a deep and nonperipheral way, giving serious consideration to issues of representation. In effect, I cannot imagine sustaining your otherwise sagacious arguments about the relations between the federal and provincial governments, between legislatures and courts, between francophones and anglophones, between aboriginals and whites, and among multiculturals, in the absence of some learned references to representation—to what it means or should mean, to how many meanings it has or might have and, ultimately, to the relevance of those various constructs for our options such as they are right now at this stage in our constitutional and political life as a country.

Since I had initially expected the political scientists among you to locate their explanations within the existing literature on the concept of representation, and since that did not happen, I became uneasy. Was I, a disciplinary interloper, somewhat naive? Or was it just that the political scientists among you preferred to take the concept of representation for granted? That said, perhaps it had, albeit implicitly, informed all of your discussions; indeed, perhaps you just assumed, and felt perfectly entitled to assume, that everyone else would understand this to be so.

Well, politesse to the rest of us aside, I am not convinced. Partly I am sceptical that all of the political scientists in this room conceptualize representation in the same way. If so, it has to be the first thing that they all have agreed upon in the past two days. That vision aside, I think that there are real differences among them;

which is to say that, collectively speaking, they represent (or, if that word is too contumelious, let me use "embody") more than one way, perhaps not a myriad but certainly two or more ways, of conceptualizing representation. If I am right however, how can I—a disciplinary outsider—identify (and not just guess about) who among them speaks for which conceptualization? And if I am wrong, that is if all of the political scientists in this particular room do share (if nothing else) the same conception of representation, I would still have to say, with respect for disciplinary boundaries notwithstanding, that partly I am sceptical simply because such scholarship is so troubling.

The problem is that while the definitional process delimits, nowhere does it necessarily mandate monomial conceptualization. Of course it is easier to distinguish federal from provincial politics, or legislative from judicial activity, or francophone from anglophone discourse, or aboriginal from white society, and among multicultural peoples, when only one conception of representation holds sway. Tempting or not, however, the costs of this approach are too high. Privileging one and only one of the components in each of these dyadic relationships simply replicates, and with distinctively preferential consequences, the existing competitive forces in society. Put bluntly, unless or until this competitive mentality is itself justified, we should not conduct scholarly inquiries as if the only issue were one of better representation. Researchers who ask only whether the people are better represented by the federal government or the provinces—or, as the Charter-phobes phrase it, the legislatures or the courts—fail to plumb the complexities of our political (and scholarly) lives.

In fact, life is undeniably the richer for what in the absence of better nomenclature I shall designate as the forces of coexistence. More specifically, such forces are invoked every time we refer to our governance as federal and provincial, or as legislative and judicial; and they also underlie our picture of Canada as a society that includes both francophones and anglophones, or aboriginal and white and multicultural peoples. Given the nature of coexistence, however, it cannot be expected to survive the application of a process of monomial conceptualization, whether in the context of representation or otherwise. To the contrary, not only must there be more than one such conceptualization, simultaneously available as it were; as well, they must be capable of egalitarian (or at least nonprejudicial) application. Therefore, while the approach that I propose is both novel[21] and conceptually demanding, it has at least one important virtue that is not available to its monomial rivals. It does not, in short, foreclose any other, otherwise viable, and not insignificant, constitutional options.

Perhaps now you understand why I expected more of the political scientists. But I am a lawyer with at least pretensions to egalitarianism and this, in turn, means explaining why my unease also extends to the lawyers who are present. In effect, I would like to know how they can justify failing to discuss the relevance of representation-based issues. After all, representation is not a concept that is foreign to lawyers given what practitioners do every day. Indeed, with the range of solicitor and client relationships available to the profession, lawyers should be among the first to recognize that representation could present more than one face to the world. Think, for example, of law teachers who endeavour to make this point in their first-year criminal law courses when they validate the roles both of crown attorney and defence counsel. While it is a sad commentary on contemporary legal education that such discussions may be few and far between, this does not obviate the significance of that concept for practising and, hence, academic lawyers.

In sum, with the cosponsorship of the conference and the disciplinary mix of the participants, I had expected interdisciplinary scholarship—at least with respect to the concept of representation. With one significant exception,[22] that is not what obtained; which is not to say that no one referred to representation. Some did.[23] But it is to say that I did not hear any of the latter orchestrate their references, leaving me able only to speculate about their hermeneutics. I found myself wondering, for example, if Professor Stevenson's throwaway reference to "good old territorial representation" might nonetheless evoke the concept of "procedural representation" that Professor Smith had earlier described more meticulously and sympathetically. Of course, publication may allay my concerns, which may be due entirely to the exigencies of oral presentation.

Given what they said, however, or more accurately did not say, the most charitable conclusion is that the scholarly presenters at this conference (whose work I previously qualified as archetypal) are not critical of the conceptual status quo (the actual contours of which remain unclear) insofar as representation is concerned. That conclusion might not seem so disquieting, even for critics, were it not for its subsidiary corollary. Unfortunately, it follows as well from the dearth of any evidence to the contrary that these scholars must also subscribe to the assumption prevailing among politicians—who, as I noted earlier, appear to believe that men can and should represent the interests of women. This scholarly complicity may be due to their lack of awareness of the evidence and arguments to the contrary, the findings of the 1970 royal commission notwithstanding. Yet such reasoning is suspect if only because, as scholars, they are expected to be familiar with work, particularly critical work, published in their own, and sometimes even in cognate, fields.

At a minimum, therefore, I have to assume that the political scientists present have or should have read the research studies published in Canada by such recognized authorities as Professors Bashevkin, Brodie, Gingras, Maillé, Tardy, and Vickers.[24] Hopefully they would be familiar as well with the work of international scholars such as Bonder, Haavio-Mannila, Klein, Mandel, Shapiro, Sinneau, and Skjeie.[25] Nor do these names exhaust the scholarship available under the rubric of the political and constitutional representation of women. Moreover, it goes without saying that much if not all of this scholarship is critical.

Recently, for example, Concordia University political scientist Chantal Maillé released a study in which she referred to the decade of the 1980s as a "turning point."[26] But she was no more sanguine about the future than had been the members of the royal commission two decades before her, and for good reason.

Pointing to recent federal election results, she noted that "the rate of progress remains very slow and random."[27] As she explained:

If women continue to increase their number of seats at the same rate as between 1984 and 1988, and the number of MPs remains constant at 295, it will take nine elections, or nearly 45 years, until an equal number of women and men are elected to the House of Commons.[28]

Observing that growth is not necessarily continuous, she then concluded that "in reality, some steps backward will likely occur unless specific measures are taken to increase the number of women elected."[29]

Maillé's reference to "specific measures" and the royal commission's call for a "special effort" were based on very similar concerns. Both cited obstacles such as prejudical stereotypes, unequal family responsibilities, and the inequities of campaign financing.[30] However, only the royal commission counselled women to "show a greater determination to use their legal right to participate as citizens."[31] In contrast, since several indepth research studies had revealed the institutional and societal nature of the obstacles by 1990, Maillé was able to be more realistic about the reasons for women's chronic underrepresentation. Accordingly, she attributed it to "the political parties' failure to make provision for gender roles and women's family responsibilities, the organizational culture of political parties, and the socio-economic conditions of the average woman."[32]

Identifying these factors meant, in turn, that Maillé considered some remedial measures that were not raised in the earlier royal commission report. Three of these measures—proportional representation, dual member constituencies, and quota systems[33]—are by no means novel, but their context is. With the enactment of the Charter in 1982, there now is a provision in the constitution giving "every citizen ... the right to vote."[34] In the absence of litigation, however, it is impossible to know with any certainty whether the three remedial measures Maillé identified will be adjudged consistent, or not, with this new Charter provision. It must be kept in mind, nevertheless, that this lacuna has only expanded the constitutional implications of reforming our system of gender representation; it did not create them. Gender representation has been a constitutional issue, albeit not necessarily acknowledged as such, for a very long time.

Indeed the lawyers present also should be aware of the existence of legal studies questioning the current state of gender representation. In 1983, for example, Dalhousie University Professor Christine Boyle published a thoroughly cogent and challenging article in which she argued that women "are de facto unenfranchised, and that, for this reason, it is necessary to embark on a reassessment of our current electoral system."[35] Also noting that the Charter constituted a "possible legal setting for such a reassessment,"[36] she provided a detailed explanation of why there was a need for change.[37] Finally, she considered and rejected "dual-member constituencies, with one man and one woman elected,"[38] advocating instead "female constituencies" in which sex would "be a factor in the drawing of electoral boundaries."[39] Under these circumstances, surely it is self-evident that her argument raised serious constitutional issues. Yet no one present even acknowledged its existence, let alone responded to its challenges.

Other Canadian legal scholars including Backhouse, Cano, Cossman, Eberts, Gavigan, Greschner, Lahey, Mahoney, Mossman, Sheehy, and Sheppard—to name only a few—have also published research studies that call into question the prevailing assumption about men representing the political and constitutional interests of women. [40] I too have argued, for example, that male judges misrepresented the meaning of sex equality throughout the course of the 20th century before the Charter was enacted, the 20-year life of the Canadian Bill of Rights notwithstanding. [41] More specifically in the context of Meech Lake, I compared the final *Report* of the first of the male-dominated federal committees with the published transcripts of their proceedings, only to learn that the committee report seriously misrepresented the submissions made by five national women's organizations. [42]

Under different circumstances, perhaps I might find it unseemly to refer at such length to the existence of the foregoing scholarship—but not here. Not when a sizeable and ever-growing body of critical scholarship has simply been stonewalled, and not by the time-honoured, albeit themselves questionable, academic methods of repartee. No, the presenters here have resorted instead to the more insidious policy of sheer silence, opting not even to acknowledge, let alone examine, the issues raised by the constitutional reform of gender representation—issues already clearly identified in the scholarship that I have been forced to cite in detail. Nor does this surprise or "upset" me; [43] rather it convinces me that the very scholarship that most disdains it actually is replete with personal political perspectives.

Which brings me, finally, to the second of my two related concepts, gender— about which I want to say very little, albeit more than and differently from what has been said at this conference thus far. Based again on what I have heard as well as not heard, I must report that no one has talked about gender representation as the constitutional issue that I and other feminist [44] scholars have identified, which is not to say that no one talked about gender. At least two presenters did in some detail [45] and several others less so (albeit much more agreeably). [46] Since the former also located their gender-talk in the context of their understanding of the issues posed by representation, I must explain the void as I identify it. Put bluntly, when they talked about gender and about representation, they neglected to talk about gender representation as an issue of constitutional reform. [47]

Insofar as those may be construed as harsh words, I want to redirect their impact by telling a short but not apocryphal story. A particular scholar, who is both a colleague and former teacher, [48] recently wrote a short introduction to a monograph on Meech Lake that included my aforementioned study of gender and the federal committee, along with papers written by three other academics. [49] His introduction cast no aspersions on my scholarship, indeed to the contrary; but still his words chilled me, less for their silence on women or gender and rather more for the way in which they forged connections among the four contributors. In effect, he adopted the gendered metaphors of Pollyanna and Hobbes to characterize our work. However, it would be unfair to require you to guess whether

I was a Hobbesian or had the propensities of Pollyanna. Even though the other three, need I say male, contributors covered the spectrum, I was not on it.[50] What more can I say? That it seems I have no gender and, lacking that, am not representative? Or, that there really are men—both the author of the continuum and the contributor assigned to the Pollyanna end—who represent the political, constitutional, and scholarly interests of women?

Another way to hear my story is to ask: what more could I have done? In this particular context, the answer was clear (and I often heard it in related contexts as well); I could have either opposed or advocated the passage of the Accord, thereby easily qualifying either as a Hobbesian or as a Pollyanna respectively. I could have, in other words, adopted the agenda of that scholar, of many other academics, and of most politicians—the vast majority of whom were men. It was never self-evident to me, however, that reducing the multiplicity of issues that otherwise surrounded the Accord to the singular one of passage or failure was necessarily in the best interests of Canadian women. Indeed, I believed to the contrary and advocated accordingly.[51] On reflection, moreover, I came to realize that this pressure to take a single outcome-oriented stand on Meech Lake had very serious implications for my scholarly work in the field of gender theory. Effectively, I was being told to include men (viz. adopt their agenda) in my gender theorizing;[52] or, to put it differently, I was being enjoined from theorizing only about women.

Interestingly enough, I have not heard anyone present disparage gender scholarship that focuses only on women. Without anticipating such an eventuality, I nevertheless intend to explain very briefly why it should be resisted. Put succinctly, proscribing women-centred research belies the distinction that is fundamental to the architecture of some gender theories. Consider, for example, the following statement which is no less theoretical for having been made by an MP: "There are two races only: men and women. The rest is just colour."[53] As theory, this statement may be interpreted as encouraging research that focuses on the distinctiveness of gender. Thus, it follows that researchers who subscribe to it must be free, should their research so indicate, to respect this underlying distinction by concentrating their inquiries solely on one side of the gender divide. That is to say, just as some research projects are no less scholarly for being limited to the francophone culture, or to Québec society, or to the aboriginal peoples, so too must it be acknowledged that research can centre on women's issues and still have the potential to qualify as good scholarship.

At this juncture, perhaps some of you will nod agreeably, subject of course to the usual caveats—prominent among which is the stipulation that men are not the enemy.[54] But that is your stipulation, not mine.[55] For me, the conjunction between men and enemy simply articulates one of the relationships that characterizes and sometimes encumbers theories of gender distinctiveness such as the one exemplified above.[56] Therefore, stipulating its eschewal from my scholarship would be tantamount to requiring my colleague, Bill Lederman, to renounce his respect for the independence of the judiciary.[57]

Even when gender theorists are not told that they must include men in their

214

theories, as obtained here they may well be required to include all women. That was how I understood the presenter who questioned "the democratic and representative credentials of those who speak for women and others";[58] and as well, another who contended that the women who spoke out during the Meech Lake process were not representative of women generally.[59] According to the latter this was partly because they did not qualify as "procedural" representatives and partly because the representation they did qualify for, which was mirror representation, is not a "compelling" form of representation.[60] Both arguments reminded me of the allegation that Madame Justice Wilson had failed to understand that the "views of a few vocal feminists" did not represent the views of all Canadian women,[61] although the contexts were considerably different.

And here, context was and is everything, which brings me full circle back to where I began. Assuming that judges do represent (and I so assume), who was Madame Justice Wilson supposed to represent, given the existence of eight other presumably representative judges on the Supreme Court of Canada? Similarly, why were the women speaking out on Meech Lake supposed to represent women who might have been, and in some cases clearly were, members of other lobby groups,[62] always assuming representation is a concept relevant to lobbying (and this seems to be more readily assumed than justified)? Then, since neither lobbyists nor judges are legislators, are there enough concepts of representation available to cover all three? Finally, can these self-same concepts be extended, expanded, or even transformed sufficiently to encompass the newly evolving suggestions for aboriginal representation, for the representation of Québec's distinct society and, last but never least, women?

NOTES

1. W.H. McConnell, correspondence, 11 July 1990.
2. E.g., Peter Westen, "The Empty Idea of Equality," 95 *Harvard L. R.* (1982): 537.
3. *Edwards and others* v. *Attorney-General for Canada*, [1930] A.C. 124.
4. Beverley Baines, "Women and the Law" in Sandra Burt, Lorraine Code, and Lindsay Dorney, eds., *Changing Patterns: Women in Canada* (Toronto: McClelland and Stewart, 1988), ch. 6.
5. E.g., Carol Smart, "Law's Power, the Sexed Body, and Feminist Discourse," 17 *Journal of Law and Society* (1990): 194.
6. To date, the Supreme Court of Canada—which is usually considered the final, although not necessarily immovable, arbiter of constitutionalized norms in Canada—has issued only one precedent-setting decision in this context, namely *Andrews* v. *Law Society of British Columbia*, [1989] 1 S.C.R. 143. However, aside from the inferences that might be derived from the fact that the court refused leave to appeal in *Blainey* v. *Ontario Hockey Association* (1986), 58 O.R.(2d) 274, we have no indication of the direction that the court will take when it begins to decide cases involving Charter-based sex equality claims.
7. See e.g., Penney Kome, *The Taking of Twenty-Eight: Women Challenge the Constitution* (Toronto: Women's Educational Press, 1983).

8. Gwen Brodsky and Shelagh Day, *Canadian Charter Equality Rights For Women: One Step Forward or Two Steps Back?* (Ottawa: Canadian Advisory Council on the Status of Women, 1989).

9. E.g., Senator Lowell Murray, *Minutes of Proceedings and Evidence of the Special Joint Committee of the Senate and of the House of Commons on the 1987 Constitutional Accord*, 4 August 1987, Issue No. 2, 16.

10. Contrary to the view expressed above, note 1.

11. E.g., Stephen Allan Scott, " 'Meech Lake' and Québec Society: 'Distinct' or Distinctive?" in Michael D. Behiels, ed., *The Meech Lake Primer: Conflicting Views of the 1987 Constitutional Accord* (Ottawa: University of Ottawa Press, 1989), 161.

12. Gil Rémillard, "Address" in Peter M. Leslie, *Rebuilding the Relationship: Québec and its Confederation Partners* (Kingston: Institute of Intergovernmental Relations, Queen's University, 1987), 41.

13. Ibid., 46.

14. Eg. Fédération des femmes du Québec, "Are Women's Rights Threatened by the Distinct Society Clause?" in Michael D. Behiels, ed., *The Meech Lake Primer: Conflicting Views of the 1987 Constitutional Accord* (Ottawa: University of Ottawa Press, 1989), 295 at 296.

15. See note 10.

16. For the actual text, see the Constitution Act, 1982, section 35(4), as amended by the Constitution Amendment Proclamation, 1983.

17. Telephone communication with an anonymous male Senate information officer, 14 June 1990.

18. Royal Commission on the Status of Women in Canada, *Report* (Ottawa: Information Canada, 1970), 355.

19. Ibid., 356.

20. With 40 seats, women currently constitute only 13.5% of the membership of the federal House of Commons. In the provincial legislatures, women have the most seats in Ontario (28 seats constituting 21.5% of the membership) and the fewest in Newfoundland (1 seat constituting 1.9% of the membership. See: Chantal Maillé, *Primed for Power: Women in Canadian Politics* (Ottawa: Canadian Advisory Council on the Status of Women, 1990), 7, 12–13.

21. I assume most academics understand that "novel" claims always have scholarly precursors, although some proponents do not believe in identifying—or is it locating—them. Mine, at any rate, derive from Hanna Fenichel Pitkin's path-breaking treatise, *The Concept of Representation* (Berkeley: University of California Press, 1967). In this study, Pitkin set out three conceptualizations of representation; where we differ is that she perceived her constructs sequentially. By contrast, I want to suggest that with some additional work they may well become available for simultaneous application, especially in federal states at constitutional moments.

22. See the paper by Professor Jennifer Smith.

23. See the papers by Professors Cairns, Russell, Stevenson, and Whitaker.

24. All but one of these Canadian authorities, and some others as well, are referred to in the footnotes to Maillé, see note 20, 35–38.

25. Ibid.

26. Ibid., 5.

27. Chantal Maillé, see note 20, 10.

28. Ibid.

29. Ibid.

30. Ibid., 3–4; Royal Commission on the Status of Women in Canada, see note 18, 355.

31. Royal Commission on the Status of Women in Canada, see note 18, 356.

32. Chantal Maillé, see note 20, 3.

33. Ibid., 33. These measures had at least one precursor in the *Report* of the Royal Commission on the Status of Women which recommended "that two qualified women from each province be summoned to the Senate as seats become vacant, and that women continue to be summoned until a more equitable membership is achieved"—see note 18, 341.

34. Canadian Charter of Rights and Freedoms, section 3.

35. Christine Boyle, "Home Rule for Women: Power-Sharing Between Men and Women," *Dalhousie Law Journal* (1983): 790 at 791.
36. Ibid. She referred specifically to combining sections 3 and 15(1).
37. Ibid., 793–799, including therein her conclusion that "it is impossible for men to represent women" at 797.
38. Ibid., 799.
39. Ibid., 800. Noting "the practical difficulties of abandoning geographical constituencies completely," she simply suggested that they be redrawn "to permit the separate election of both male and female representatives from each constituency ... preferably through the use of the system of proportional representation" or "alternatively, each province could simply become one constituency." She also posed the intriguing "question of whether there would be a separate geographical element or totally self-selecting constituencies."
40. For a relatively recent bibliography, see Susan Boyd and Elizabeth Sheehy, "Feminist Perspectives on Law: Canadian Theory and Practice," 2 *Canadian Journal of Women and the Law/Revue juridique 'La femme et le droit,'* (1986): 1 at 41. Many articles in subsequent numbers of this Journal also contain relevant arguments.
41. Beverley Baines, see note 4; also, "Women, Human Rights and the Constitution" in Audrey Doerr and Micheline Carrier, *Women and the Constitution* (Ottawa: Canadian Government Publishing Centre, 1981), 31.
42. Beverley Baines, "Gender and the Meech Lake Committee," 94 *Queen's Quarterly* (1987) 807, reprinted in Clive Thomson, ed., *Navigating Meech Lake: The 1987 Constitutional Accord* (Kingston: Institute of Intergovernmental Relations, 1988).
43. After I posed a question from the floor in which I tried (or so I thought) to encourage a presenter to develop his theoretical perspective, he privately inquired of me whether I was "upset" with him. I could be "upset" with him only if I felt the need to live (or is it share?) his life, which I certainly do not.
44. I have not used this so-called "f" word to date although it describes all of the arguments on which I have relied and much of what I do. If it now sticks in your craw, stopping up your ears as it were, I have to conclude that I was right to restrict my discourse to gender instead, especially given that I had hoped to encourage you to focus only on issues of substance and not to be distracted by their form. This choice is not without scholarly and personal costs for me, however, and sometimes I just decide not to pay them.
45. See the papers by Professors Cairns and Smith.
46. See the papers by Professor Kathy Brock and Deborah Coyne.
47. Professor Donna Greschner has identified this same, apparently somewhat pervasive, phenomenon in a different context, asking: "How democratic is a system which reduces women to another lobby group attempting to exert influence on democratic institutions from the outside?"—see "Abortion and Democracy for Women: A Critique of *Tremblay* v. *Daigle*," 35 *McGill Law Journal* (1990): 633 at 640.
48. As I consider how conventional those words are in academe, I am struck by how remote it is that I could ever apply them to a woman. Even though I took all the requisite courses to qualify for a four-year honours BA at McGill and for a three-year LLB degree at Queen's, not to mention the myriad of graduate political science/studies and law courses on my McGill, Queen's, and Yale transcripts, the sad fact remains that only two were taught by women (for the mildly curious, both were at McGill in the 1960s, one being introductory sociology and the other, an advanced economics course).
49. See note 42. (The editor of the monograph and the author of the introduction are not one and the same.)
50. His words were: "Beverley Baines's subject does not allow us to judge in which direction she is leaning, although her article makes it difficult to visualize the author as sharing many of Pollyanna's traits. No reader, however, is likely to find it difficult to place the other three contributors on the Pollyanna-Hobbes continuum." Of course, given that he also referred to "the curmudgeon and the bleeding-heart poles," perhaps it is wiser not to demur.

51. Beverley Baines, "'An Alternative Vision of the Meech Lake Accord," 13 *Queen's Law Journal* (1988): 1, especially at 28 where I concluded the article with the words "the only solution is to re-envision the Meech Lake Accord now."

52. Contrariwise, women may be attacked for including men within the purview of their analysis. This happened recently to Madame Justice Wilson when she concluded that there is "a distinctly male perspective" to some aspects of, for example, criminal law—a male perspective that led, in turn, to legal principles that "are not fundamentally sound," being based as they are "on presuppositions about the nature of women and women's sexuality that in this day and age are little short of ludicrous" (see: Madame Justice Bertha Wilson, "Will Women Judges Really Make A Difference?", The Fourth Annual Barbara Betcherman Memorial Lecture, Osgoode Hall Law School, York University, 8 February 1990). As a result of her words, R.E.A.L. Women complained, albeit unsuccessfully, to the Canadian Judicial Council that her views constituted a bias that should disqualify her from sitting on the Supreme Court of Canada. They contended, in short, that she should not have included men in her gender-talk.

53. Ethel Blondin as quoted in William Johnson, "Opposition parties fail to rise to occasion in Oka debate," *The Gazette*, (Montréal), 26 September 1990, B3.

54. I have also been asked how I could justify perceiving men as the enemy while continuing to live with one. When I struggle to find the credibility in this *ad hominem* question, I figure it must rest in the improbable hypothesis, unevenly applied, of some sort of correlation between household arrangements and scholarship.

55. The best I can say is that there may be a difference between saying that men are the enemy and hating them. Sometimes I have hated men. Last year after a man methodically massacred 14 women at Ecole Polytechnique, I hated men. Right now, living in Montréal where so many women were murdered by men in 1990 as a result of what we so misleadingly label "family" violence, I am again close to hatred. But mostly I just think that men are the enemy. For a comprehensive exegesis of men as the enemy from an academic lawyer's perspective, see: Catharine A. MacKinnon, *Feminism Unmodified: Discourses on Life and Law* (Cambridge: Harvard University Press, 1987).

56. See the text accompanying note 52.

57. He won't and neither will I; the difference between us is that only I risk losing my job, a job that requires me to teach men as well as women. This notion leads me, in turn, to wonder whether representation should be conceptualized more in terms of personal risk rather than by the test suggested yesterday by Professor Cairns when he said that "you don't mind having someone represent your interest if you think they are doing a good job." Some further light might be shed on this question by considering Hanna Fenichel Pitkin's reflections on representation as "the making present of something that is nevertheless absent"—see note 21, 237.

58. Professor Cairns.

59. Professor Smith.

60. Ibid.

61. See note 51.

62. Knowing Bill Lederman appeared before several Meech Lake committees, I am led to speculate about his response had he, Charter-phile that he is, been told that his presentation would have to include as well the views of his copanelist, who might best be described by contrast as a Charter-phobe. That Bill could do it, good lawyer that he is, is undoubted; what is more questionable is whether his copanelist would accept his representation.

Aboriginal Peoples
and the Constitution
OVIDE MERCREDI
ASSEMBLY OF FIRST NATIONS

In my more lucid moments, I think that until the prime minister and Senator Lowell Murray begin to listen to the aboriginal peoples and to other Canadians, there will be no future for constitutional change in this country. I say that not to be impolite or trite, but if you look at the mystery of Meech Lake and the style and the approaches taken by these very powerful men in our country, you can't help but come to the conclusion that they need to approach constitutional developments with a totally different set of values. That is what I want to talk about here, in relation to aboriginal peoples.

The way I see it, and it may be very simplistic, is that what evolves as a future for First Nations in Canada will not be determined by the visions or the lack of vision of Canadians—or, for that matter, the elected or provincial leaders. The future of our people in this country will be ultimately determined by what we do, or what we fail to do, to protect our distinct way of life and our collective rights and freedoms. Of course, I realize, being a realist and being pragmatic, that the future decisions or choices that we make for ourselves as First Nations will be influenced by the values Canadians and their governments adopt in their dealings and in their relationships with us. Respect, for instance, for our people and our collective rights will elicit one kind of response. Rejection and exclusion of both our people and our collective rights will elicit a different response.

Assimilation, paternalism, racism, exclusion, oppression are not, in our view, the cornerstones that will dictate to us our future as distinct peoples in Canada.

We have already rejected those values. And that is why we are in a continuous struggle with your governments in trying to attempt to come to some consensus for a different relationship based on different values.

Our indigenous spirit to survive and develop in the future as distinct people with collective rights and freedoms is stronger than the pressures we now face, and historically have faced, to conform and comply with the will and the power of the dominant society. It is up to the Canadian people and their governments to discover and embrace the realization that more appropriate and positive human values are needed to govern future relationships between Canada and aboriginal peoples. The exclusion of our people from deriving any social or economic benefits from the exploitation of aboriginal land and resources must be replaced by fairness and equity with regard to territorial jurisdiction and wealth generation. This would mean that the Canadian people would have to accept the value of sharing, which our ancestors attempted to teach the new settlers who came to what we call Turtle Island. A denial and rejection of our collective freedom of self-determination must likewise be replaced by respect and acceptance.

This, I believe, would have resulted had the new settlers adopted, as we had hoped they would, the value of coexistence our ancestors attempted to teach them. Indeed, the deliberate misrepresentation and the selective adoption of interpretations to provisions of treaties by federal and provincial governments could have been avoided had the settlers and their descendants regarded these nation-to-nation arrangements with the equal commitment and sacredness our people accorded to their treaties and still do. After all, from our perspective, the treaties were made in the full view and in the presence of our Creator.

Our future as aboriginal peoples in Canada will not be decided by the prime minister or the premiers. Nor, for that matter, will public opinion be the final arbiter of aboriginal destiny.

At the end of our struggle for self-rule in Canada, our liberation will be decided by our people. It is what we do, as I said earlier, or what we fail to do, that will be the blueprint for aboriginal destiny. No one needs to take this comment in a negative context. It may be best interpreted as a declaration by our people to take better care of themselves by acting in their best interests within the context of their rights to exist as distinct people. Just as, our elders tell us, the Creator had intended. In that context, it is not a threat. It is not an absolution of federal or provincial government obligation to responsibility either. Nor can it be seen as a statement rejecting other Canadian people.

How quickly we achieve respect for our cultures and people will, of course, be determined by the values Canadians and their governments choose to apply in their dealings with us. For instance, a policy of exclusion or rejection would retard but not diminish our resolve to exercise our rights and powers of self-government. Under this kind of policy we can expect political confrontations, costly litigation, increasing national disharmony, and moves by more and more First Nations toward independent sovereignty. The end result of such a policy may well be to drive our people, the aboriginal peoples, into rejecting the very society that systematically rejects and excludes them now.

On the other hand, we could instead adopt a policy of respect. Under this policy neither the federal nor provincial governments would remain our adversaries. We could even expect, from time to time, the Federal Departments of Justice and Indian Affairs to act as advocates as opposed to adversaries of our treaty and

220

aboriginal rights. And as you know, there is nothing preventing these government departments from interpreting section 35 of our constitution in the positive terms it was intended to be interpreted, which is to affirm and recognize our rights and freedoms.

A policy of respect would also mean that the decisions that have been made by the Supreme Court of Canada in recent months would be accepted and applied by politicians and lawyers alike. The end result of such a policy would mean that finally after years and years of rejection and exclusion our people would begin to fully enjoy their treaty and aboriginal rights, including the right of self-determination. This latter policy would create harmony in our country. More important, for us, it would permit our people to concentrate their energies and resources in activities that would accelerate our healing process and the reconstruction of our own distinct society. It would be far more enjoyable for us and more constructive for everyone if we had the time and energy to build for a better future rather than involving ourselves in racial disharmony and confrontations.

What is the future for constitutional reform in Canada? This will depend on the values people choose to use in amending their supreme law. The prime minister recently announced that he had found a way in which he could get people to start talking about what is important to them in this country. The difficulty that we have as aboriginal leaders in terms of accepting and embracing this idea of a Citizens' Forum is that we are being lumped together with the rest of Canada and, therefore, our distinct rights and freedoms are not, once again, being acknowledged by the prime minister. We are being treated as if we were just mere individuals in Canada who have no distinct status, no collective rights. We are expected to appear before so-called "average" Canadians to talk to them about what is important to us as aboriginal peoples and on what we think Canada should do.

The prime minister had an option. It was an option he chose not to exercise. That was to simply reconvene the First Ministers Conferences on aboriginal peoples and having done that, he would have provided us with the forum that we need to move toward the kind of constitutional arrangements that would bring about the kind of harmony and unity he is looking for in this country. For him to expect us to simply run forward and embrace the Citizens' Forum suggests to me that he has not learned very much from the last First Ministers Conferences or, for that matter, from Meech Lake or the Oka incident.

Our people want to deal with the federal government on a government-to-government basis, on a nation-to-nation basis. We don't want to give a committee any power to recommend for us what the government should do. We feel we should be there to negotiate for ourselves what we believe is in our best interests. A constitutional process where we can negotiate with the government would provide us with that opportunity. A committee would treat us as mere individuals and not acknowledge our collective status in Canada.

I think, in light of those comments, that we will have some difficult decisions to make as to whether or not we will participate in this committee in the coming months.

Someone has said that the Meech Lake Accord was an instrument that would have brought into our country the French-Canadians who felt alienated by Canada. The question is—can you allow a constitutional amendment that distorts the fundamental characteristics of Canada? And the reason why we took such a hard stand against the Meech Lake Accord in the province of Manitoba was because we realized that the concept of a founding nation was being entrenched into the constitution and that the place of our people and our history in Canada were not being respected and, in fact, we were being ignored.

It is not as if no one made proposals for changes. We made numerous proposals for amendments to the Meech Lake Accord. The problem was not that people didn't come forward with options. The problem was that the people with power in this country did not want to see or accept any options from anybody. That is why we have now, across Canada, a constitutional impasse and that is why we have Canadians demanding from their politicians some kind of accountability, some involvement in future constitutional reform.

Canada is a big country. It is also not a weak country. I don't share the view many people have that we are in a state of crisis in terms of the future of Canada. What we do have is a lot of uncertainty. People are questioning their place within our society. But that doesn't mean that the country is on the verge of breaking up. What it means is that we have the opportunity in light of that uncertainty across the land, to come up with a new arrangement for the nation-state called Canada, that will accommodate not only the concerns of the province of Québec but the concerns and the interests of aboriginal peoples as well. Unless aboriginal concerns and interests are incorporated into the constitution of this country, then, in my view, and only then, will we really be in a crisis. As stated earlier, the way Canada treats the aboriginal people in this country, the values used to deal with us, is what will determine the fate of this country. If it cannot come to terms with the rights and freedoms of aboriginal peoples, it will never come to terms with the rights and interests of people that created the nation-state.

The aboriginal concerns must be of foremost and primary importance to everybody. The very first constitutional conference that we have in the near future has to deal with aboriginal rights, not the place of Québec in Canada. Because if we don't do it on that basis, as I said earlier, we will never be able to deal with the rights of Québec simply because, even in that province, they have to come to terms with the rights and the aspirations of the aboriginal people there. Québec cannot separate without, first of all, resolving issues with aboriginal peoples. They have no right to take all the land and resources when aboriginal peoples in that province have standing rights to land and resources. Québec has to realize that they have to deal with the aboriginal peoples in a just way and that they have to come to some consensual arrangement with the aboriginal peoples there before they start talking about a new deal with the rest of Canada.

COMMENTARY

DONNA GRESCHNER

UNIVERSITY OF SASKATCHEWAN

I have surprising and disquieting news for the conference participants. Our event is not the major happening in Saskatoon today. Fourteen thousand people are congregating in the city to hear a rock band, New Kids on the Block. Rock bands as a method or expression of national unity may be an idea worth exploring. It is especially appropriate that this band is playing on the same day as this panel, since aboriginal peoples and women are the new kids on the constitutional block, not permitted to be in the neighbourhood until recently and still treated with suspicion by the long-time residents.

Recently, I have been thinking about the two groups—women and aboriginal peoples, together. What are the connections and dissimilarities between them? What aboriginal peoples and women have in common, obviously and primarily, is aboriginal women. For two reasons, I suggest that we keep aboriginal women in the forefront of our minds as we think about the constitution.

First, they remind us, simply by who they are, that everyone has multiple identities at one and the same time and all the time. Their treatment by government for decades—the injustice of section 12(1)(b) of the Indian Act by which they were told they could either be Indians or mothers and wives in the family of their choice—illustrates shamefully that it is unrealistic and profoundly damaging to force people to select one facet of their identity. Professor Laforest made this point eloquently in his paper when he said that Quebeckers must not be forced to choose between their identity as Quebeckers and their identity as Canadians. If we want a unified Canada, our search must be for methods of governance that permit and foster multiple identities, as federalism once did and may do still. If it does not, then it has outlived its usefulness.

Second, aboriginal women are the worst-off of the worst-off. We should ask whether every constitutional proposal helps them—whether it improves the conditions of their lives. Any examination of the current constitutional structure and evaluation of suggested change is undertaken from a particular perspective. It is critical to identify one's perspective and to hold it up for scrutiny; otherwise experience tells us, as feminists, that the unstated and unquestioned perspective will be that of the most powerful. For productive dialogue, we must not only acknowledge our specific perspectives but attempt seriously to move beyond them, to consider the point of view of others. Taking the perspective of aboriginal women as the standard of assessment for constitutional proposals is consistent with the feminist method of looking to the bottom, of asking who is buried beneath the social heap, why and what can be done about it. At the least, constitutional change should meet the Rawlsian standard of not making worse the position of the worst-off.

If we cannot do good, at least we should not do harm.

What aboriginal peoples and women have in common generally is that neither has been able to exercise much political or economic power. Both have as their objective a redistribution of power in order to enhance the lives of their members. Constitution making is about power: who has it, who has too little of it, and how it can change hands. We have heard much talk about constitutions being symbols, myths, articulations, and discourse. A constitution is all of that but it is first and foremost about power. The faddish use of voice as metaphor must not obscure the reality of voice as command. The question of who gets to speak for others is the question of who gets to command others, who gets to exercise power over others. That words and speech are orders is the reason why representation, as Beverley Baines has argued so well, is a fundamental question. When we do not talk about power openly, we are implicitly accepting the existing power arrangements which have kept both groups out of any effective exercise of power within Canadian society. So let us be upfront about what we are talking about.

Participants in this conference have spent much time discussing the process of constitution making. They have recognized that both groups, aboriginal peoples and women, share the status of outsiders in the process. The larger and less-acknowledged point is that neither group created the process of government that we live with today and does not to this day participate in adequate numbers in that process. It is because of their exclusion from political forums, first formally and completely by law and now effectively by practice, that women and aboriginal peoples have turned their attention to the constitutional forum in trying to ensure that their perspectives and interests will not continue to be ignored. It is also because of this exclusion that the two groups are organized into national associations such as the National Action Committee and the Assembly of First Nations. The Charter of Rights and Freedoms did not create these groups, it recognized them. Existing political processes necessitated the formation of the two groups as political forces external to the dominant political mechanisms, the forums for the interest group of the white privileged men that are called legislative assemblies. To call women and aboriginal peoples "interest groups" in a disparaging tone and to argue that they subvert the democratic process displays a blindness to the histories of exclusion and the imperfections of the so-called democratic process. Such blindness will not help resolve the difficult issues in our constitutional future.

One big constitutional challenge from aboriginal peoples and women is the reshaping of democratic processes and practices in such a way that they are more comprehensive and effective. The parliamentary process is adversarial and majoritarian, the antithesis of a process that not only hears all voices but takes all experiences and aspirations into account. Parliament in its structure ensures the existence of losers, who are somewhat euphemistically called the Opposition. It is surely evidence of a fundamental flaw in the parliamentary process that politicians go outside of it if they want to achieve a consensus, as Prime Minister Mulroney has announced he will do by establishing the Spicer Commission. Constitution making will continue to be piecemeal and persistent unless the underlying political practices are changed. In this regard, aboriginal peoples have lessons to offer us, such as the practise of consensus decision making used by the Assembly of Manitoba Chiefs. What would our political system look like if aboriginal women were its chief architects? If the question seems silly, consider that aboriginal women constitute in all likelihood a greater percentage of the population than did the lords in Britain who created and shaped Parliament in protection of their interests. If Canadians could labour for over 100 years under a system modified from British aristocratic practice, maybe we ought to consider labouring for a while under a system modified from aboriginal practice. My bet is that we would have a much better chance of having a truly democratic system.

THE FUTURE OF CONSTITUTIONAL REFORM

What Future for Canada?

GORDON ROBERTSON

I t would be comforting to believe, as some of our political leaders have suggested we should, that the question of the role and place of Québec in Canada poses no problem for the future. The so-called problem is just a car stuck in the snow. You rock and rock; the car gets out; you are back on the road and off you go. No change—just happy driving thereafter. It is a comforting metaphor, but we would be fools to believe it.

Of course we would like to believe it. There is nothing most of us want less than another run at the problem that has given rise to so much emotion, vexation, and distress and has absorbed so much of our national energy. But it cannot be avoided for long. The question is not whether we again address this central question of our union, but when, how, and with what result.

There are, of course, other problems that relate to our constitution. As a boy in Saskatchewan I was brought up on Western alienation. It is greater now than it was in the worst years of the thirties, partly because nothing fundamental has been done to alleviate it in the past 50 years. Senate reform seems the only change that could lessen the West's sense of having too little weight in our federation, but it received no serious attention outside the West until it became a possible factor in the success or failure of Meech Lake. The question is bound to rise again—that is, if our federation survives with its "sea to sea" dimension.

Mohawks on the TV screen, night after night last summer at Kahnesatake and Kahnawake, made the problem of aboriginal rights more real to more people than ever before. That question will not go away. It is one of the most complex and difficult questions facing us. There are other problems in our constitution, however, the "Québec question" is unique. It is the only one that can and, unless we are very careful and resourceful, will tear this country apart.

I am aware that in referring to it as the "Québec question" I am putting the problem in "English Canadian" terms. It was in the 1960s that people began asking "What does Québec want?" After the Parti Québécois came to power in the 1970s, the question became more urgent, but after the referendum of 1980 and the apparent success of the Constitution Act, 1982, it seemed to go away. We now know it did not, and, if the events surrounding the agony of the Meech Lake Accord tell us anything, it is that the problem is not just what Québec wants. What does the rest of Canada want this country to be?

On 1 November 1990 the prime minister announced the establishment of a "Citizens' Forum on Canada's Future." It is to "launch a dialogue with and among people across the country and encourage the creation of a new consensus about Canada." It is a wise initiative. Canadians are invited to say what they "value most about their country," and what should be done "to renew and reinforce the values Canadians share." Mr. Spicer and his colleagues should have our prayers for it will be a formidable task.

Many English-speaking Canadians have said they want Canada to be a country where there are no hyphenated Canadians—where we are all Canadians together. That is no answer to our basic problem. Québec is different, whether we like it or not. Is Canada to be a country where a Québec that is 80% French-speaking can feel secure and at home? Many Quebeckers feel it is not that kind of country today. If the pride of nearly 25% of our population in their French culture and their very different institutions leads them to want to be recognized as a distinct society within Canada, is that too great a price to pay to keep Québec in Canada? Or would we rather see Québec go, hoping that will bring a less stressful political life with a uniform federal structure and every province the same as every other? These are the kinds of questions that emerge from the painful national soul-searching that led to the failure of Meech Lake last June and that should be probed by the new forum.

It is worthwhile, I think, without anticipating the dialogue in the Citizens' Forum, to try to discern what the three years of the Meech Lake debate and the 22 years of constitutional effort since prime minister Pearson started the review process in 1968, suggest about some attitudes in this country that are relevant to our future.

As far as Québec is concerned, the basic point surely is that the constitution, as it emerged from the First Ministers Conference of November 1981, and as amended by the Constitution Act, 1982, is not acceptable. Except for the Equality Party, which is English-speaking only, no provincial party in Québec supports it or can be expected to in the future. It is regarded as an imposition and an insult. The status quo may be a legal fact but is utterly dead as the basis for Québec's continuation as a part of Canada. The only realistic question is whether our present constitution can be amended so our federal system can survive or whether it must be replaced by something quite different. Unless I am very wrong, these views will be reflected in the discussions of the Québec commission on the future of Québec.

As we know, Mr. Bourassa's government, after coming into office in 1985, put forward in May 1986 its "five points" of change to make the constitution of

1982 acceptable. The five points were revised considerably at Meech Lake in the interest of the other provinces to produce a package they would agree to. Premier Bourassa made it very clear that the Accord was a minimum for Québec. Last June the Accord failed. Whatever one may say about nine Canadian governments accepting the Accord between 1987 and 1990, and about English Canada not really rejecting it, it died—and to many French-speaking people of Québec both the Accord and they as a people were rejected.

All opinion polls in the last year or more have shown a dramatic swing of opinion in Québec away from federalism and in favour of "sovereignty." From 39% in the referendum of 1980, support for sovereignty had dropped to around 25% in the mid-1980s. As criticism of the Accord grew in English-speaking Canada early this year, the support for sovereignty also grew month by month in Québec. After the death of Meech Lake it rose to 65% in Québec opinion polls. The Bloc Québécois candidate, standing for sovereignty, got 68% of the vote in the federal by-election in Laurier-Ste. Marie in mid-July of this year. The only federalist candidate got about 16%. Laurier-Ste. Marie was not a separatist constituency in the past: the previous MP had been a Liberal. Recent polls indicate that the surge of support for sovereignty was not an emotional reaction of the moment. According to polls in the fall of 1990, it is still the preferred option of two-thirds of the people of Québec.

The death of Meech Lake was not the only factor in the increase of support for sovereignty. The "English only" position in Sault Ste. Marie and other Ontario municipalities, the rise of APEC (Alliance for the Preservation of English Canada) and COR (Confederation of Regions Party), the stomping on the Québec flag in Brockville, and an impression of animosity in English-speaking Canada against Québec and against the French language and culture, had the result one would expect. Many people in Québec now feel that neither they, nor French, nor perhaps their province, are understood or even wanted in Canada.

In such a climate in Québec there is little if any prospect of a proposal emerging in 1991 or 1992 from the extended legislative Committee of Québec that will be even close to the moderation of the five points of 1986. Moderation did not seem to pay off; many Québécois think it was a recipe for humiliation. There will almost certainly be some proposal from the committee, or some of its members, for a much revised federalism, in which there would be specific powers for Québec to protect those things essential to its identity, especially its language and culture. Premier Bourassa has indicated repeatedly that a revised federalism is his preferred option and there is still a substantial federalist wing in the Liberal Party of Québec. It is equally certain that we must expect to see an alternate option for some form of "sovereignty-association" as the best arrangement for the future of Québec.

If these are the kinds of things, relevant to the solution of the "Québec problem," that we have learned about attitudes in Québec as they have developed during the Meech Lake experience, what have we learned about Canada outside Québec?

One thing is that most Canadians in the other nine provinces profoundly hope not to have to revisit the question of constitutional reform for years—preferably never. People in English-speaking Canada are fed up with the whole issue. There is little understanding of why Québec really cannot accept the 1982 constitution and little sympathy for Québec's concern over its French language and culture. There is virtually no acceptance of the proposition that it may not be an unreasonable invasion of the rights of anglophones in Québec to take measures to protect the language of 80% of the population there, if French is seen to be threatened by the enormous surrounding "English" majority of North America. Bill 178, banning outside signs in English in Québec, was condemned and resented in English-speaking Canada. Yet in our cities we readily accept municipal by-laws for building restrictions, for controlling signs on streets, and other restrictive regulations that are in the interest of a municipal majority, and that are probably resented by an interested minority just as Bill 178 is by the English-speaking minority in Montréal. We do not recognize such restrictions as protection of "collective rights" in our communities, yet they are. French-speaking Québec has a collective right it seeks to protect—the right to preserve its unique identity in North America.

With this lack of sympathy for Quebecker's concern about their language and culture, it is not surprising that the distinct society clause in the Meech Lake Accord raised strong objection—and it is not surprising that that lack of sympathy was seen in Québec as a rejection of its values.

The relevance of all this is that language, culture, and the distinctive character of Québec are not marginal items to the French-speaking people of Québec: they are fundamental. If we could not accept them in the moderate form of Meech Lake, can we accept any modification of our federalism that will accommodate and protect them in the future?

Related to all this is the myth that has taken so strong a hold in English-speaking Canada in the last 20 years that our constitution must treat all provinces in all respects in exactly the same way—"a province is a province is a province." Four of Québec's five points of 1986 had to be generalized at Meech Lake in April 1987, and made applicable to all provinces to make them acceptable. The one that was not generalized—the distinct society clause—became the focal point of objection. This strong feeling for treating all provinces the same was not the prevailing attitude as late as the Victoria Conference in 1971. The "Victoria formula" for constitutional amendment was accepted there, with vetoes for Ontario and Québec but for no other individual province. Provinces could then be different in weight and in power in our constitution. It was after the Victoria Conference that homogeneity took over as a rule of constitution making. If we cling to this concept of utter uniformity for provinces, we will sharply curtail our capacity to meet Québec's legitimate concerns within our federal system.

If, as seems virtually certain, the government of Québec will seek more specific powers to protect its language and culture, and a more clearly defined distinctive status for Québec, and if we cannot afford such arrangements without giving every province the same powers and the same status, the result will be to decentralize our federalism much more than Meech Lake would have done. Any substantial decentralization in an already much-decentralized federalism might be extremely unwise. I would hope it would be unacceptable to Canadians in all parts of Canada who have a fundamental interest in effective government in this country.

Utter provincial equality and no distinct society, as rigid principles of our federalism, will end up either with the status quo, which Québec has said is not acceptable, or with some new structural arrangement that departs from our federalist system. The remaining solution would be for Québec to become a totally separate state and for the rest of Canada to reorder its affairs to produce a new Canada minus Québec.

It seems to me that there are at least two other things of relevance for the future revealed by the Meech Lake drama.

One is the revulsion against the amending process that was used from 1987–1990, with the very limited degree of effective and timely public participation. Clearly that will not be repeated. No government will risk it in the future. However, it would be, a mistake to assume that public participation is going to make resolution of the "Québec problem" any easier; it may do just the opposite. The public sessions in Manitoba and New Brunswick heard the views of the people of those provinces. It was not, and it could not be a process of accommodation and adjustment. The reports tended to become restraints on the political leaders when they engaged, as they later had to, in the effort to reach compromises at the national level. If public participation in 10 provinces ends up in 10 reports with 10 rigid positions what chance will there be for agreement?

Adjustment and compromise are unavoidable in a diverse country like Canada. It is not clear how we can accommodate this need in a political climate where privacy for political negotiators is condemned as secrecy and where compromise is damned as deal making. Real negotiation, and the tradeoffs necessary for compromise and agreement, cannot happen in front of a television camera.

The other thing that has been shown is that English-speaking Canada tends to underestimate the capacity of Québec to "go it alone" economically and politically, while some sovereignty enthusiasts in Québec underestimate the value of having the broader economic and political base that the Canadian federation provides. There is little question that Québec, if it considered it worthwhile to accept some reduction in its GNP and some increased economic risk, could be a thoroughly successful independent country. But on the other hand, the economic and financial instability of a transition could be lengthy and painful and a solitary future would be less secure than one that linked Québec with the rest of Canada.

If these thoughts are more or less correct about what 1990 has shown to be relevant attitudes in this difficult country, what may be probable constitutional options for our future?

As I have said, I am convinced that the status quo cannot last. The constitution, as it now stands, will not be tolerable for a Québec that has been dissatisfied with it since the 1960s and saw none of its concerns addressed by the changes made in the Constitution Act, 1982. If a total separation of Québec from Canada is left aside, in the hope that there is still enough good sense in this country for something better to be worked out, there seem to me to be three likely possibilities—each with a wide spectrum of specific provision within it.

Two would be modifications within our federal system. One of these would see constitutional adjustments for Québec related to its basic "difference" within Canada. It would provide arrangements that would meet Québec's essential concerns—in a sense, a new, more specific and more extensive version of the approach involved in the five points of 1986. The provisions would not apply to other provinces. To balance these special arrangements for Québec, and to make them acceptable to the rest of Canada, there likely would need to be adjustments in the rights of Québec representatives in the House of Commons and in a reformed Senate, and perhaps in some other central institutions of government. These would be tricky to work out but in principle it does not seem an impossible task.

The practical feasibility would depend, in part, on the character and extent of the powers Québec sought. The other major questions would be how to fit the differences into the operations of Parliament: the voting on bills and financial measures and, especially, questions of confidence. If such a plan could be devised and was acceptable to the other governments and legislatures whose agreement would be necessary under our present amending formulas, the result would be an asymmetrical federalism: one province different in several defined respects from the other nine and having a somewhat different place and weight in some agencies of our national government.

The second possibility, still within our federal system, might follow the pattern of the Meech Lake Accord in generalizing the changes needed to meet Québec's legitimate concerns. In this hypothesis, with a much more nationalist climate in Québec than prevailed in 1986–87, the changes would be greater than in the Accord. The result would be more decentralized federalism than Meech Lake would have produced, had it been approved.

The third option, as I see it, would arise if neither of the first two options could be agreed upon—or if either, on the only terms capable of agreement, seemed less desirable than moving to a solution outside our federalism. The solution in that case might be some form of sovereignty-association that would try to achieve the advantages of a continuing relationship between Québec and the rest of Canada while giving up the political and constitutional unity we now have.

Sovereignty-association has always had a calamitous ring about it. It has seemed to be sophistry to see a distinction between it and "separation," pure and simple. Yet there could be a profound difference both in substance and in the quality of the relations that might prevail in future between a "Canada of nine" and a new state of Québec. In a sense, an agreed "association" arrangement would be political separation but with the type of practical cooperative arrangements that the European Community has been increasingly establishing over the last 30 years and more.

As has been shown as the European Community has evolved, there are any number of degrees of association and integration possible. At the most integrated of them, "sovereignty" can be so merged in factual cooperation and formal commitment that, as Mrs. Thatcher fears, it ceases to be the concept of autonomous independence it has been in the past and that she so treasures. It could be, in our case, an "association" option in which each partner accepted a reduced individual sovereignty in order to achieve important benefits, mostly but not exclusively economic. This kind of arrangement need not be hostile, as a separation without agreement or with a rancorous and resentful one probably would be.

A Québec-Canada association would not be easy to devise. It would be more difficult between two partners of disparate size and weight than among 12, as in Europe. Québec could not expect to have complete parity in whatever institutions and policies might be established for the community. Nor could the rest of Canada expect complete domination in such areas. The talent for compromise we used to have in this country would have to be applied to new institutions and arrangements.

I recognize that there are other options than the three I have sketched— plus the complete separation of Québec. In theory, a reordering of Canada on a regional basis, with four or five regions instead of 10 provinces, is a possibility. I doubt if it is a practical one. If one were to attempt to take the federal structure of Canada apart in this way, and depart so much from our provincial history and tradition, I doubt very much if Humpty-Dumpty could be put together again.

For similar reasons I have grave doubts about approaching our problem by means of a national constitutional convention that would throw our doors open to all sorts of intellectually ingenious schemes of theoretical possibility. Confederation was a nearly miraculous achievement. It has produced enormous benefits for Canadians. We should, I think, view with caution any method of arriving at consti- tutional change that would vest the task in some new and untried agency, whether elected or not. We are not revolutionary France nor are we the postrevolutionary Thirteen Colonies, rejecting a past seen as vile and repressive and setting up something totally new. We are a country with a history of great accomplishment trying to retain as much as we can of the benefits that 123 years of political experience and economic development have given us. In short, we should build on what we have and not throw it away without any guarantee we can substitute something better.

Why do I not include a fourth option—a completely revised, modernized, and clarified BNA Act—a brand new federal constitution for Canada? In logical terms, this would be highly desirable. It is so logical that the 11 governments of Canada agreed in February 1968 to try to achieve it. Years were spent in negotiation from 1968 to 1979 and two more years in 1980 and 1981. On the distribution of powers alone only one simple change could be agreed upon—jurisdiction over nonrenewable resources. As a participant in that exercise for over 11 years, I cannot be other than pessimistic about the practical feasibility of this option.

So, to summarize, I would suggest that the constitutional future of Canada, if we are constructive, will not see an attempt to preserve the status quo on the one hand, nor complete separation of Québec from Canada on the other. There is a range of possibility between the two within which we should be capable—

Québec and the rest of Canada—of finding a better solution for both of us. It is likely, as I have said, to involve one of three things: an asymmetrical federalism, or a more decentralized federalism, or a structured association of Québec with a "nine-province Canada"—a Canada-Québec community.

As I have thought about these prospects I have, of course, asked myself which solution I would prefer. I have no problem. An asymmetrical federalism, that accommodated the reasonable needs of Québec to protect its French language and culture, with recognition of the reality of its genuine distinctiveness, while preserving the political and economic unity of Canada: that would be the option I would seek. I emphasize the words "reasonable needs" and the relation to the protection of the French language and culture. There would have to be a clear principle to determine legitimate areas of difference and a test of reasonableness about their scope. Without such a basic principle, I doubt if special arrangements would be acceptable at all.

Such a federalism, with a carefully devised and balanced asymmetry, could preserve the great benefits that have come to all Canadians from our political and economic union. It could avoid the inefficiencies of a looser federalism that might be unable to cope with a highly competitive world in the next century. It would avoid the dreadful problems that separation could entail, with angry disputes over boundaries, the sharing of the national debt, entitlement to federal assets, rights to federal employment and accumulated federal benefits, and a host of other things. Perhaps most of all, it would avoid the defeat of the transcendent purpose we have inherited of two peoples of different language and culture sharing and building a great country together. These, to my mind, are objectives that are worth all the effort, all the mutual tolerance, and all the talent for compromise we can summon.

Does the fate of the five points and the failure of Meech Lake mean that there is no hope for such a federalism? Perhaps not. The alternatives to such a solution may be clearer by 1992 or 1995 than they were in 1987–1990. They may be seen to be less palatable than an asymmetry that balanced the distinct society and defined powers with adjustment in some of our central institutions. In addition, a more acceptable procedure in developing a new plan, with a greater opportunity for public participation, might produce different results.

If, however, asymmetrical federalism cannot be made acceptable both to Québec and to English-speaking Canada, it seems to me not impossible that the "association option" in some form might be better than a more decentralized federalism. An important question would, I think, be whether the "association" could be established in a way that would preserve the monetary and economic effectiveness that a new Canada would require while still providing the degree of political autonomy Québec would seek.

If it comes, as I hope it will not, to a situation where no adjustment within our federal system seems possible, I would hope that neither we nor the people of Québec would become mesmerized over "sovereignty" as such. As never before, sovereignty is a matter of degree in this world—except perhaps for Myanma (the former Burma), and Albania. They have full sovereignty, untrammelled by commitments to any other state. They also have two of the lowest standards of political, social, and economic living on earth.

Political independence, with fairly substantial sovereignty, is undoubtedly attainable by Québec if the people of the province at some time clearly choose that option. But it might provide a dubious gain and a poor trade for advantages that might be achieved in other ways if the rest of Canada also brings good sense to bear. There is a tremendous common interest, in a cruelly competitive world, in not prying apart the economic and social union that has served us so well and a political system that, with all its faults, has provided stability and freedom.

We are the envy of most countries and most people on earth. We have too much to lose—all of us, English-speaking and French-speaking—to press with rigid logic or emotional fervour for solutions or shibboleths that may not fit tomorrow's world.

The glass is very unclear. Nothing about the Canada of 10 or 20 years from now is certain except that it will be very different from what we have known thus far.

The Future of Canada's
Constitutional Reform Process

JOHN D. WHYTE

QUEEN'S UNIVERSITY

The nation of Canada is not bound to flourish in the near future. More precisely, and more damaging to long-term national well-being, the idea of nation in Canada may not flourish. We should recognize that Canada's struggle for self-reformation is not doomed to succeed and that Canada's evolution falls within a general ongoing historical process in which national structures are commonly fragile and transitory.

Political forces within Canada and political values at play in Canada may not permit a resolution which would avoid a serious splintering of the nation. The bases for, and expressions of, nationalism are feeble while the political energy behind Canadian minority communities and minority nations seems potent. Even if there were a countervailing political force on behalf of the whole nation, there is no clear and obvious route by which the Canadian nation, as we know it, can find expression and be maintained. At our current juncture, there is no credible prescription for national wholeness and the more coherent programmes of constitutional reform are those that develop the idea of two separate successor states—Québec and Canada without Québec.

The usual range of solutions to constitutional malaise—reform of central institutions to better represent diversity, alteration in the federal division of powers to better reflect the modern context for governance, and changing the content of citizens' rights and privileges to match varying states of collectivist interests—have run up against radically different ideas about how the Canadian state needs to evolve. There are strong new forces within Canada that are striving to reform the national Parliament so that all regions of the country will have sufficient power to force national political processes toward decision making based on forming region-by-region coalitions. In fact, it was the rich potential for parliamentary reform contained in the Meech Lake proposals (even without further constitutional amendments) that made them appealing to some western provinces. In the view of others, namely provincial leaders in Québec, this sort of alteration of national politics would merely exacerbate the potential for tyranny by national majorities over the Québec minority.

On the other hand, strengthening the traditional means of checking national majorities through increasing the scope of exclusive provincial authority will, for others, undermine our ability to maintain a level of national self-determination requisite to meet both global challenges and internal disparities. Devolution of power is equated with abandonment of the many instruments that support the concept of nation.

Finally, there is deep conflict over the issue of whether the interests of communities, especially the interest of the province of Québec in maintaining a distinct political community, should have ascendancy over other claims based on group needs, or on fundamental human rights. For many Canadians, retrenchment from the rights base that has been created by the Charter would be unacceptable. For Québec, and perhaps for aboriginal communities, the Charter of Rights represents a serious source of erosion of political autonomy.

These illustrations of the pattern of irreconcilable visions for a restructured country show how difficult it will be to respond to the imperative to reform constitutionally. Despair is sometimes described as living with the demand that one be something that one cannot be. Perhaps that is why despair is such a prevalent tone in the talking and writing about post-Meech Canada. Many believe that a constitution must express the basic values common to the whole population and describe the basic structures that enjoy universal confidence.[1] We are told that we need to reconstitutionalize ourselves in order to sustain ourselves as a nation, yet we sense that we cannot satisfy what is regarded as the basic condition for any constitutionalizing process—we cannot speak as a people.

In this paper, I want to advance the argument that Canada was not formed under, and has never enjoyed, a single coherent set of national political values— there has been no single organizing political ideology around which Canada has developed. We have always constructed ourselves as a nation around diverse and unresolved conceptions of political community.[2] Our best hope for the future is to recognize this and to accept that changes to the constitution, particularly those that relate to Québec's role within Canada, will reflect political beliefs that are simply inconsistent with the ideas that lie behind other constitutional provisions and will represent ideas of statecraft that do not follow pure forms.

The most obvious points of the current dissonance come from different conceptions of the appropriate role for national political authority and the absence of a uniform commitment to the liberal values of equality and personal liberty which the Charter of Rights has expressed and solidified. We are being challenged to accommodate Québec's sense that it requires special powers—powers that other provinces are not seeking to remove from the national government and powers that many Canadians believe should not be placed beyond constitutional review.

In short, Canada is faced with demands for legal and constitutional pluralism that before now it has not had to accept in order to maintain its historic cultural pluralism. The question we face is whether codification of power that matches the actual differences in the experiences of the peoples of Canada is possible without destroying the underlying commitments of citizens that allow Canada to continue as a nation.

What follows are eight observations that may be of help as we begin to develop a response to this challenge.

THE IDEA OF NATION IS A MORAL CHALLENGE

The coercive authority of the state over its inhabitants is not inherently a matter of virtue. Legitimacy for state authority may be rooted in ideas other than the idea of a cohesive nation. Some justificatory notions for authority are social contract, divine will, the need for social order, and protection from outside destructive forces. These justifications seem no longer relevant for Canada, if they ever were.

The moral problem of justifying state authority is more acute when we know, as we now know in Canada, that there are people who feel that they are trapped within our country. We cannot answer the clamour for liberation by appeals to common experience, past romantic visions of a distinct nationhood, or our past fear of outsiders. Historic commitments to nationhood can become spent and lose their relevance and when that happens it is specially problematic to insist that the commitments made by foreparents bind the current generation. Although constitutionalization is a process in which the decisions made at a single point in time bind successive generations, that binding must expect to be challenged by the claim of distinct minority communities to exercise self-determination, at least to the extent of acquiring political authority over processes and functions that are central to social and political self-definition.

On the other hand nations cohere not simply because all of their parts share a common vision of the future. Nations are often formed in the most unromantic of circumstances and in the absence of any illusions about creating a common history. These states (perhaps they are not, in one sense, nations) also have an integrity that needs to be protected. One might argue that the purpose behind the creation of a state is not the pursuit of a particular destiny but only the creation of a polity in which conflict can be resolved and ideas of the socially good can be fashioned. Success in continuing the polity—in continuing the process of acting for the social good of all—is jeopardized when one segment of the state raises the stakes too high through the threat of secession. When elements of a nation respond to political frustration by breaking away—by leaving the polity—the stability necessary to form and execute the next generation of policies is gone. Countries like Canada are formed according to some sense of geopolitical realities and it is serious business to ignore those realities. The withdrawal of unhappy and disaffected minorities from a nation represents disintegration—the possibility of successive withdrawals and, ultimately, collapse. Separation means the weakening (or destruction) of those national institutions that Canada has formed for the good of all its citizens. Perhaps, therefore, states have the right to resist the processes of disintegration and consequent reformation. They are processes that will produce a weaker and less-coherent nation.

From one perspective, then, Québec cannot expect the rest of Canada to adopt a facilitative stance in response to its struggle for liberation. But from another perspective, a policy of confounding Québec's search for a new level of political autonomy amounts to no more than the oppression of a minority people. Hence, Canada is not only faced with a political challenge that taxes the imagination and goodwill of its citizens, it is faced with a moral dilemma.

HOW WE TREAT THE KAHNESATAKE WARRIORS REVEALS SOMETHING ABOUT THE MATURITY OF OUR STAGECRAFT

The Mohawk warriors at Kahnesatake allegedly committed serious crimes—possibly, culpable homicide and possession of dangerous weapons. They will need to be charged and tried for the criminal acts that may have occurred. How should we proceed to deal with these possible criminal acts? In September 1990, the federal minister of justice, in response to a request that there be an investigation into the most appropriate legal regime for trying these cases, told the House of Commons that under Canadian law there was only one possible criminal and prosecutorial regime to be used.[3] She was referring to the criminal law of Canada and the system of provincial prosecution under the provinces' jurisdiction over the administration of criminal justice.

Developing international law supports greater legal pluralism. So, too, do some aboriginal treaties. It has been judicially suggested that section 35 of the Constitution Act, 1982, could exempt some aboriginal activity from provincial regulatory regimes and, instead, make it subject to the authority of aboriginal governments.[4] Neither recent Canadian case law, nor the older American case law recognizing distinct governmental powers for aboriginal peoples, denies the capacity of the dominant state to intrude into aboriginal processes to protect vital state interests.[5] The recent Supreme Court of Canada decision in *Sparrow* makes it clear, however, that the burden of justifying such intrusions (by showing the close relationship between the intrusion on aboriginal government and the vindication of a vital state interest) falls on the government of the dominant state.[6]

The question Canada faces is whether its strong liberal conception of justice (one law and one administration for all the members of the nation) can be deviated from to the extent of permitting a distinct sub-national group to enjoy independent administrative regimes. We have, in fact, accepted independent regimes for education and child welfare, but we seem not to be able to tolerate legal pluralism with respect to crimes, or land use, or the rights of citizens. If our liberal sense is so deeply ingrained that we cannot give specific content to the general recognition of aboriginal rights, and cannot contemplate that that might include an aboriginal regime of social control, then we shall need to recognize our innate difficulty in accepting any significant special political arrangement for any minority community within Canada.

240

THE LIBERAL TRADITION IN CANADA ALTHOUGH NOT NECESSARILY HISTORICALLY ROOTED IS NOW DOMINANT

It would be folly not to recognize the extent to which the two Liberal prime ministers of the 1960s and 1970s generated a national consciousness that can fairly be equated with generating a liberal sensibility. This equation probably needs justification. Liberalism, it is often argued, stands in conflict with communitarianism.[7] Federalism is an attempt to permit distinct ordering regimes for distinct communities. The greater the focus on provincial capitals for the vindication of political interests, the more distinct the various provincial communities are likely to be and the less likely the whole population will subscribe to a nationalist political ethic. If there is no strong national political identification then differences in the treatment of, programmes for, and regulation of, different populations will be regarded as normal and acceptable. A low presence of national values and a low sense of national commitment are connected, therefore, with a pattern of different legal fates for individuals who find themselves in radically different political communities. In this way, the development of strong sub-national communities is a form of illiberalism and, correspondingly, the development of a national political sensibility is threatening to a continuing role for, and legitimacy of, distinct province-based polities.

This linkage between a strong federalist regime and communitarianism may, however, be suspect in the Canadian context. Professor Robert Vipond of the University of Toronto has argued that all those lawyers, political scientists, and philosophers who have arranged Canadian history into the conflict between the competing ideas of community and decentralized democratic participation, on the one hand, and atomistic liberalism rooted in the rights of national citizenship, on the other hand, have missed an important truth about Canadian federal theory. What they have missed is the strong connection that has been historically made between provincial rights (strong provincial authorities) and the traditions of legal liberalism.[8] In his account, Vipond suggests that the important element in weakening national government was the delegitimization of the federal government's overarching power to reserve and disallow provincial legislation. This occurred through a steady resort by promoters of provincial rights to the liberal ideas of legalism and equality. Vipond observes:

> Beneath the important superficial differences there is actually a deep affinity between the claim for provincial autonomy mediated by the rule of law and [the] "rights model". At the level of political rhetoric, for instance, it is useful to remember that provincial governments still couch their claims to power in terms of rights, and they still reinforce these claims by comparing provincial rights to individual rights.[9]

This version of Canadian intergovernmental history may cast doubt on the fit of the traditional dichotomies but it does serve to support the claim that liberal values are deeply embedded in Canadian political consciousness.

The claim for the influence of liberalism in the development of the Canadian nation is reinforced by other scholars. George Grant in his 1974 Josiah Wood lecture, "English-Speaking Justice," maintained that the English-speaking world, including most of Canada, has been dominated by liberalism simply because we, and our institutions, are the product of 18th and 19th century English political thought. Grant pointed out that for a considerable time, certainly since the midpoint of the 19th century, "liberalism is the only political language that can sound a convincing moral note in our public realms"[10] and "it is the only political thought which can summon forth widespread public action for the purposes of human good."[11] In other words, it has been our unexplained, unexplored, and unjustified political philosophy.

On the other hand, some Canadian political scientists have been at pains to understand our ideological roots as anything but liberal. Gad Horowitz in a famous essay,[12] argued that:

The key to understanding Canadian politics is the elusive distinction between a tory corporate—organic—collectivist conception of the common good, preserved in socialism, and a liberal individualist conception, illustrated above all by the United States.[13]

The Horowitz thesis that Canada can best be understood as an expression of tory collectivism has been doubted on much the same basis relied upon by George Grant: Canada's intellectual origins are undoubtedly Whiggish; that is, based on faith in the liberal instruments of supreme parliament and open market.[14]

Gerald Vano has argued that such a derivative form of ascendancy for liberalism in Canada is a weak argument easily swept aside by the consistent nonliberalism and nonautonomy of the Canadian state.[15] Canada, from its inception as a political unit, adopted feudalistic European thinking in which there is no real social dynamism, people are located by estate, status, and function. Canada was designed with a highly fragmented state structure and there has been no appreciable movement or single organizing authority at either a political or philosophical plane. This failure can be blamed in part on the rejection of nationhood by the Judicial Committee of the Privy Council in terms of the phenomenon of being willing to by-pass the national court for nearly three-quarters of a century, and by its assertion of continuing authority (against Canadian preferences to the contrary) for the last quarter century of its role, and finally by the actual decisions it made with respect to national powers.

Under this analysis, elements of continuing extraterritorial constitutional structure facilitated the ascendancy of community interests, which, in Gerald Vano's words, means exclusive and divisive ethnicity and its prevalence over integrating liberal principles such as individual merit and freedom.

The pattern in Canada of preserving local authority, either as a matter of imperial policy, or domestic illiberal policy, or equally plausibly, as an expression of un-Americaness guaranteed, for some time, the dominance of social pluralism—discrete centres of power dominated by special limited and nonnational interests.

Whatever the ambiguity of our past, the tide has now turned. The Pearson national welfare programme and the Trudeau national rights programme were decisive in the establishment of liberal values in Canada. Trudeau adopted a number of other measures that helped develop strong national citizenship. Bilingualism was a programme to enhance the substantive content of Canadian citizenship. His veto in 1983 of a constitutional amendment to allow provinces to by-pass provincial Superior courts in the administration of laws was done in recognition that the rule of law, and the constitutional vesting of a minimum entrenched jurisdiction for courts, were elements of a national identity. Even the invocation of the War Measures Act in 1970 may have been the product of ulterior nationalist motives in the sense that nationalist sentiment is formed most successfully in rallying against threats to the stability of the state. In fact, one of the reasons for Canada's low level of nationalist sentiment is that Canada has not been greatly threatened by an identifiable subversive force. We have so often had to adopt the enemies of other nations; we adopted Britain's enemies in the two World Wars and American enemies during the Cold War. The FLQ represented a moment for forming a nationalist sense so long, that is, as truly national instruments were deployed to meet the threat. Hence, we had the War Measures Act and not the simpler, less drastic, and more obvious deployment of police forces to the site of social disorder.

The greatest triumph for liberalism was the 1982 Charter of Rights. The Charter did not so much create a liberal vision as reflect a changing sensibility. It found resonance in a liberalized world—a world that, as a result of the Second World War, learned to be sceptical of state conceptions of the morally correct. There grew a desperate sense that state power cannot be counted on to reflect virtue and that it is individual moral claims that provide the most morally compelling check to state power. This produced in Canada a yearning for constitutionalized rights that was captured in the voices of, first, John Diefenbaker and, then, Pierre Trudeau. Constitutional values in a nation cannot be constitutionalized by text alone but by the matching of text with the ethical perceptions of the population. In the case of the entrenchment of rights such a constituting has taken place.

Of course, we could choose to see the Charter of Rights as not truly liberal—as, instead, expressing a high level of ambivalence about the relative ranking of fundamental, universal, and inherent rights and rights which are based on actual historical claims—rights that are contingent on history. The Charter, after all, grants both group rights (based on language, religion, ethnicity, and nativeness) and individual human rights. Although the text of the Charter supports the claim of ambivalence, the history of the past eight years tells us that what has been constituted as basic are individual rights. Through the words of Canadian courts, they are granted a higher place than group rights, which have been seen as contingent, bargained for, and ultimately trumpable.[16] Even section 1 of the Charter, the most open invitation possible to rob the Charter of its underlying liberal quality, was not used to defend the interests of the minority group in Ford v. Québec[17]—the most significant Supreme Court of Canada case to date dealing with how to reconcile claims of individual right with sub-nationalist interest.

There is, in addition, the evidence of a growing appreciation of the full meaning of a constitutional vested judicial authority. W.R. Lederman's ground-breaking article on the independence of the judiciary in 1956[18] has been followed in recent years by judgments[19] which affirm the inviolability of the judicial role in assessing the legality of governmental action. These cases underscore, for Canada, one of the underlying conditions of liberalism—the resort to legalism to locate the legitimacy of public authority.

The experience of the last decade, if not the whole of Canada's history, provides us with little basis to doubt that liberalism represents the dominant organizing idea of the Canadian political make-up. Insofar as the accommodation with Québec requires Canada to recognize special political authority for Québec—requires us to deviate from the liberal ideals of one Parliament and one Charter of Rights for all Canadians—the road to constitutional renewal will be difficult.

THE REJECTION OF THE MEECH LAKE ACCORD IS FURTHER EVIDENCE OF A LOW TOLERANCE FOR ILLIBERALISM

The rejection of the Meech Lake Accord is further evidence of the presence of a number of public values. It could be said that Meech Lake was rejected because it ignored the tension between strong regionalism and effective national self-determination. Part of the fabric of Canadian political value is belief in the national role, through central institutions, in shaping the welfare of citizens, the system of laws, and the constitutional future of the country. The Meech Lake Accord seemed to erode the national role in these matters and Canadians resented the abandonment of this element of national integrity.

We know, however, that that was not likely the actual sticking point. The feature of the Accord that was widely problematic was the distinct society clause and the form of cultural establishmentarianism that that clause represented. True liberals will always question any arrangement under which special state authority can be directed to social processes to drive them toward certain outcomes. Liberals of the old breed were not pleased that the modern activist state began to intrude on the freedom of contract and the rights of property owners. Modern liberals don't accept state intervention into questions of religious faithfulness and the development of culture. Meech's main "fault" was its perceived empowerment of the Québec National Assembly to dictate language practices and, hence, to allow the state to shape the social climate of a free society.

Since the main theme of future constitutional reform in Canada is bound to be devolution of political authorities to minority nations so they can act to promote and preserve their distinct cultural communities, the militant liberalism that may have been at play in the rejection of Meech underscores the serious problem in developing novel constitutional arrangements devised to permit Québec nationalism to find expression within Canada.

INSISTING ON IDENTICAL CONSTITUTIONAL ARRANGEMENTS FOR ALL PROVINCES IS AN ELEMENT OF LIBERAL THOUGHT THAT WILL STAND IN THE WAY OF CONSTITUTIONAL REFORM

The federal structure was adopted for Canada because national uniformity would undermine the separate political communities that joined confederation. Diversity of laws, programmes, and administration was anticipated and welcomed. Even the coming of the Charter of Rights, with its national standards with respect to the administration of criminal justice, has not eroded the commitment to diversity in criminal and penal regimes.[20] However, as has already been suggested a strongly federalized nation with powerful and distinct communities will be illiberal in, at least, the sense that not all citizens are entitled to the same rights.

It might be asked if different legal regimes are acceptable (as they are in a federal country) why are different constitutional regimes also not acceptable? Different legislative and executive powers for different provinces should not produce a different theoretical problem than federalism itself. Both lead to diversity, and disparity, in regimes of ordering but this feature is not necessarily accentuated because it is explicitly created by the constitutional text.

On the other hand, the recognition of different constitutional powers for different provinces will produce serious practical problems. For example, the elected representatives to the national legislature will have varying categories of responsibility. If the solution were to preclude legislative participation in a matter by members from a province that did not admit to federal authority in that matter, there would be the problem of the government not enjoying the confidence of the Commons as certain members, from time to time, were excluded from participation. Similar problems arise with respect to the role of the prime minister and federal cabinet. The members of the government assume responsibility for the full executive function at the national level. If some of the members of the government were from Québec they would be exercising authority beyond that mandated by the electors of Québec whose interests in choosing representatives to Parliament are limited by virtue of the greater governmental role played by Québec.

An equally serious problem arises with respect to the passage of acts that apply to Québec but do so on a considerably different basis than those that operate in the rest of Canada. For example, federal tax measures would presumably impose significantly different burdens on taxpayers from Québec for whom the Canadian government has relatively little responsibility and those from other provinces who benefit from higher transfers under the full range of federal programmes. Given the drastic difference in taxation likely, it is difficult to see how Québec members could properly participate in tax legislation, yet as representatives of taxpayers at some level they must. It is not a solution to create two Parliaments—one for Québec members and one for other members—to deal with this problem since, for equity reasons, the tax regime has to be based on a common sense of tax base and tax rate.

These problems are undoubtedly acute but the problems of disparity in representative responsibility are not impossible to work out. Solutions will require both the suspension of concern about power being absolutely congruent with authority and the invention of new parliamentary institutions. For instance, it would be possible to resort to the use of conferencing between members from Québec and other members to come to a common position with respect to legislation that needs to be passed by a bifurcated Commons. There could be new formal rules relating to votes of confidence so that special votes, permitting the participation of all members, will be conducted to establish the level of legislative confidence in the government.

Both the fact of making adjustments and the substance of the adjustments will be seen as favouring Québec and it is quite possible that the rest of Canada is driven by political imperatives that will make these sorts of adjustments impossible. This resistance goes beyond the problem of a deeply rooted liberal hostility to legislative pluralism, it represents a limit to political manoeuvrability with respect to the Québec agenda.

PUBLIC PERCEPTIONS SHAPE OUR CONSTITUTIONAL AGENDA, AS WELL AS THE RANGE OF TERMS FOR CONSTITUTIONAL RECONCILIATION

There is nothing revelatory about the connection between public opinion and policy options; it is to be hoped that in a democracy public perceptions will form and will guide public choices. It is, however, concerning that so much of public perception around constitutional reform centres on tolerance within Québec and the rest of Canada for each other's politics and each other's dominant language. Furthermore, there seems to be a passion to note all the signs of low tolerance and disrespect. The 1982 Constitution has been consistently presented as the product of a process that excluded Québec and, even, deliberately held Québec at bay. The critical debate on Meech Lake was represented as hostility to Québec. The support of Meech rested virtually entirely on the basis that failure to support would be taken as further rejection. And the failure of Meech was taken as precisely that. (The government of Canada systematically presented an account of events that minimized other bases for understanding the lack of acceptance of the Meech Lake Accord.)

This trend continues. Voices within Québec suggesting forms of integration are not being repeated within the rest of Canada and events in Canada (for example the NDP election victory in Ontario) have been presented in Québec as instances of anti-Québec sentiment.

This practice, which is not just a press practice but the habit of expression of political sophisticates (in fact, this practice is often taken as the hallmark of that sophistication) has limited the opportunity for creating a discourse of integration.

A FORM OF INTEGRATION BETWEEN QUÉBEC AND THE REST OF CANADA IS ESSENTIAL TO BOTH QUÉBEC AND THE REST OF CANADA

The recent history of the flourishing of Québec, as both an economic community, and a political community has occurred in the context of integration—integration with Canada and integration with the rest of the world as a result of its membership in the Canadian nation, as well as in its own right. Continued political and economic integration is as important to Québec as it is to any advanced state and there can be no more cost-effective way of sustaining the necessary level of integration than through continuing political engagement with the rest of Canada. Of course, membership with Canada may produce such a degradation of Québec nationalist spirit so that Québec might prefer to seek less cost-effective forms of integration.

Hence, an argument based on necessary levels of political and economic integration for Québec does not necessarily make a compelling case for remaining in Canada.

With respect to forms of integration, if we start with the concept of a form of economic union we would grow very quickly to making the case for political union.[21] There are many reasons for this, one being the necessity of a national political imperative to blunt domestic protectionist forces within Québec. In other words, arguments for political disengagement quickly translate into arguments for economic separation. The holding of power creates political demands that are hard to resist in the absence of a set of constituted restraints.

These are not mysterious processes; they are understood and, in fact, widely feared. This means, I believe, that the energy of Québec nationalism will be carefully channelled into political separation which is rhetorical, safe, and does not place special constitutional status on a slippery slope leading to the abandonment of essential elements of economic and political integration.

THE REST OF CANADA NEEDS A STRONG SENSE OF SELF-CONFIDENCE AND A STRONG SENSE OF THE VALUE OF CANADA IN ORDER TO RESPOND CONSTRUCTIVELY TO QUÉBEC'S DEMANDS FOR DEVOLUTION

I do not subscribe to the view that Canada needs to articulate the essential core of Canadianism or else we are doomed to disintegrate. There is, I believe, a sense of being part of Canada which is held sufficiently strongly in all parts of the rest of Canada that there is probably sufficient will to continue as a nation regardless of levels of regional frustration. The real question is whether the rest of Canada will have enough of a sense of national cohesion to be able to receive from Québec proposals for specialness (or rhetorical separation) with openness. There is no chance that Québec can continue without expressing, in some form, its liberation from the rest of Canada. There can be either a constructive or destructive response to this from the rest of Canada. A constructive response requires recognition that special status, and special constitutional regimes for Québec, do not violate fundamental constitutional principles. It also requires the sense that other regional alienations do not have to be dealt with in similar ways and at the same time. These two conditions can only be met if the rest of Canada has taken the opportunity to express its commitment to the Canadian nation prior to dealing with Québec's proposals.

For a variety of reasons the government of Canada, regardless of how consultative its proposed constitutional review process, cannot credibly manifest the necessary commitment to Canada. It must come from those who, although presently dubious about the relevance of Canada, are not willing to abandon their commitment to its continuation. It is only through bringing the people of Canada into constitutional commitment, through local processes (by which I mean provincial processes), that there will be generated a national will directed toward Canada's future that will permit the largeness of spirit to see Québec's need for instruments of Québec nationalism. As I have indicated already, the tolerance for this will vary depending on whether the new Québec powers are directed against citizens (in which case the tolerance will be low) or are directed against elements of the corporate and public sectors (in which case tolerance should be higher). This means that arrangements under which special Québec authority is accepted will have to be accepted. These can include special authority over internationally significant economic development (but does this mean special Québec authority over environmental protection?), education (but does this mean special Québec authority over the claims of minorities?), instruments of culture (but does this mean special Québec authority over the language of public media?), domestic savings and investments (but does this mean special Québec authority over the mobility of the capital of Quebeckers?), and the protection of the community social and welfare environment (but does this mean special Québec authority to create penal regimes?). These elements of enhanced autonomy would not be intolerable in a nation, the bulk of the membership of which accepts the value of national identity. I think Canadians have not lost sight of Canada and its role and that Québec's requests for special accommodation will not cause us to question the underlying and fundamental value of our nation.

NOTES

* This paper is drawn in part from the author's "Nations, Minorities and Authority," the Viscount Bennett Memorial Lecture delivered at the University of New Brunswick, Fredericton, New Brunswick, 25 October 1990.

1. See, e.g., D. Owram, "The Historical Context of Meech Lake," 2 Constitutional Forum Constitutionnel (1990–91): 23, at 23.

2. See J. Whyte, "Constitutional Aspects of Economic Development Policy," in R. Simeon, ed., *Divisions of Powers and Public Policy* (Toronto: University of Toronto Press, 1985), 29 at 29–30.

3. Canada, Parliament, House of Commons, *Debates*, 34th Parl., 2nd Session, vol. 131, No.215B, 13390 (25 September 1990).

4. See the Supreme Court of Canada decision in *R. v. Sparrow* (1990), 70 D.L.R. (4th) 385, in which the court recognized that section 35(1) of the Constitution Act, 1982, is rooted in historic colonial policy, which, while recognizing the sovereignty and legislative authority of the Crown also, per *Johnson v. M'Intosh* (1823), 8 Wheaton 543 (U.S.S.C.) accepts inherent sovereignty (or political authority) in Indian tribes (404). The court's earlier decision in *Guerin v. The Queen*, [1984] 2 S.C.R. 335, also limits governmental authority in order to give content to aboriginal rights that are derived from the historic relationship between the Crown and aboriginal peoples; that is, are derived from the concept of political community.

5. *Sparrow*, ibid., 409.

6. Ibid., 410.

7. See, e.g., M. Sandel, "Justice and the Good," in M. Sandel, *Liberalism and Its Critics* (New York: New York University Press, 1984), 159–176. But, cf. W. Kymlicka, *Liberalism, Community and Culture* (Oxford: Clarendon Press, 1989). Kymlicka argues that the protection of minority nations in pluralist societies is consistent with liberal theory; see c.10 "Minority Rights and the Liberal Tradition," 206–219.

8. R. Vipond, "Alternative Pasts: Legal Liberalism and the Demise of the Disallowance Power," 39 *U.N.B. Law Journal* (1990): 126.
9. Ibid., 156.
10. G. Grant, "English-Speaking Justice" (Sackville: Mount Allison University, 1974), 5.
11. Ibid., 13.
12. G. Horowitz, "Conservatism, Liberalism and Socialism in Canada: An Interpretation," 32 *Cdn. Journal of Economics and Political Science* (1966): 143.
13. This summary is found in H. Forbes, "Hartz-Horowitz at Twenty: Nationalism, Toryism and Socialism in Canada and the United States," 20 *Cdn. Journal of Political Science* (1987): 287 at 305.
14. R. Preece, "The Myth of the Red Tory," 1 *Cdn. Journal of Political and Social Theory* (1977): 3, cited in H. Forbes, ibid., 300–301.
15. G. Vano, *Neo-Feudalism: The Canadian Dilemma* (Toronto: Anansi, 1981).
16. See, e.g., *Québec Association of Protestant School Boards v. Attorney General of Québec* (1982), 140 D.L.R. (3d) 34 (Que. S.C.) in which C.J. Deschenes at 61–65 blends collective rights with individual rights and asserts that the denial of a right to a single individual represents the defeat of the collective right. See, also, *Société des Acadiens du Nouveau-Brunswick v. Association of Parents* (1986), 27 D.L.R. (4th) 406 (S.C.C.) in which J. Beetz, in speaking for the majority, stated that legal rights are seminal in nature while language rights are based on political compromise. The significance of this distinction for J. Beetz was that although the latter rights are not immune from judicial interpretation, "the courts should approach them with more restraint than they would in construing legal rights" (415).
17. (1988), 54 D.L.R. (4th) 577 (S.C.C.).
18. W.R. Lederman, "The Independence of the Judiciary," 34 *Cdn. Bar Review* (1956): 769, 1139.
19. *Crevier v. Attorney General of Québec* (1981), 127 D.L.R. (3d) 1 (S.C.C.); *McEvoy v. Attorney General of New Brunswick and Attorney General of Canada* (1983), 148 D.L.R. (3d) 25 (S.C.C.).
20. See, *R. v. S.(S.)* (1990) 57 C.R. (3d) 273 (S.C.C.) in which C.J. Dickson, speaking for the court, said "The division of powers not only permits differential treatment based upon province of residence, it mandates and encourages geographical distinction" (299).
21. The inexorable linkage between economic integration and the development of integrating political instruments is explored in D. Soberman, "The Parti Québécois and Sovereignty/Association," in *The Constitution and the Future of Canada* (Law Society of Upper Canada Special Lectures) (Toronto: Richard DeBoo, 1978), 65–85.

After Meech Lake
IAN SCOTT
ONTARIO, MPP

For all of you gathered here another conference on the constitution is *no* novelty. At weddings they give a prize for the guest who has come the farthest distance; at constitutional conferences they should give a prize for the lawyer, political scientist, or politician present whose record of constitutional conference attendance is highest. The competition for such a prize in this room would be intense.

But just as this cannot be the first conference to discuss constitutional arrangements in Canada for any of you it clearly will not be the last. Questions about how we govern ourselves are important in this country if the expectations of Canadians about economic well-being, social service delivery, and minority and majority interests are to be addressed. Beyond these concrete concerns, constitutional arrangements as well have a symbolic character that makes addressing them harder, not easier.

If academics and political scientists approach this weekend with enthusiasm, it is an enthusiasm not shared by your fellow Canadians.

Some months have passed since the death of Meech Lake on 23 June. That memorable, if slightly ridiculous, week in which dozens of us were closeted at Union Station in Ottawa has begun to recede from the national consciousness. It was a week when, pollsters tell us, the problems of national unity were regarded everywhere as the most important issues facing the country. In the intervening four months events at Oka, the Persian Gulf, and the Senate have dominated the national news. Canadians have had a surfeit of debate about constitutionalism; the summer has been a welcome respite from it all.

If further confirmation of this present disinterest is required, it can be found in a *Globe and Mail*/CBC News poll (October 1990) which reported that 56% of English Canadians believed that our political leaders should get on with other matters; only 39% were prepared to envisage the start of new negotiations with Québec.

Perhaps, the reason for this disinterest is that 72% of English Canadians believed that the possibility of Québec's separation from Canada was unlikely.

This conference will be the first of many opportunities to discuss what happened between 1980 and 1990—to analyse why the process failed, and to propose new guidelines for a renewal of the exercise. May I take a moment to express the views, not expert or scholarly, of a practising politician, now sitting on the sidelines.

When we discuss what went wrong I think it is important to remember that the Meech Lake Accord was the first amendment to our constitution proposed under the rules for amendment fixed by the 1982 Constitution. Prior to that, constitutional amendment was a unilateral exercise managed by the federal government; though consensus of some kind was desirable it was not until the repatriation case that the Supreme Court of Canada established a standard of provincial support against which any amendment had to be measured.

The new rules established in 1981–82 through which the Meech Lake proposals were forced to proceed can only be characterized as rigid and unwieldy. The unanimity requirement established in 1982, which applied to at least two of Québec's five conditions, would itself have wrecked the negotiations of 1982 and in 1990 permitted two provinces with less than 10% of the national population to block passage of the Accord. As well, the three-year time limit had the paradoxical effect of assuring that the process would take longer than if there had been no time limit at all. The result was that changes in government in two provinces within the three-year time limit permitted withdrawal of support for the Accord.

The requirement of legislative enactment which could only be practically achieved by the support of presiding governments, and the absence of any method of brokering 11 potentially different legislative resolutions within the requisite time frame led to the political assertion that the Accord was a "seamless web" which could not be amended. This created the perception among the Accord's critics, and even among some of its friends, that the process was undemocratic.

Looking back, it is clear that parts of the process and its death throes clearly exhibited opéra comique features. The premiers, their attorneys general and assorted aides huddled in what could only look to the average TV-viewer like a giant necropolis, but was in fact a railway station; each trooped one by one to the microphones at odd hours of day and night, like marionettes doing their set pieces, but saying nothing of consequence. The early surrender of the government of New Brunswick, which had a major responsibility for the very initiation of this last phase; the endless and tiresome waiting as Filmon, barracked by Doer and Carstairs of Manitoba and Wells of Newfoundland, postponed for days the answer 'Yea' or 'Nay' to the single question that was before the conference; the prime minister's fatal interview with *The Globe and Mail*; the determined blockade conducted by a single member of the Manitoba legislature against the interests of his own and two other political parties, which in the end made him a national hero; and the refusal of Premier Wells at the last moment even to permit the will of his legislature to be tested by a vote because "He knew the result."

252

But the remarkable fact overlooked in this bizarre process is not that the Meech Lake Accord failed but that it came so close to succeeding. The first proposed amendment to our constitution was in fact supported at one time or another by each government in the country; it had passed the federal Parliament and nine legislatures; and a coalition of parties in the tenth province were committed to its passage.

The genesis of the Meech process was a near-universal recognition by Canadians that following the 1982 constitutional round an accommodation with Québec was required. This was the price of the decision to proceed over the objections of Québec in 1982. The decision to proceed over those objections was of course perfectly legal, and perhaps even wise, but political legitimacy was properly seen to be important. As the 1987 process began, no one inside or outside the province of Québec seriously suggested that an accommodation with Québec and its symbolic adherence to the 1982 Constitution was in any sense superfluous.

Early in 1987, the Mont Gabriel Conference clearly outlined the elements of the strategy that would achieve this accommodation. The agenda must be limited to the five conditions; a preliminary set of informal discussions should take place behind closed doors in order to identify whether a consensus was possible—only when that consensus was achieved and identified should first ministers' negotiations begin.

These two guidelines proposed by the Mont Gabriel conference as a basis for proceeding have been severely criticized lately. They were seen by single interest groups and rights protagonists in a variety of communities as entirely inimical to their interests, as if the Québec round would be the last round of negotiations ever undertaken. The political assurance that other agendas would have their place at a later date was simply not compelling.

The second requirement, the necessity for a consensus arrived at in private, was necessary to assure Premier Bourassa the flexibility at home that public discussions would not have permitted. But once the consensus had been achieved it became politically impossible for the government of Québec to agree to any amendments. The only remaining issue was said to be the willingness of English Canada to meet the conditions in a formal way that it had agreed to through private consensus. There was no practical possibility of the Accord being amended after 23 June and being reratified by the province of Québec. Those who think there was are clearly dreaming in technicolour.

For those who think a more open, a more democratic process would have produced a better result the experience of the Charest Committee must have been disappointing. At first, the appointment of this committee was hailed as a break-through, an abandonment by the prime minister of the seamless web theory; via a companion resolution the interests of the rights protagonists would be advanced and concerns in English Canada about Senate reform and other matters could be addressed. But in the end, the Charest Committee recommendations satisfied no one. Not Bourassa, not Wells, not Filmon. The committee recommendations made the prospects of ratification more remote in part because it gave intellectual credibility to the dissentients and created the illusion that amendments to the Accord were still possible in 1990. The hope of amendment was held to tenaciously, but as Professor Patrick Monahan has said, "It took six days and nights in the Ottawa railway station to finally convince Gary Filmon, Sharon Carstairs, Gary Doer, and Clyde Wells of the true nature of the choice they had to make."

Whatever the validity of any criticism of this first attempt to use the 1982 constitutional amendment process—that it was undemocratic, that it was surrounded by too much secrecy, that it was too narrow and excluded the legitimate interests of other groups—in the end I think it can be said that even had these concerns been addressed from the beginning, the prospect of accommodating Québec, although it could not have been attempted at a better time, was always a long shot.

As one of the participants, now relegated to the sidelines, what do I draw from this experience?

First, the chance of securing a formal constitutional amendment under the general amending formula in the Constitution Act is not good. The Meech process began in a period of relative calm and a consensus was reached supporting the most modest requests for accommodation advanced by the province of Québec in a generation. The very failure of Meech Lake itself will make the next round more difficult, and the next series of proposals from Québec will not be as modest as those that initiated the Meech process. Another stalemate will confirm and exacerbate any determination in Québec to abandon the constitutional process and proceed through bilateral negotiations with the federal government or by unilateral declaration.

Recently, Premier Bourassa indicated that he is prepared to undertake bilateral negotiations with Ottawa. At the end of the day this will, I believe, permit successful resolution of only some minor administrative matters and should be seen as a short-term political posture. It is to me inconceivable that Canadians can accept the proposition that the province of Québec can negotiate its constitutional concerns bilaterally with a federal government in Ottawa, leaving it to that federal government to negotiate an acceptance of those terms in the other nine provinces. Even assuming that this was a permissible process, it could only be undertaken with a federal government in place with a clear mandate to do so and the requisite moral authority to act. For the foreseeable future, that seems unlikely.

If then one is obliged to conclude that, without a unilateral declaration of Québec intention, a renewal of multilateral negotiations in support of constitutional change must be undertaken sooner or later. The question is how can that be done in a regime that maximizes the opportunities for success? In short, what are the lessons we have learned that we would seek to apply to the next round?

Certain factors seem from my perspective unalterable. *One*, the 1982 amending formula requiring unanimity, legislative resolutions, and the existing time limit cannot be changed. *Two*, the ultimate brokerage in support of an agreement inevitably will occur behind closed doors. *Three*, the determination of Québec to be accommodated within our constitution if federalism is to survive will not, absent shattering economic changes, be reduced. *Four*, the pressure from other provinces

254

and groups of Canadians, the West, aboriginals, and others to address their agendas will increase.

I make only two rather commonplace suggestions for your consideration. They are founded upon the proposition that the Meech Lake Accord failed because it did not attract popular support. Indeed at the end of the day the two who opposed it with most public vigour—Premier Wells and Elijah Harper—became in certain parts of the country national heroes by the simple and effective, if somewhat undemocratic strategy, of preventing its merits from being voted on in their respective Legislative Assemblies. Without public support behind the Accord this undemocratic strategy was permitted to prevail.

I believe popular support for the Accord was withheld for two reasons: first, the formulation of the distinct society clause, and second, the legitimacy of the process by which the Accord was achieved.

I hasten to assure you that I am a supporter of the distinct society clause. I believe it was a moderate accommodation of the need in the province of Québec for a largely symbolic gesture and represents, at most, a modest attempt to assure legitimacy to Québec arguments in support of legislative enactments aimed at protecting or enhancing language and cultural concerns unique to that province. But almost from the beginning, it was misunderstood. Critics of the Accord believed that it provided the Québec National Assembly with powers that no other Legislative Assembly in the country possessed; that it had the capacity to usurp federal legislative authority under section 92 (notwithstanding the explicit assertion in the Accord that it did not); and the uniqueness of the Québec distinct society clause (because no other community in the country was similarly identified) seemed to many an assertion of a superior right or entitlement in the legislative arena.

The problem engendered by this misunderstanding was exacerbated by a host of single interest groups who would not permit their claims, often legitimate, to be postponed in favour of a Québec round.

The practical trouble for politicians who supported the Accord was that because the provision would ultimately be interpreted by the Supreme Court of Canada, the lie could not be put to these arguments or these fears. What the distinct society clause meant was always seen as a question of conjecture. If we could not be absolutely certain what it meant what were we doing putting it in the constitution anyway? At the end of the day the distinct society clause promoted a climate of fear in many parts of English Canada. There was no clear-cut or assured way to eradicate those fears. The clause itself as the principal focus of the public debate served the interests of neither Québec nor English Canada.

In the next round, if there is one, I believe a different tack must be taken. Instead of talking about distinct society we must talk affirmatively about the powers that the province of Québec legitimately believes are necessary to protect and assure the continuance and growth of its language and culture. The focus of the renewed negotiations must be around sections 91 and 92 rather than around an ambiguous and precatory recital. Renegotiating the distributions of powers for the benefit of Québec's unique language and cultural concerns will not be an easier task for politicians; it will in fact be a harder one.

But at least the debate will be grounded in real not theoretical choices. If the negotiations about what renewed powers should be produces a consensus, it will at least be a consensus that Canadian politicians supporting it can rationally and definitively expound in concrete terms. If there is an important value supporting Québec's place in the federal system these are the renewed powers that Québec needs in order to assure that it remains Québec, that is to say, a province with a unique and fragile linguistic and cultural identity in a country committed to an historic duality. As a practical politician I believe I will have an easier task advancing such an argument to my constituents (even if the renewed powers are not shared by other provinces) than I did when I attempted in two general elections to explain the meaning of the distinct society clause.

The second suggestion relates to process: public opinion throughout Canada even among adherents of the Accord rejected its legitimacy. By this I do not mean that there was concern about the criteria for amendment that the 1982 Constitution established; about this there was little debate and in any event there is no prospect of altering it. The problem was that Canadians felt they were shut out from the exercise from the beginning and they simply did not trust their politicians to reflect the public's legitimate concerns.

It is indeed a perplexing question to determine how legitimacy can be obtained for a process that is confined by a constitutional amending formula that inevitably involves politicians, in an environment where the normal give and take of political discussion is vested with enormous symbolic value.

May I make one tentative proposal? For purposes of discussion, I suggest a national convention composed of delegates equally selected by the 11 governments and from a wide variety of interest groups and community representatives. Its task over a period of time (and it may take a year or two) will be twofold: first, to devise a recommended constitutional agenda, perhaps involving a recognition that constitutional reform can only be advanced in bite-sized chunks.

The constitutional convention's second task will be to submit to governments one or more preferred forms of amendment. Thereafter, the more traditional governmental brokering role will resume as the constitution seems to anticipate.

This proposal is advanced as a start for my own thinking about what should be done. It is in no sense a fully fleshed out concept. I propose it (although I recognize that many may regard it as radical) for a number of practical reasons: it does not require legislative or constitutional change; it recognizes that elected democratic governments have a fundamental constitutional responsibility; but most of all it is founded on the proposition that Meech Lake failed not merely because Canadians are cynical about politicians or dislike backroom brokering, but because Canadians themselves were not obliged to directly address the hard choices that constitution making in a country like Canada requires. For me the most compelling argument in support of Meech Lake was that it represented the best that we Canadians could do in the year 1990 in addressing an important national problem.

I was convinced that this was so, but most Canadians were not. As I say, I am not at all certain that a convention of the type I propose will produce a better result or a fuller consensus, but I am certain that it will achieve some level of satisfaction that the public interest is being protected and the sense in the Canadian public mind that the proposals at hand are the best we as a nation can do.

Finally, I have two last words for my compatriots in English Canada.

First, I hope all English Canadians will take the constitutional crisis in which we are now thoroughly immersed with utmost seriousness. Our French-speaking compatriots in Québec clearly do. Whatever the outcome may be, the impact of this crisis on our systems of government, our commitment to quality of life, to education, health, and social services, and our search for a distinct cultural identity, as well as our very place in North America will be profound. It is now clear that the status quo cannot be maintained; fundamental change is inevitable. I suggest that if we are truly committed to the existence of a non-American presence on this continent English Canadians must accept fully and unreservedly the Laurendeau principle of duality if we want Canada to survive as a nation. Special powers must be conceded if the principle of duality requires them, failing which we in English Canada as individual provinces face the future alone.

Second, while it may be unpalatable or even inappropriate for a guest in western Canada to say so, it would, in my opinion, be a gross misreading of our history to believe that the separation of Québec will for long leave nine united English Canadian provinces. The history of English Canadian life on this continent has been, since at least the American Revolution, an attempt to forge alliances with others to make viable a non-American presence with all the values that I believe it represents. The history of Upper Canada, and subsequently Ontario, in building alliances with the province of Québec in the period from 1673 to 1867 is illustrative. Following separation, it is inevitable, after a mourning period, that Ontarians will welcome and then forge an alliance, economic at first and then, (if possible) political with Québec.

At the end we must ask: Will the reality of this crisis for our country focus the minds of English Canadians? We will know the answer to that question before the decade is out.

CONTRIBUTORS AND EDITORS

BEVERLEY BAINES is Associate Professor of Law at Queen's University. She has written a number of articles on the Meech Lake Accord and the constitutional status of women, has taught women and the law and feminist jurisprudence courses since the mid-1970s, and was among the legal advisors to several of the national women's organizations that responded to the Meech Lake resolution.

ALLAN E. BLAKENEY is a former NDP Premier of the province of Saskatchewan. For the academic year 1990–91, Mr. Blakeney holds the Law Foundation of Saskatchewan Chair in the College of Law, University of Saskatchewan, where he teaches advanced constitutional law and current issues in Canadian federalism.

KATHY L. BROCK is an Assistant Professor at the University of Manitoba and was Research Director of the Manitoba Task Force on Meech Lake, 1989–1990.

ALAN C. CAIRNS is Professor of Political Science at the University of British Columbia. Past-president of the Canadian Political Science Association and a recipient of the Molson Prize Awarded annually by the Canada Council, he is the author, co-author or editor of a number of noted books and articles on Canadian federalism and the constitution. Several of the essays for which he is best known appear in *Constitution, Government and Society in Canada* (1988).

THOMAS J. COURCHENE is Director of the new School of Policy Studies at Queen's University where he holds the Stauffer-Dunning Chair. A former chairman of the Ontario Economic Council (1982–1985) and a Senior Fellow of the C.D. Howe Institute since 1980, he is the author of many books and articles on Canadian policy issues, including *Equalization Payments: Past, Present and Future* (Ontario Economic Council) and *Economic Management and the Division of Power* (Macdonald Royal Commission).

JOHN C. COURTNEY is Professor of Political Studies at the University of Saskatchewan. In 1990–91 he was the William Lyon Mackenzie King Visiting Professor of Canadian Studies at Harvard University.

DEBORAH COYNE is a lawyer and co-founder of the Canadian Coalition on the Constitution, a coalition of groups and individuals opposed to the Meech Lake Accord. She has taught law and public policy, and is currently the Director of Constitutional Policy in the Government of Newfoundland and Labrador.

GRAHAM FRASER is the Ottawa Bureau Chief of the *The Globe and Mail*. Educated at the University of Toronto, he is the author of three books: *Playing for Keeps: The Making of the Prime Minister 1988* (1989); *PQ: René Lévesque and the Parti Québécois in Power* (1984); and *Fighting Back: Urban Renewal in Trefann Court* (1972).

DONNA GRESCHNER teaches constitutional law and legal theory at the University of Saskatchewan and has been a constitutional advisor to national and provincial women's organizations. Most recently, she was counsel to the Assembly of Manitoba Chiefs and Eiljah Harper in their successful efforts to stop the Meech Lake Accord.

259

GUY LAFOREST is Assistant Professor of Political Science, Université Laval. He is currently working on a book-length manuscript on the fate of political duality in Canada. His articles have been published in journals such as *Government and Opposition, Les Cahiers de Droit, Canadian Journal of Political Science, Recherches sociographiques, Politique.*

WILLIAM R. LEDERMAN is Professor of Law and former Dean, Faculty of Law, Queen's University. A frequent member of or consultant to royal commissions and advisory committees on constitutional matters, he is the author of *Continuing Constitutional Dilemmas: Collected Essays on the Constitutional History, Public Law and Federal System of Canada* (1981) and co-author and co-editor of *Canadian Constitutional Law: Cases, Notes and Materials* (1977).

PETER MACKINNON, Q.C. is a native of Prince Edward Island. Educated at four different Canadian universities, he was admitted to the Bar of Ontario in 1975 and to the Bar of Saskatchewan in 1979. A past president of the Canadian Association of Law Teachers, he has been dean of the College of Law, University of Saskatchewan since 1988.

ROBERT MARTIN is Professor of Law at the University of Western Ontario. He teaches constitutional and comparative constitutional law. In addition to being a columnist for *The Lawyers' Weekly,* he is editor of *Critical Perspectives on the Constitution* (1984) and of *A Source Book of Canadian Media Law* (1989).

JOHN MEISEL is Sir Edward Peacock Professor of Political Science, Queen's University. Most of his research and publications have dealt with elections and political parties, regional and ethnic tensions, cultural policy and the relation between politics and communications. He is a former chairman of the Canadian Radio-Television and Telecommunications Commission.

OVIDE MERCREDI, elected Manitoba Regional Chief in 1989, is a member of the executive committee of the Assembly of First Nations. Called to the Manitoba Bar in 1979, he was subsequently legal advisor and co-ordinator of the Manitoba Constitutional Committee of Chiefs, as well as the Manitoba representative on the Assembly of First Nations Constitutional Working Group.

EDMOND ORBAN is Professor of Political Science at the Université de Montréal. He has written extensively on the subjects of comparative politics and federalism. His publications include *La Dynamique de la centralisation dans l'Etat fédéral: un processus irréversible?* (1985) and a forthcoming collaborative work *Cours suprêmes (ou constitutionelles) et Fédéralisme.*

VAUGHN PALMER is a political columnist for *The Vancouver Sun.* He has been writing about British Columbia provincial politics for the last seven years.

MARC RABOY is an Associate Professor in the Departement d'information et communication, Université Laval. A former journalist with the *Montreal Star* and CBC radio and television, his major publications include *Movements and Messages: Media and Radical Politics in Québec* (1984) and *Missed Opportunities: The Story of Canada's Broadcasting Policy* (1990).

GORDON ROBERTSON, a member of the federal public service between 1941 and 1979, was closely associated with federal-provincial relations after 1963, as Secretary to the Cabinet and as Secretary to the Cabinet for Federal-Provincial Relations. He is the author of *A House Divided: Meech Lake, Senate Reform and the Canadian Union* (1989).

PETER H. RUSSELL teaches constitutional and judicial politics at the University of Toronto. An author and editor of several works on the Canadian federal and judicial systems, he is currently President of the Canadian Political Science Association.

IAN SCOTT is currently member of the Ontario Legislative Assembly for St. George-St. David. Between 1985 and 1990, as Attorney General in the Liberal government of David Peterson, he was directly involved in the constitutional reform process. His responsibilities as minister have also included women's issues, Native affairs and race relations.

DAVID E. SMITH is Professor of Political Studies at the University of Saskatchewan. His most recent publications include *Jimmy Gardiner: Relentless Liberal* (1990), co-authored with Norman Ward, and "Perennial Alienation: the prairie west in the Canadian federation" in Michael Burgess, ed. *Canadian Federalism: Past, Present and Future* (1990).

JENNIFER SMITH is Associate Professor of Political Science at Dalhousie University. She is currently writing a biography of Robert Stanfield. Her recent publications on the theme of this conference include "Confederation and the Influence of American Federalism" in *Canadian Journal of Political Science* (1988) and "Political Vision and the 1987 Constitutional Accord" in K. Swinton and C. Rogerson, eds. *Competing Constitutional Visions: The Meech Lake Accord* (1988).

GARTH STEVENSON is Professor of Politics at Brock University. He is the author of *Unfulfilled Union: Canadian Federalism and National Unity*, now in its third edition.

DAVID TARAS, a political scientist, is Director of the Canadian Studies Programme at the University of Calgary. His publications touch on several of the themes of the conference. He is author of *The Newsmakers: The Media's Influence on Canadian Politics* (1990) and associate or co-editor of *Meech Lake and Canada: Perspectives from the West* (1988 and 1989) and *A Passion for Identity: Introduction to Canadian Studies* (1987 and [1992]).

REG WHITAKER is Professor and Director of the Graduate Programme in Political Science at York University, Toronto. He is the author of a number of books on Canadian politics, including *A Sovereign Idea: Essays on Canada as a Democratic Community* (McGill-Queen's University Press, 1991).

JOHN D. WHYTE is Dean of the Faculty of Law, Queen's University. Appointed constitutional coordinator, Department of the Attorney General, Government of Saskatchewan in 1979, he became Director of that Department's constitutional branch in 1981, a position that led him to act as advisor to the province's Premier and Attorney General during the 1979–1982 constitutional reform process. He is a co-author of *Canada ... Notwithstanding: The Making of the Constitution, 1976–82* (1984).

Printed in Canada